critical
vices
the myths of
postmodern
theory

Critical Voices in Art, Theory and Culture
A series edited by Saul Ostrow

This book is part of a series. The publisher will accept continuation orders which may be cancelled at any time and which provide for automatic billing and shipping of each title in the series upon publication. Please write for details.

nicholas zurbrugg
essays

critical
vices
the myths of
postmodern
theory

commentary
warren
burt

Australia · Canada · France · Germany · India · Japan · Luxembourg
· Malaysia · The Netherlands · Russia · Singapore · Switzerland

G+B
ARTS
INTERNATIONAL

Copyright © 2000 OPA
(Overseas Publishers Association) N.V.
Published by license under the G+B Arts International imprint,
part of The Gordon and Breach Publishing Group.

Amsteldijk 166
1st Floor
1079 LH Amsterdam
The Netherlands

British Library Cataloguing in Publication Data
Zurbrugg, Nicholas
Critical vices : the myths of postmodern theory.
(Critical voices in art, theory and culture — ISSN 1025-9325)
1. Postmodernism
I. Title II. Burt, Warren
700.4'113

ISBN 90-5701-062-3

contents

Commentary   Warren Burt

introduction
to the series

CRITICAL VOICES IN ART, THEORY AND
Culture is a response to the changing
perspectives that have resulted from the
continuing application of structural
and poststructural methodologies and
interpretations to the cultural sphere. From the ongoing processes of deconstruction and reorganization of the traditional canon, new forms of speculative,
intellectual inquiry and academic practices have emerged that are premised on
the realization that insights into differing aspects of the disciplines that make up
this realm are best provided by an interdisciplinary approach that follows a discursive, rather than a dialectic, model.

In recognition of these changes, and of the view that the histories and
practices that form our present circumstances are in turn transformed by the
social, economic, and political requirements of our lives, this series will pub-
lish not only those authors who already are prominent in their field—or those
who are now emerging—but also those writers who had previously been
acknowledged, then passed over, only now to become relevant once more.
This multigenerational approach will give many writers an opportunity to
analyze and reevaluate the position of those thinkers who have influenced

their own practices, or to present responses to the themes and writings that are significant to their own research.

In emphasizing dialogue, self-reflective critiques, and exegesis, the Critical Voices series not only acknowledges the deterritorialized nature of our present intellectual environment, but also extends the challenge to the traditional supremacy of the authorial voice by literally relocating it within a discursive network. This approach to text breaks with the current practice of speaking of multiplicity, while continuing to construct a singularly linear vision of discourse that retains the characteristics of dialectics. In an age when subjects are conceived of as acting upon one another, each within the context of its own history and without contradiction, the ideal of a totalizing system does not seem to suffice. I have come to realize that the near collapse of the endeavor to produce homogeneous terms, practices, and histories—once thought to be an essential aspect of defining the practices of art, theory, and culture—reopened each of these subjects to new interpretations and methods.

My intent as editor of Critical Voices in Art, Theory and Culture is to make available to our readers heterogeneous texts that provide a view that looks ahead to new and differing approaches, and back toward those views that make the dialogues and debates developing within the areas of cultural studies, art history, and critical theory possible and necessary. In this manner we hope to contribute to the expanding map not only of the borderlands of modernism, but also of those newly opened territories now identified with postmodernism.

Saul Ostrow

acknowledgments

I would like to offer particular thanks to Elinor Shaffer, John O'Brien, Ken Ruthven, Sydney Lévy, Michel Pierssens, Paul Foss, Ross Harley, John Caughie, John H. Astington, Mike Gane, Douglas Kellner, Stuart Koop, Ric Allsopp and Claire MacDonald, whose generosity and enthusiasm first helped these essays into print; to J.G. Ballard who endorsed this publication; to my editors Saul Ostrow, Liza Rudneva and Brian Bendlin who prepared the present volume, and to Warren Burt, for his visionary final essay.

This book is dedicated to all those artists, writers, critics, theorists and friends whose writings and conversation provoked its pages in the first place, and to everyone who shared Paris Street oysters, passion fruit, and another bottle of wine, back at Drake Street, Brisbane, as these essays slowly began to enter subtropical orbit.

Nicholas Zurbrugg

one or two final thoughts (a retrospective preface)

0

Draw yourself back ... and say in a cold nasal whine: "You think I am innarested to contact your horrible old condition? I am not innarested at all."

—William S. Burroughs,
Dead Fingers Talk

The essays in this book attempt to identify those "critical vices" confining postmodern cultural theory and leading the best minds of our generation to miss their mark, betray their object, and institutionalize the tired mythology that "modern civilization" is at best an "irremediable mistake" before which "we can only retain our humanity in the degree to which we resist its pressures."[1] Adventurous investigations of contemporary culture should surely resist the perils of this "horrible old condition."[2]

As Warren Burt observes in his commentary upon these essays, contemporary culture shock prompts two responses: the defeatism of those embracing "the philosophy of giving-up," and the creative persistence of those *giving themselves up* to the challenge of understanding and implementing new creative possibilities.[3] Eloquently commending this second aspiration in a manifesto of some half-century ago, the modernist avant-garde film-maker Germaine Dulac observed, "Occasionally, an idea with no precedent springs from a prophetic brain, with no preparation, and we are surprised. We do not understand it and we have difficulty accepting it. Should we not, then, contemplate this idea religiously, from the moment it appears to us in the light of its dawn, contemplate it with a fresh intelligence, stripped of all tradition, avoiding reducing it to our own level of understanding, in order, on the contrary, to raise ourselves up to it and expand our understanding with what it brings us?"[4] But as Dulac also acknowledges, prescient understanding, "born of both the criticism of the present and the foreknowledge of the future,"[5] invariably disquiets critics conditioned by tradition. Successive technological innovations increase such disquiet incrementally, as pre-institutionalized practices emerge more or less immaculately, not merely *against* but *beyond* the flow, "born technically, occasionally even aesthetically" (as Roland Barthes remarks), long before they are "born theoretically."[6]

"Take the easy way! Go by the book! Don't stick your neck out!"[7] As Burroughs observes, institutional training may well prompt discrete distantiation from the new. But as Félix Guattari argues, the question of whether to be, or not to be, open to the slings and arrows of outrageous innovation should be both axiomatic and unproblematic: "This is the dilemma every artist has to confront: 'to go with the flow,' as advocated, for example, by the Trans-avant-garde and the apostles of postmodernism, or to work for the renewal of aesthetic practices relayed by other innovative segments of the Socius, at the risk of encountering incomprehension and of being isolated by the majority of people."[8] Guattari's reference to "the apostles of postmodernism" principally targets those complacently over-institutionalized architects, artists and theorists whose work gives postmodernism a bad name, rather than those contemporaries whose innovation "engenders unprecedented, unforeseen and unthinkable qualities of being."[9] Lambasting the worst minds of his generation, he grimly concludes that "The prostitution of architecture in postmodern buildings, the prostitution of art in trans-avant-garde painting, and the virtual ethical and aesthetic abdication of postmodernist thought leaves a kind of black stain upon history."[10]

For many younger critics the apparent paucity of contemporary creativity makes theory far more attractive than practice, and as Hal Foster indicates, prompts the decision "to treat critical theory not only as a conceptual tool but as a symbolic, even symptomatic form." Such an approach, Foster stipulates, "will not address art directly." Rather, it attempts "to see how historical shifts may be registered in theoretical texts—which will thus serve as both objects and instruments of my history."[11]

While Foster qualifies his enthusiasms as those of "a second-generation initiate" (as opposed to "the zeal of a first-generation convert"), his autobiographical sketch below typifies the susceptibility of his generation to the seductive bondage of what Guattari calls the "structuralist straitjacket"—or indeed, to what we might now think of as the "poststructuralist straightjacket."[12]

Whereas Burt comments, "although I possess quite catholic tastes in artistic activity, I have quite narrow ones when looking at criticism," Foster rather differently observes that, "Like others in my milieu, then, I have some distance on modernist art, but I have little on critical theory," adding, "In particular I have little distance on the semiotic turn that refashioned much art and criticism on the model of the text in the middle to late 1970s . . . for I developed as a critic during this time, when theoretical production became as important as artistic production. (To many of us it was more provocative, innovative, urgent—but then there was no real contest between, say, the texts of Roland Barthes or Jacques Derrida and new-image painting or post-historicist architecture.)"[13]

The ludic superficiality of new image painting and posthistoricist architecture may well pale before the poetic provocations of Barthes and Derrida. But it is hard to ignore the almost unfailing abstraction and imprecision of Barthes's and Derrida's key concepts (for example, Barthes's evocation of "punctum" as an "effect" that seems "certain, but unlocatable . . . acute and yet muffled," and Derrida's enthusiasm for the "trace of the implacable," or "something like that—not what I love, but what I would like to love, what makes me run or wait, bestows and withdraws my idiom").[14] Alluding to, and *very generally* rebounding from, prior discourse (rather than identifying specific instances of present intertextual and intermedia innovation), Barthes's and Derrida's text-based speculations and systems, and anti-systems, seem oblivious to what Foster terms the "new aesthetic experiences" of "ambitious art."[15]

As Baudelaire suggests in his essay, "The Universal Exhibition of 1855," cultural theory predicated upon previous cultural theory usually proves incommensurate with the complexity of its object, and culminates in minuscule exercises in "backsliding" (rather than affording the kind of "fresh" understanding advocated by Dulac),[16] leaving the user "imprisoned in the blinding fortress of his system":

> Like all my friends I have tried more than once to lock myself inside a system, so as to be able to pontificate as I liked. But a system is a kind of damnation that condemns us to perpetual backsliding; we are always having to invent another, and this form of fatigue is a cruel punishment. And every time, my system was beautiful, big, spacious, convenient, tidy and polished above all; at least so it seemed to me. And every time, some spontaneous unexpected product of universal vitality would come and give the lie to my puerile and old-fashioned wisdom. . . . In vain did I shift or extend the criterion, it could not keep up with the universal man, and it was for ever chasing multiform and multicoloured beauty, which dwells in the infinite spirals of life.[17]

If Baudelaire's references to the "infinite spirals of life" sound remarkably similar to Barthes's and Derrida's allusions to "unlocatable" and "implacable" sensation, his research differs from that of Barthes and Derrida in terms of its specific analysis of contemporaries such as Eugène Delacroix (whom Baudelaire finds "decidedly the most original painter of both ancient and modern times"), and Constantin Guys (whom he finds still more interesting perhaps, as an artist "looking for that indefinable something we may be allowed to call 'modernity'").[18] Put another way, Baudelaire is a cultural critic both willing and able to extricate himself from "systems," in order to discuss "some spontaneous unexpected product of universal vitality."[19]

As Foster remarks, much post-seventies cultural theory elaborates hypotheses based "on the model of the text,"[20] and by the late eighties this mythology attained such epidemic impact that for Fredric Jameson, at least, it seemed indisputable that "the available conceptualities for analysing the enormous variety of objects of study with which 'reality' present us (now all in their various ways designated as so many 'texts') have become almost exclusively linguistic in orientation."[21]

Arguing that "the older language of the 'work'—the work of art, the masterwork—has everywhere largely been displaced by the rather different language of the 'text,' of texts and textuality," Jameson still more chillingly advises that "the hegemony of theories of textuality and textualisation means, among other things, that your entry ticket to the public sphere in which these matters are debated is an agreement, tacit or otherwise, with the basic presuppositions of a general problem-field."[22] At best, such suppositions typify the inflexibility and intolerance of academia's "public sphere"; a subculture patently at odds with the vitality of radical postmodern creativity.

For example, commenting upon this book's critique of "the limits of inter-textuality,"[23] the poet, artist and Burroughsian sidekick, Brion Gysin, made it abundantly clear that he had very little sympathy for the alleged hegemony of theories of textuality and textualization. Remarking "how much I appreciated your article in the *Review of Contemporary Fiction*," Gysin's letter continued: "I wish I knew of some way to have it printed here in French. It would cause quite a furore . . . if furore can still be caused. It sets straight in my mind the careerist opposition I and we get from the New Establishment . . . here in France. . . . Fuck the intertextualists!"[24]

Gysin's conclusions offer a welcome riposte to the three articles of poststructuralist/intertextual faith approvingly outlined by Jameson:

> 1. that "full postmodernism" is an era in which "the philosophical priority of language itself and of the various linguistic philosophies has become dominant and wellnigh universal."

> 2. that "the older language of the 'work'—the work of art, the masterwork—has everywhere largely been displaced by the rather different language of the 'text.'"

> 3. that this mythology affords a legitimate "imperialising enlargement of the domain of language to include non-verbal—visual or musical, bodily, spatial—phenomena."[25]

Interweaving verbal and nonverbal materials, and generating the distinctively *post-linguistic* register that Jameson himself diagnoses as postmodern culture's "emergent mediatic conceptuality," the finest works of the multimedia avant-garde consistently discredit such hypotheses.[26] Reconsidered in the nineties, "full postmodernism" evinces both the self-evident submonumentality of its lower depths and the unexpected monumentality of innovative techno-arts commanding appraisal in the "older language of the 'work'—the work of art, the masterwork."

Once we look beyond the misleading presuppositions of what we may now warily regard as the quaintly "older language" of seventies and eighties inter-texual dogma, the most significant examples of late-twentieth-century creativity begin to fall more clearly into focus as symptoms of the extraordinary multimedia renaissance brought about by those visionaries sharing William S. Burroughs's sense that it is now "Time to leave the Word-God behind."[27] As Burroughs's early novel, *The Ticket That Exploded* (1962), cryptically hints, new kinds of multimedia creativity require new kinds of multimedia consciousness acknowledging the mutation of word culture into new compounds of "Word," "image track," and "sound track": "Now some words about the image track . . . whenever the sound track is run the image will literally come alive in your flesh—Word with heavy slow motion image track *is* flesh—You got it?—Put on any image at 35 frames per second and play the sound track back and see the image sharp and clear. . . . Play the sound track back and the image will rise out of the tape recorder—Slow motion sound track is flesh. . . . Subliminal slow flesh out of the tape recorder—Word with heavy track *is* flesh—"[28]

Perhaps this kind of multimedia sensibility will only really begin to inform cultural theory when theorists finally share the media of their subjects, by working digitally with word, image track, and soundtrack, rather than shuffling textual quotation in the manner of these pages. As Warren Burt concludes, it may well ultimately prove to be a mistake "to even use contemporary word-based critical theory," when addressing multimedia creativity meriting—but still awaiting—"a new criticism, one that is completely comfortable with the new technological tools and cultural expressions at hand."

In this respect, these essays may well appear "mistaken" if (like Burt) the reader prefers their author to "tell us about those things he enjoys," rather than "dealing with critics who fail to get to the point of those things he is enthusiastic about." But what can one do? Writing on the new arts, one inevitably questions those theoretical mythologies that obstruct illumination, in order to clear the way for more productive consideration of those creative initiatives that one most admires.

Ranging from the early eighties to the late nineties, these essays might initially appear to offer alternating currents of enthusiasm before visionary, "positively postmodern" creativity, and frustration before myopic, "negatively postmodern" theory. But gradually (and to some extent, to my own surprise) they increasingly reflect the pleasure of discovering new waves of more enlightened theoretical debate during the past decade, as theorists such as Baudrillard and Guattari advocate "a more subtle form of analysis," sensitive to technology's potential as "an instrument of magic," and identify "aesthetic machines" as "the most advanced models—relatively speaking—for the blocks of sensation capable of extracting full meaning from all the empty signal systems that invest us from every side."[29]

Nevertheless, one constantly hungers for discussion of specific examples of such "magic" alternatives to "empty signal systems," and more often than not one finds that even the most affirmative currents in contemporary cultural theory fail to exemplify their claims. Perhaps the essays in this book gesture in the right direction. Certainly they attempt to identify the most lucid currents in contemporary theory and practice, in order to identify those artists who, in Marshall McLuhan's terms, "[pick] up the message of cultural and technological challenge decades before its transforming impact occurs ... anticipating and avoiding the consequences of technological trauma."[30]

This book begins by outlining the ways in which the electroacoustic postmodern avant-garde has realized and revolutionized the modernist avant-garde's dream of an art "multiplied by the machine,"[31] and by suggesting the ways in which avant-garde practices such as the cut-up experiments of William S. Burroughs and Brion Gysin point to the limitations of Roland Barthes's early intertextual theory.

Subsequent essays question three of the most prevalent mythologies of postmodern theory: Achille Bonito Oliva's invention of the death of the avant-garde and discovery of its replacement by a trans-avant-garde; Jean Baudrillard's invention of the "abyss" between European culture and the radical modernity of America; and Fredric Jameson's invention of the supposedly post-monumental qualities of video art (in particular) and of postmodern media culture (as a dark whole).

Finally, discussion of Robert Wilson's innovative multimedia collaborations with Heiner Müller prefaces reconsideration of the monodimensionality of most critiques of Baudrillard's writings; of the unexpectedly lucidity of Baudrillard's and Paul Virilio's most recent writings on photography, video and technoculture; and of Baudrillard's engagingly ambiguous accounts of radical illusion in *The Perfect Crime*.

According to William S. Burroughs's essay "Remembering Jack Kerouac," the writer has to have "*been there,*" or "he can't write about it".[32]

It is surely equally imperative that contemporary cultural theorists resist the ranks of card-carrying cadres modestly monitoring parochial fluctuations within the microcosmic rhetoric of confined, predefined problem-fields, and *be there*, out there, as informed, ambitious, critical observers, familiar with unfamiliar practices within the macrocosmic reality of emergent multimedia, and prepared to evaluate the effectiveness of dominant theoretical presuppositions in terms of their capacity (or incapacity) to address radical cultural transformation.

"Be there or be square." There is no other solution.

marinetti, boccioni and electroacoustic poetry

futurism and after

1

ONE OF THE MOST DIFFICULT TASKS FOR the comparatist is the definition and categorization of successive phases in the art of the contemporary avant-garde. A worse nuisance than small children, such creativity is often assumed to be best seen and not heard, or if possible, neither seen nor heard. Thus while D. J. Enright, the editor of the recent *Oxford Book of Contemporary Verse*, happily countenanced an international, comparative "juxtaposition of British writing with American and Commonwealth," this impulse encompassed only relatively conventional writing.[1] Sweeping experimental poetry under the global carpet, Enright argued that: "However modish on the international circuit ... a 'sound' poem ... can be a good deal more trivial than a conventionally metrical sonnet: the effects may be striking, but they do not strike very deep" (xxvi).

Enright does not exemplify the kind of sound poem he has in mind, though his association of the term with the "Lautgedicht" (xxvi) certainly compounds the ambiguity of his argument by equating sound poetry as a genre with one of its earlier, more primitive, variants. Had Enright considered the subsequent, highly sophisticated, technological orchestration characterizing later variants of the genre than the *Lautgedicht* (a predominantly phonetic and syllabic poetry, dependent upon live declamation), then his response to the entire genre might have been more sophisticated in its turn.

Enright's narrow frame of reference exemplifies the key problems attending anyone attempting to analyse avant-garde literature: the frequent inaccessibility of exemplary works and the absence of any conceptual framework for their analysis. A number of recent publications have claimed to deal with postmodernity and the avant-garde, yet few of them even discussed the experiments which—to this writer at least—constitute the most exciting and interesting creations of the contemporary avant-garde: the successive phases of "electroacoustic" literature.[2]

If *avant-garde* trends may be differentiated from contemporaneous *mainstream* trends in terms of what Walter Benjamin defined as their characteristic aspiration toward "effects which could be fully obtained only with a changed technical standard, that is to say, in a new art form,"[3] electroacoustic literature might be defined as an avant-garde postmodern genre characterized by its dependence upon recording technology, both as a means of *production* and as a means of *reproduction*. Anticipated by László Moholy-Nagy's *Vision in Motion*, of 1947, as "a literature of phonograph record and of radio," electroacoustic literature is still aptly qualified by Moholy-Nagy's phrase, "not yet accepted but in the making."[4]

What is the best way of defining such a bewildering movement, still "in the making"? One solution might be to trace its history carefully, thereby situating contemporary developments in terms of their immediate and less immediate predecessors, within a network of causes and influences. Far from constituting the book that might unravel this complex history, this article attempts to identify certain distinctions and creative patterns, borrowed both from Futurist theory and from analyses of other avant-garde postmodern genres, which might serve as parts of a framework for differentiating the successive phases—or "languages"—of electroacoustic literature. No attempt is made here to identify any causal patterns or any questions of influence between Futurism and electroacoustic literature. Nor indeed is it my primary intention to locate symptoms of cause and influence between electroacoustic literature and other avant-garde, postmodern genres. It is simply suggested that such comparative approaches to electroacoustic literature reveal a number of helpful analytical concepts, contexts and distinctions.

As recently as 1971, the American critic Michael Kirby was able to claim that "Futurist Performance is virtually unknown in the United States."[5] Today, some ten years later, the same could be said of electroacoustic literature, both within and without the United States, and in such circumstances it is scarcely surprising that most existing studies of Futurism make very little contribution to an understanding of the postmodern, literary avant-garde. Quite simply, the authors of these studies seem unaware that a contemporary, technological, literary avant-garde even exists. Accordingly, most attempts to distinguish between the modernist visions of Futurism and the postmodern, technological compositions of the present day have been in terms of non-literary creativity.

For example, just as Walter Benjamin concluded that "Dadaism attempted to create by pictorial—and literary—means the effects which the public today seeks in the film" (239), Michael Kirby's *Futurist Performance* likewise suggests that the literary innovations of Futurism finally attain their predestined *filmic* apotheosis, noting that: "Many recent avant-garde films could be described quite accurately as 'cinematic *parole in libertà*'" (141). It must be added that Kirby, like many subsequent theorists and practitioners of "performance art,"[6] also identifies the more literary parallels between Futurist theory of the theater and postmodern performance art, observing: "Many of the concerns of this new theatre may be traced to Futurism, making the theories and performances of the Futurists of great interest and importance" (7). With the hindsight afforded by such recent anthologies and surveys of sound poetry as the Italian poet Arrigo Lora-Totino's *Futura: Poesia Sonora* and the French poet Henri Chopin's *Poésie Sonore Internationale,* Futurist theory now appears important not only in the relatively familiar context of postmodern film and postmodern performance art, but also in the additional literary context of postmodern electroacoustic poetry.[7]

The most telling of all Futurist assertions is surely their repeated claim to be "i primitivi di una sensibilità completamente rinnovata" (the primitives of a completely renovated sensibility).[8] This claim is predicated not only upon the concomitant avowal that "Noi italiani moderni siamo senza passato" (228) (We modern Italians have no past [176]), but also upon an active hatred of "archaic" variants of the primitive and barbaric. Elaborating these notions in his manifesto "Che cosa ci divide dal Cubismo," of 1914, Umberto Boccioni reflected:

> Lo studio e la conseguente influenza degli antichi arcaici, dei negri, delle sculture in legno, dei bizantini, ecc., ha portato nei quadri dei nostri giovani amici

di Francia, una saturazione di arcaismo che è un'altra piaga passatista, un'altro fenomeno di cultura come le influenze greco-romane. Queste influenze d'arti rudimentali se si fanno accettare per le novità, se hanno servito a liberarci dal classico, sono però dannose allo sviluppo di una pura coscienza plastica moderna. È in questo senso che noi ci dichiariamo primitivi. Nessuno di noi futuristi ... è affetto di quell'arcaismo che porta con sé una immobilità ieratica di solenne antico che ci ripugna. Ripeto ancora: Vi è un *barbarico* nella vita moderna che ci ispira.(229)

The study and therefore the influence of the archaic art of antiquity, of the Negroes, of wood carvings, of Byzantine art etc., has saturated the paintings of our young friends in France with the archaism which is another evil brought about by this obsession with the past, a cultural phenomenon related to the influence of the classical world. Even if these influences from rudimentary arts are accepted for what they have that is new, and even if they have helped to free us from classicism, they are still harmful to the development of a completely modern plastic outlook. That is why we call ourselves primitives. None of the Futurists ... is tainted by that archaism which brings with it a hieratic immobility and an antique solemnity which repel us. I repeat: there is a *barbaric* element in modern life in which we find inspiration. (176)

Some indication of what the Futurists understood by this "barbarism" appears in F. T. Marinetti's "Fondazione e Manifesto del Futurismo," of 1909, which enthuses over the noise of double-decker trams (44), just as Luigi Russolo's 'L'arte dei rumori', of 1913, celebrates the noises of trams, back-firing cars and crowds (129). It thus seems possible to distinguish between two modernist impulses: the archaic, pretechnological primitivism of the African and oceanic art inspiring the Cubists and the Expressionists; and the machine-age, prophetic "primitivism" of artists and writers such as the Futurists—and, to a considerable extent, the Dadaists—who wished above all to employ, evoke and emulate the dynamism of the early twentieth century.[9]

In many ways the same dichotomy informs the oral impulse in contemporary poetry. On the one hand a number of American poets loosely grouped around Jerome Rothenberg are presently elaborating "ethnopoetic" poetry: a poetry based upon primitive chanting and ritual, which in Rothenberg's terms returns to "the Indian *poesis* as our primary ground."[10] Introducing and documenting this *poesis* in his influential anthology *Technicians of the Sacred*,[11] Rothenberg has defined his cultural ambition as the desire "to break or alter the dominance of the literal, civilized culture over our poetics" and to "bring in the primitive, the tribal, the oral," if need be by employing "a simpler technology perhaps of ritual acts."[12] According to Rothenberg's polemics: "The model—or better, the vision—has shifted: away from a 'great tradition' centered in a single stream of art and literature in the west, to a *greater* tradition that includes, sometimes as its central fact, preliterate and oral cultures throughout the world."[13]

This impulse has led Rothenberg to a relatively abstract poetry often based upon such primitive literature as the chants of North American Indians and usually only employing recording technology as a means of reproduction (rather than as a means of production). Typical of Rothenberg's work is the following extract from one of his most popular poems: a 'version' of a Seneca longhouse song, entitled "Old Man Beaver's Blessing Song: Notations for a Chant." This begins:

OLD MAN BEAVER'S BLESSING SONG
    all i want's a good 5 cent seegar
    heeheeHOHOheeheeHOHOheeheeHOHO
    all i want's a good 5 cent seegar
    heeheeHOHOheeheeHOHOheeheeHOHO[14]

Repeating the two basic lines five more times, the poem ends as it began, with the titular opening line. Slight as the text may seem upon the page, it becomes an engaging mixture of nonsense and vocal energy when performed by Rothenberg; indeed, the most important trait of the poem is that it is very much a score for authorial performance and improvisation within the *live* dimension of "real time."[15] Both literally and metaphorically, this variant of contemporary oral poetry is a far cry from the electroacoustic poetry pioneered by such "primitives" of postmodern recording technology as Henri Chopin and Bernard Heidsieck—two of the many poets who have realized Marinetti's ideal of "L'uomo moltiplicato a macchina" (145) (Man multiplied by the machine [97]).[16]

In the work of Henri Chopin, this multiplication of the voice leads to a semi-abstract poetry existing in a peculiar no poet's and no musician's land *between* poetry and music, but very definitely *on* recording tape. Describing his work, Chopin specifies: "*La poésie sonore*, faite pour et par le magnétophone appartient à des microparticules vocales, plutôt qu'au verbe que nous connaissons … et … cet art se codifie mieux par des machines, par l'électricité ... que par les moyens de l'écriture." (*Sound poetry* made for and by the tape-recorder, is a matter of vocal micro-particles, rather than the Word as we know it ... and ... this art can be more easily codified by machines and electricity ... than by any means proper to writing.)[17]

For the critic, Chopin's sound poetry poses enormous problems. Is it poetry? Is it music? Is it sound sculpture? Chopin simply suggests that his compositions derive from, and exemplify, the crucial innovation of "machine poetry," and his manifesto entitled "Machine Poem," of 1964, proclaims "L'important c'est d'avoir vaincu la machine. C'est d'avoir par la voix d'un seul être trouvé des possibilités infinies d'orchestration, timbrales et sonores dues à un homme seul" (The important thing is to have conquered the machine. And with the voice of just one being, to have found infinite possibilities of orchestration, timbre and sound).[18]

The compositions resulting from this orchestration of fragmented words and vocal micro-particles are very difficult to describe, save as a dense sonic texture, often with many superficial resemblances to electronic music. While the occasional presence of recognizable words gives these compositions some claim to be poetry,[19] Chopin distinguishes them from electroacoustic music on the grounds that they are made with the human voice, a "warm" instrument in comparison with "la musique électroacoustique qui est souvent froide" (electroacoustic music which is often cold).[20] The warm or cold quality of Chopin's work is perhaps a distinction best tested personally by the curious comparatist, but the compositional technique of his work is more susceptible to precise description. As the Swedish poet and composer Bengt-Emil Johnson has remarked, "For Henri Chopin, the new technology signifies an opportunity to discover, reach and gain control over the tiny fragments of vocal sounds which, otherwise, one does not consciously perceive, and to exploit microphone technique for the registering of very weak mouth sounds, as well as the possibility of superimposing such sounds upon one another in up to as many as fifty superpositions."[21]

As I have observed, it is not my intention to speculate upon causal links between the modernist and postmodernist avant-gardes. Yet at the same time, it cannot be denied that the terms with which Johnson describes Chopin's work—and indeed the terms with which Chopin defines his experiments—offer uncanny echoes of Marinetti's more audacious proposals. In this respect, Chopin's achievement can not only be conceptualized with reference to Boccioni, in terms of his distinction between archaic and modern variants of primitivism, but can also be defined with reference to Marinetti's meditations, as a postmodern avant-garde *realization* of a modernist avant-garde *aspiration*. To some extent then, Futurist theory anticipates postmodern practice, just as postmodern practice vindicates Futurist theory.

In the context of electroacoustic literature, Marinetti's most startlingly prophetic aspirations appear in one of his least-known manifestos: "La Radia," of 1933. Seldom anthologized, and, it seems, untranslated,[22] this manifesto fascinatingly proclaims the potential of "The pure organization of radiophonic sensations": a new dimension of "radiophonic" creativity which Marinetti's deliriously visionary prose associated with the "Captazione amplificazione e trasfigurazione di vibrazioni emessa da esseri viventi da spiriti viventi o morti . . . Captazione amplificazione e trasfigurazione di vibrazioni emesse dalla materia." (Picking up, amplification and transfiguration of the vibrations emitted by living beings, living or dead spirits . . . The picking up, amplification and transfiguration of the vibrations emitted by materials.)[23] Bizarre as this proposal to capture, amplify and transfigure such immaterial material as the vibrations of dead spirits may be, its basic ambition, and its tripart formulation, offer a striking premonition of Chopin's subsequent ability to "discover, reach and gain control over tiny fragments of vocal sounds."[24] Similarly, Marinetti's patriotic claim that "noi futuristi perfezioniamo la radiofonia destinata a centuplicare il genio creatore della razza italiana" (we Futurists are perfecting radiophony destined to multiply one-hundredfold the creative genius of the Italian race) offers equally extravagant, but equally startling, prefiguration of Chopin's more convincing claim that the tape recorder allows the individual poet's voice "infinite possibilities of orchestration."

While Chopin has worked with the tape recorder for much of his career as a means for producing and orchestrating predominantly abstract sounds, Bernard Heidsieck exemplifies the corresponding tendency for sound poets to use the tape recorder to modify and orchestrate both abstract sounds *and* language as recognizable semantic material. Heidsieck's work is best exemplified by his poem "La Poinçonneuse,"[25] a narrative work dramatizing the confusion of a commuter as he reads a love-letter given to him by "la poinçonneuse"— a lady ticket puncher—in a *métro* station. Juxtaposing the plaintive, and relatively unorchestrated, voice of Christine Tsingos, who reads the ticket-puncher's letter, with both Heidsieck's repetitive narration of the story and his explosive declamation of the commuter's confusion, this work con-

textualizes and counterpoints these interacting discourses with the monotonous humming of variously arriving and departing trains, and the staccato
clanging of the metallic barriers as passengers arrive and depart in their turn.
As Gérald Gassiot-Talabot has remarked, "La Poinçonneuse" constitutes "une
brève notation aussi pénétrante qu'une nouvelle de Tchekhov" (a brief text,
poignant as a story by Chekhov).[26]

Clearly illustrating the limitations of D. J. Enright's assertion that sound
poems "may be striking, but they do not strike very deep," and demonstrating
that the sound poem need not be limited to meaningless phonetic or syllabic
materials, Heidsieck's work forcefully substantiates his observation that "le fait
de sortir de la page n'implique pas obligatoirement l'abandon de la séman-
tique" (the decision to leave the page does not necessarily imply that semantic
values are abandoned).[27] Employing new recording technology as "un nouveau
support... un nouveau instrument de travail" (a new aide... a new tool) (364).
Heidsieck quite literally realizes Ulrich Weisstein's metaphor of the, "artist-
engineer" who may "add, subtract, dismantle and reassemble" his materials.[28]
As the following extract from "La Poinçonneuse" reveals, this poem's exploita-
tion of such symptoms of technological editing as "repeated echoes," "superimposed echoes," and "progressive fragmentation" lends itself—like Chopin's
work—to conceptualization in terms of Boccioni's distinction between archaic and modern primitivism, insofar as Chopin and Heidsieck are both "primitives" of postmodern electroacoustic literature. (fig.1.1) Significantly, Chopin
has been described as "the barbarian of the tape recorder" by the American poet
Larry Wendt—whose use of computers, synthesizers and micro-processors
characterizes him as belonging to an altogether different generation of postmodern electroacoustic poets.[29]

Like Chopin's work, Heidsieck's experiments can also be defined as a postmodern realization of Futurist aspirations, particularly the aspirations of
Marinetti's "Synthesist Theatre." Marinetti's "Manifesto del teatro sintetico," of
1915, insisted that "la realtà ci vibra attorno assalendoci con raffiche di frammen-
ti di fatti combinati tra loro, incastrati gli uni negli altri, confusi, aggrovigliati, coal-
izzati" (251) (reality throbs around us, bombards us with squalls of fragments of
inter-connected events, mortised and tenoned together, confused, entangled, coa-
lesced [194]); and as a combination of superimposed fragments of verbal and
nonverbal sounds evoking a sudden incident in the *métro*, Heidsieck's "La
Poinçonneuse" perfectly reflects this "reality."

il lui tendit . . .   Oh! Monsieur! vous avez laissé
                                                        tomber ce papier!

lui tendit . . .   (échos répétés)
lui tendit . . .
lui tendit . . .
lui tendit . . .
lui tendit . . .   Oh! Monsieur! vous avez laissé
                                                        tomber ce papier!

elle, mûre et poinçonneuse, encore que
ce matin, fébrile et tendue
elle, mûre et poinçonneuse, encore que
ce matin, fébrile et tendue
elle, mûre et poinçonneuse, encore que   Oh! Monsieur! vous avez laissé
ce matin, fébrile et tendue   tomber ce papier!

comme chaque matin   (35 seconds   )
comme chaque matin   (avec:)
comme chaque matin   (échos répétés)
comme chaque matin   (échos superposés)
comme chaque matin   (décomposition)
comme chaque matin   (progressive   )
comme chaque matin   (rapidité   )
comme chaque matin   (croissante   )
comme chaque matin   (mécanisation)
comme chaque matin   (des mots et   )   Oh! Monsieur! vous avez laissé
comme chaque matin   (sifflements   )   tomber ce papier!
                                                        (avec échos et répétitions)

arrivées et départs de rames de métros
arrivées et départs de rames de métros

---

he handed her . . .   Oh! You've dropped this piece
                                                        of paper, Sir!

handed her . . .   (repeated echos)
    ,,   ,,
    ,,   ,,
    ,,   ,,
    ,,   ,,

she, a ticket-puncher of middle years,
today, strained and tense . . .

today as usual   (35 seconds with:)
                      (repeated echos)
                      (superimposed echos)   ,,
                      (progressive fragmentation)
                      (increased speed)   ,,
                      (words and noises becoming)
                      (more mechanical)   ,,

                                                        (with echos and repetitions)

arrival and departure of Métro trains
arrival and departure of Métro trains

Extract from Bernard Heidsieck's "La Poinçonneuse."

It might be assumed that the following extract from Heidsieck's poem indicates the raw materials of its recorded, version, in much the same way that the extract from Rothenberg's "Old Man Beaver's Blessing Song" gives some indication of Rothenberg's raw materials. But whereas a recording of Rothenberg reading this poem would merely duplicate a verbal performance which might just as well be heard live, complementing the printed text with the revelation of Rothenberg's live—or "uncooked"—verbal mannerisms, the recording of Heidsieck's text reveals a performance attained only after the technological *haute cuisine* of studio editing. It is precisely this "cooking" of the poetry books which distinguishes electroacoustic literature born of what might be termed "reel-time" from the "oral impulse in contemporary American poetry" recently discussed in the review *Boundary 2,* which derives from acoustic performance in real time.[30]

As Michel Benamou observed in his introduction to a series of papers on *Performance in Postmodern Culture,* it is tempting to consider postmodern culture in terms of "two visions, one shamanistic, the other futuristic."[31] This distinction certainly helps to demarcate the basic dichotomy that I have already discussed in terms of Boccioni's polarization of archaic and modern modes of primitivism, and additionally coincides with my thesis that primitives of the "new" postmodern sensibility often technologically realize the aspirations of Marinetti's more extravagant manifestos (be these toward an abstract "radiophonic" literature, or toward "synthetic" narrative juxtaposing "squalls of fragments of inter-connected events"). Predictably, these distinctions have become less and less clear in recent years, as poets who once seemed to epitomize "pure" models of electroacoustic impulse have moved more and more into what Michel Chion might call "hybrid" acoustic dimensions of real time performance.

For example, rather than presenting his work to the public by simply playing tapes to audiences in purely audible performances, Bernard Heidsieck has combined prerecorded sound of his tapes with live declamation and gesture, creating a combination of "reel-time" and real-time materials. In his own words:

> Mais ce que je recherche et souhaite toujours, c'est offrir la possibilité à l'auditeur/spectateur de trouver un point de focalisation et de fixation visuelle.... Sans aller jusqu'au happening, loin de là, je propose toujours un minimum d'action pour que le texte se présente comine une chose vivante et immédiate.... Il ne s'agit donc pas de lecture à proprement parler, mais de donner à voir le texte entendu. (361)

> But what I'm always looking for and always want, is a way to offer the listener/spectator the possibility of finding a fixed visual focus point.... For without wishing to

create a happening, far from it, I always offer a minimum of action so that the text may be presented as something living and immediate. . . . It doesn't consist of a reading in the strict sense of the term, but of visually projecting the audible text.

Such performances mark a fascinating turning point in the evolution of electroacoustic literature. Commencing as a genre defined by contrast with live performance, it now displays every sign of repudiating its most singular characteristic in response to the acoustic "call of the wild." How does the critic come to terms with such transitions? How, for example, should the critic categorize the work of the American poet Charles Amirkhanian? In 1971 Amirkhanian seemed the model "studio" poet, making such helpful comments to this writer as: "My sound poems derive from texts . . . which are first read by me in a control room and then altered in various ways . . . the works are not fully scored in advance of working in the control room."[32] Yet despite the fact that the letter containing the lines above also observed "I am particularly uninterested in producing scores of my word/sound pieces for printed media," Amirkhanian has subsequently produced scores such as "dutiful ducks," of 1977, which clearly exist for the page, as the following extract demonstrates. This poem begins

> *dutiful ducks*
>
> dutiful
> the drano ducks collide
> *and mercy*
> gather-collide-like
> *fancy tension*
> pow-wow
> *dutiful dutiful ducks*
> than double Elly
> *Macy*
> treetops pray
> the signal
> hay in May
> says
> *dutiful*
> —
> *dutiful*
> *ducks*
> —
> *dutiful*
> —
> *dutiful*
> *dutiful*
> *ducks*[33]

Emphasizing the acoustic properties rather than the semantic dimension of its components, "dutiful ducks" transfers the dynamic, rhythmic editing techniques that Amirkhanian first developed in the control room into the realm of live performance, thereby attaining the effect that Marinetti's manifesto "Lo splendore geometrico e meccanico e la sensibilita numerica," of 1914, envisioned as "l'entusiastica imitazione del'elettricità e della macchina" (212) (the enthusiastic imitation of electricity and the machine[154]). To be exact, Amirkhanian allows this text both to imitate the machine in live, real time performance, and to exploit the machine, with edited, "reel-time" recorded orchestration—or indeed to combine both possibilities, via one or more performers. According to its author, it is a work for "solo voice, multiple voices, or voice(s) with pre-recorded voice(s) on tape."[34]

Confronted by such works, the critic might well despair of differentiating the different "languages" of electroacoustic literature and retreat to the less vertiginous pastures of the conventionally metrical sonnet. For as helpful as Boccioni and Marinetti are for establishing general contexts for electroacoustic literature, their assumptions cast little light on the seemingly eccentric creativity of Heidsieck and Amirkhanian. Guidance can be found, however, by updating the principles of that most lucid of modernist critics, László Moholy-Nagy. According to Moholy-Nagy, the student of modernist literature "must be acquainted ... with ... the tendencies of contemporary composers" (592), and by the same logic, the analysis of electroacoustic literature (which we shall continue to exemplify primarily in terms of electroacoustic poetry), is greatly facilitated by reference to criticism of other forms of postmodern technological creativity.[35]

In this respect, the French composer and theorist Michel Chion's article, "Vingt années de musique électroacoustique," of 1972, is doubly inspiring, both as an example and as a catalyst of such critical cross-fertilization.[36] Analyzing the relatively unfamiliar genre of electroacoustic music by analogy with the phases in the evolution of the cinema, it simultaneously suggests concepts and terms which might also be applicable to the even less familiar genre of electroacoustic literature.

The first of the four phases that Chion discerns in the evolution of the cinema and, by extension, within electroacoustic music, is "la période zéro" (the zero phase), which Chion associates with "une simple démonstration de son principe" (a simple demonstration of principles). Citing Pierre Schaeffer's "Études de Bruits," of 1948, as a musical example of this phase, Chion specifies that such works evince "plus de l'émerveillement devant un nouveau moyen de parler que d'un souci quelconque de *quoi dire*" (26) (more of an amazement before a new language than a desire *to say anything in particular*). An identical phase characterizes the first modernist and first postmodernist experiments with the acoustic and electroacoustic dimension of literature, such as the phonetic experiments of Hausmann and Schwitters, and the phonetic and noise poems recorded and "primitively" orchestrated by postmodern poets such as the Frenchman François Dufrêne, the Englishman Bob Cobbing and the Austrian Ernst Jandl.[37] Most early works by these poets are certainly more important as explorations and demonstrations of new raw materials and specific effects, than as works containing any other specific message, and thus to some extent are, in D. J. Enright's terms, "striking . . . but not . . . very deep."

Chion identifies the second phase of the cinema—and of electroacoustic music—with the innovatory genre's attempt to find "ses lettres de noblesse culturelles dans l'imitation d'arts plus anciens, dotés d'expérience et de prestige" (26–27) (its certificate of cultural nobility by imitating established arts already crowned with experience and prestige). Illustrated by Chion's reference to the way in which composers such as Pierre Schaeffer and Pierre Henry created electroacoustic *symphonies* and *suites,* this phase has its exact counterpart in experimental poetry. The Dadaist Kurt Schwitters similarly imitated the compositional conventions of classical music in his *Sonate in Urlauten* of 1919–32; while François Dufrêne collaborated with the aforementioned composer Pierre Henry, contributing material to the latter's *Le Voyage* of 1967, just as the Belgian poet, Paul de Vree, collaborated with both the composer Jan Bruyndonkx and the actor Julien Schoenaerts, when "sonorizing" his poem "Vertigo Gli," of 1963.[38] (In much the same way, a number of pop groups have flirted with classical music and orchestras, in a bid for cultural respectability.)

Chion subsequently argues that this *imitative* phase is followed by a third, *purist* phase, during which directors like Robert Bresson revealed "la volonté de faire du cinéma un art spécifique, pourvu d'un langage propre, et devant refuser à imiter les autres . . . un puritanisme esthétique" (the desire to make the cinema into a specific art, with its own language, refusing to imitate others . . . an aesthetic puritanism). Chion suggests that Schaeffer's *Études aux objets, aux allures,* of 1958, exhibits a same sort of puritan impulse, explaining: "une fois dégagé quelques principes, Schaeffer et ses collaborateurs se mettent en quête d'un langage propre, qu'ils expérimentent dans des oeuvres sévères" (27) (having established certain principles, Schaeffer and his group sought a language of their own trying it out with a number of austere compositions). Henri Chopin's "purist" concern for a sound poetry made *uniquely* by and for the tape recorder exemplifies a similarly puritan austerity in the realm of electroacoustic literature, in which works become almost exclusively a product of "reel-time."[39]

But as we have observed, this austerity gives way to more hybrid forms of verbal-visual performance, involving *recorded* sound, *live* sound and *live* gesture. In much the same way, Chion discerns an open-ended final phase both in the cinema and in electroacoustic music. Distinguishing the present multiplicity of cinematic experiments from the genre's "zero" phase, he observes:

> L'identité ayant été acquise avec le temps, garantie par un langage de base, des oeuvres fortes, des auteurs confirmés, le souci d'identité s'affaiblit, le puritanisme se relâche. Les générations nouvelles s'amusent à retrouver la saveur de l'ambiguïté de la confusion des genres et des références. Le cinéma s'incorpore tout, et s'incorpore à tout. Mais cette confusion n'est pas un retour à zéro, car elle s'appuie sur une experience, une tradition propre. (27)

> Its identity having been acquired in the course of time, and guaranteed by its own basic language, by substantial works, and by established authors, the problem of identity subsides, and the puritan impulse relaxes. New generations amuse themselves with the rediscovery of ambiguity, and of the confusion of genres and references. Incorporating everything into itself, the cinema incorporates itself into everything. But this confusion in no way signifies a return to zero, since it is based upon experience, upon its own tradition.

Of the fourth, contemporary phase of electroacoustic music, Chion similarly comments: "Tout paraît remis en cause" (27) (Everything seems thrown back into question).

The work of poets like Charles Amirkhanian makes best sense as examples of this hybrid, self-questioning creativity, coming at the end of a new genre's emergent tradition. From this point of view, at this point in the evolution of electroacoustic literature, the apparently incompatible paths of "reel-time" and real time creativity may be seen to come together unexpectedly, somewhat like Swann's Way and the Guermantes' Way, in Proust's *Rememberance of Things Past* (*A la recherche du temps perdu*).[40] The consequence of this convergence of "reel-time" and real time creativity is that definitions which previously distinguished the former from the latter now become much wider in their potential application. The Swedish poet and composer Sten Hanson has defined sound poetry as a predominantly technological art form, notable for its "combination de l'exactitude de la littérature, et la manipulation du temps de la musique" (combination of the exactness of literature and the time manipulation of music).[41] But as the American poet Larry Wendt observes in the following extract from a recent interview, an analogous quality of musical manipulation now characterizes the real time performances of poets such as Bernard Heidsieck, and Wendt's fellow American John Giorno, who enjoy the best of both acoustic and electroacoustic worlds by combining them. Discussing John Giorno's performances with stereo tapes of "multiple voices," Wendt comments:

> I think what's really important is his temporal sense. He's got a time-sense like Bernard has a time-sense. Bernard has immaculate rhythm and so does John—I saw him do this performance, like the tape is going on with his multiple voices, and he's reading along with it, and at certain parts in the performance he would not say anything, and this thing would go on, and then he'd start again right in sync, and like his timing sense is incredible, it was just wow! This is the aspect of live performance, because you don't get that in tape. You can do it, you can fake it with tape, but in live performance you can't fake it, you have to be on time, and have that sense of rhythm. These differences in timing give live performance its excitement.[42]

In the same interview, Wendt explained that the use of computers and microprocessors facilitates the production of what we have termed "reel-time" effects (or studio editing, previously achieved laboriously, in sequential "phonomontages," combining layer after layer of sound), in real time, as relatively spontaneous "phonomontage." As Wendt intimates, such creativity adds yet another "language" to electroacoustic poetry:

> The availability of microprocessors explodes certain things right open in terms of really new frontiers in vocal speech manipulation and syntax manipulation. With the use of computers you have the flexibility to do something that's very difficult to do on the tape-recorder in terms of splicing. With the computer you can splice a lot finer than you can on the tape-recorder, and so you are able to produce new words, new sounding words, out of the fragments of old words. It's a whole new bag of tricks one can play on language. With tape-manipulation you have little bits of tape all over the floor—you're removed from the actual physicality of producing that sound. New technology would give you more real time control—with a micro-processor you get more immediate control.

Distinguishing the work of the French pioneers—or primitives—of early tape-recorder poetry, and the Swedish and American, West Coast primitives of computer poetry,[43] Wendt suggests that whereas poets like Bernard Heidsieck and Henri Chopin may now be defined as masters of early recording technology, the primitives of early computer poetry still risk considerable "brain damage" in the effort to master their instruments. Alluding to the "immediate control" afforded by the microprocessor, Wendt adds:

The problem is to get to that point you have to go through all that brain dam-age programming computers, but after that whole hardware technological stage you can use that thing as a creative device, as a wand, as a paintbrush. Bernard Heidsieck has a more limited use of technology—he just uses tape echo and tape superimposition, but he uses those techniques very artistically. He's mastered his media, same as Henri mastered his instrument. It's like a per-son with a saxophone, the way he uses the tape-recorder. He's mastered the early types of tape-recorder, not those big multi-track, two inch, twenty-four track jobs, but the ones that first came out, the two channel tape-recorder.

Though this is not the place or space for such a study, a fascinating survey might be made of the differing modes of sound poetry resulting from the dif-fering accessibility of "twenty-four track jobs" to different poets. Whereas Swedish and American poets have had access to the studios of radios and uni-versities, this is less common elsewhere.[44]

It is only fair that these pages should finally confess themselves a "primitive" account of the different phases of electroacoustic literature, having liberally applied this adjective to any number of poets. Hopefully though, despite the lim-ited selection of examples on these pages and despite the necessarily hasty analy-ses of these examples in an article of this size, this comparative panorama of electroacoustic poetry has indicated that the new "languages" of the new art of sound poetry are more numerous, more sophisticated and more deserving of critical attention than conservative critics, such as D. J. Enright, have supposed.

Briefly, the "*revolution of the word*" celebrated by the American poet and editor Eugene Jolas did not come to an end with James Joyce's *Finnegans Wake,* as is commonly assumed. Indeed, if, as Jolas wrote in 1948, "The language of poetry has undergone more radical changes in the past fifty years than were recorded during the previous three hundred years,"[45] then the following thirty years, felicitously christened "l'ère du magnétophone" (the age of the tape-recorder),[46] bear witness to the evolution and revolution of a number of still more radical poetic experiments, which have been quite literally recorded with ever-more-complex postmodern technology.

As contemporary poets enter the age of the computer, a succession of even more radical poetic experiments may be anticipated, be these on the printed page, on the stage, on record, on audiotape or on videotape. Yet when considered in terms of Marinetti's aspirations, Boccioni's distinctions, and Chion's categories, these sur-prises should surely make surprising sense to the computer-age comparatist.

the limits of intertextuality

barthes, burroughs, gysin, culler

THE AMERICAN NOVELIST WILLIAM S. Burroughs and his compatriot and sometime collaborator, the poet and artist Brion Gysin, are particularly fond of alluding to Hassan i Sabbah, the "Old Man of the Mountains, Master of the Assassins," who, some thousand years ago, spread terror throughout the Moslem world from the heights of his mountain fortress at Alamout by exercising the secret powers that "enabled him to control and activate his assassins from a distance."[1] Those of his adepts who were not accomplishing remote-controlled assassination assignments remained apparently at Alamout, of which Gysin reports: "like, uh, it must be fucking cold up there in the wintertime ... uh ... very dangerous, cold and uncomfortable spot ... which I guess Hassan i Sabbah dug a lot, and he must've been very hard to live with is all I can think of."[2]

More by accident than by design, Roland Barthes appears to have become the Hassan i Sabbah of contemporary literary theory: the involuntary master of an international school of assassins pledged to the ideals they perceive in his celebrated essay on "The Death of the Author."[3] Carrying this analogy a little further, it seems that just as the followers of Hassan i Sabbah lacked the unusual ability to weather the bitterly cold conditions that their master "dug a lot," surviving only when tranquilized with liberal helpings of hashish or opium, so too Barthes's followers seem to lack their master's breadth of vision, and only "live with" his ideas by reducing them to a dogmatic, quite un-Barthesian vision that tranquilizes the tensions within Barthes's teachings by ignoring them. Yet these tensions—and conflicts—like the tensions and conflicts in the works and theories of William S. Burroughs and Brion Gysin—should surely not be tranquilized, but scrutinized, since they indicate the limitations that Barthes appears to have identified in his theory of intertextuality.

Perhaps the most revealing tension in Barthes's writing is that between his efforts to create more or less scientific analytical systems that deny the existence of the author and dismantle texts into as many codes as he had currently invented, and his conflicting compulsion to locate loopholes within these systems for symptoms of authorial presence and originality, be these the "grain of the voice" in performances, the "third meaning" in the film still, or the "accent" in works by cinematic and noncinematic authors. The implications of these are considerable, for they unexpectedly undermine two of Barthes's famous declarations: "the text is henceforth made and read in such a way that at all its levels the author is absent" (145), and "The intertextual in which every text is held, it itself being the text between of another text, is not to be confused with some origin of the text ... the citations which go to make up a text are anonymous, untraceable, and yet *already read:* they are quotations without inverted commas." (160; emphasis in the original) These two highly influential statements from "The Death of the Author" and "From Work to Text" are usually taken literally by the Barthesian "assassin"; an error of judgement that surely obscures their function and significance as prime examples of Barthes's ability to invent what Chion would term irresistibly "pure" utopian "laws" in order to legitimize reams of equally seductive, subsequent "hybrid" illuminations.[4]

There is surely something slightly ludicrous in Barthes's apocalyptic announcement that "henceforth" the text will be both made and read in such a way that the author will be eliminated from it at all levels. Indeed, this vision rings with the same all-encompassing megalomania as that more forcefully outlined in Burroughs's *Exterminator!*, when a veteran from *The Naked Lunch*, "A.J. the laughable, lovable eccentric,"[5] steps forward in his Uncle Sam suit and assures his supporters: "I pledge myself to turn the clock back to 1899 when a silver dollar bought a steak dinner and good piece of ass . . . I pledge myself to uphold the laws of

America and to enforce these hallowed statutes on all violators regardless of race, color, creed or position.... We will overcome all our enemies foreign and domestic and stay armed to the teeth for years, decades, centuries.'"[6] As the cover of Barthes's *Barthes sur Barthes* ironically demonstrates, it is impossible to stop time and then turn the clock forward to a new era in which all trace of the author is removed from every text. On the contrary, technological advances such as audiotape and videotape proliferate signs of the authorial presence as never before.

In much the same way, Barthes's equally apocalyptic suggestion that creative time has somehow stopped, and that every text, however new, is implicitly "already read," is not so much the statement of some literal truth or "law," as it is an act of conceptual provocation sharing the beguiling theoretic licence that similarly informs Burroughs's recent—and no less provocative—declaration that "Immortality is the only goal worth striving for: immortality in Space. Man is an artefact created for the purpose of Space travel. He is not designed to remain in his present state anymore than a tadpole is designed to remain a tadpole.... We are not fighting for a scrap of sharecropper immortality with the strings hanging off it like mafioso spaghetti. We want the whole tamale."[7] A master of such stimulating overstatement (though lacking the extravagance and the dry humor of Burroughs), Barthes redeems what must surely have been the self-conscious myopia of his overenthusiastic assertions regarding the permanently dead quality of the author and the already read quality of the intertextual cosmos, by offering antidotes to these claims in some of his companion pieces to "The Death of the Author" and "From Work to Text."

Thus Barthes's essay entitled "The Grain of the Voice" juggles somewhat uneasily with his speculation that upon apprehending the "grain" of a voice (or what he terms "the materiality of the body speaking its mother tongue" [182]), the listener enters into a "relation with the body of the man or woman singing," and then necessarily evaluates this performance according to "a new scheme of evaluation ... made outside of any law," and "outplaying not only the law of culture but equally that of anticulture" (188). Turning his attention to the "grain" of instrumental music, Barthes emphasises once again that his evaluation "shall not judge a performance according to the rules of interpretation, the constraints of style ... but according to the image of the body ... given me" (188–89). Contemplation of the "grain of the voice," then, triggers off a relationship between the listener and the unfamiliar "body" of the performer, rather than that between the decoder and the familiar "tissue of quotations" (146) with which "The Death of the Author" associates textual matter.

Barthes never explicitly concedes that this new relationship between the listener and the performer approximates to the reader-author relationship that he mockingly evokes as "the important task of discovering the Author . . . beneath the work" (147). But were Barthes's object to change ever so slightly from that of listening to a singer singing a song, to the experience of listening to an author reading from one of their own works—for example, Burroughs reading from *The Naked Lunch*[8]—then this experience might well have to be defined as the process of evaluating the "grain" of the authorial voice, and as the problematic rediscovery of the author "beneath" the authorial performance. Briefly, Barthes's meditations upon the extra-literary genres of the song and of instrumental music lead him to a position from which he is virtually obliged to reassess his previous assumptions about the literary text. Having identified the body of the singer and the instrumental performer, Barthes is but one step away from discovering the musical "author" in performances by composers of songs and instrumental music, and but two steps away from the resurrection of the literary author in the authorial performance of the text. Significantly, Barthes also insists that this evaluation of the "grain" of the performing voice is outside of any law.

Presumably then, this evaluative process is necessarily outside the system of prior discourses within which Barthes's "From Work to Text" locates "every text," and within which such subsequent theorists as Jonathan Culler restrict all acts of textual explication. Converting the inventions of Barthes's theoretic licence into the legislation of his *Structuralist Poetics,* Culler decrees: "A work can only be read in connection with or against other texts, which provide a grid through which it is read and structured by establishing expectations which enable one to pick out salient features and give them a structure."[9] Culler elaborates the implications of this law throughout *The Pursuit of Signs* in passages such as the following synthesis of Barthes's and Julia Kristeva's theories of intertextuality (characteristically pivoting upon "only," that most suspect of four-letter words): "literary works are to be considered not as autonomous entities, 'organic wholes,' but as intertextual constructs: sequences which have meaning in relation to other texts which they take up, cite, parody, refute, or generally transform. A text can be read only in relation to other texts, and it is made possible by the codes which animate the discursive space of a culture. The work is a product not of a biographically defined individual about whom information could be accumulated, but of writing itself."[10]

This definition hovers ambiguously between the two poles of intertextual theory. On the one hand, it specifies that intertextual relations inhabit the relatively closed discursive space between the prior literary texts of writing itself. On the other hand, it intimates that intertextual relations embrace the infinitely wider spectrum of that plurality of "codes which animate the discursive space of a culture." Culler reiterates this more open-ended concept elsewhere in *The Pursuit of Signs,* defining intertextuality as "the relationship between a text and the various languages or signifying practices of a culture and its relation to those texts which articulate for it the possibilities of that culture" (103) and suggesting that intertextuality designates "everything that enables one to recognize pattern and meaning in texts" (104). Once again, Culler faithfully paraphrases and synthesizes the theories of his forbears. Barthes, for example, equates the intertextual with such panoramic points of reference as "citations, references, echoes, cultural languages . . . in a vast stereophony" (160); while Julia Kristeva argues still more generously that "The term *intertextuality* designates the transposition of one (or several) system(s) of signs into another (*"Le terme d'*inter-textualité *désigne cette transposition d'un [ou de plusieurs] système[s] de signes en un autre."*)[11]

Like Barthes's conception of the relations between "cultural languages," Kristeva's notion of the relations between different signifying systems obviously extends beyond "writing itself." Indeed, as Laurent Jenny remarks in his oft-cited survey of intertextual theory entitled "*La Stratégie de la forme*," Kristeva's use of the term "intertextuality" is misleading insofar as it extends "beyond all literary and aesthetic problems" ("*au-delà de toute problématique littéraire ou esthétique*"), foregrounding relations between two or more systems of signs, rather than examining relations between two texts.[12] Nevertheless, in a subsequent article about literary collages, Jenny advocates the same kind of open-ended definition of intertextuality as that adumbrated in Barthes's and Kristeva's most flexible speculations, concluding that: "that which is known as 'intertextuality' is doubtless nothing other than the sum of all the procedures necessary for the decoding of every discourse" ("*ce qu'on appelle 'intertextualité' n'est sans doute que la somme des procédures nécessaires au déchiffrement de tout discours*").[13]

At this point, intertextuality becomes what Culler—paraphrasing Kristeva—defines as "the sum of knowledge that makes it possible for texts to have meaning" (104). Ironically. the implications of this catholic—or "hybrid"— approach to intertextuality are seldom realized. Culler's theoretical writings certainly acknowledge the importance of the plurality of codes animating a culture; associate intertextuality with everything facilitating the recognition of pattern and meaning in texts; and confirm Kristeva's and Jenny's suggestion that intertextuality designates the sum of knowledge permitting texts to be decoded. Yet most of the time, Culler's definitions, and—more significantly— Culler's intertextual practice, restrict this everything and this sum of codes to the written text. Rather than looking to extraliterary variants of the kind of "additional experience" and "supplementary knowledge" that he advocates in his *Structuralist Poetics* (95), or contextualizing new literary discourse within a wide range of literary and extraliterary "schemata or knowledge frames" of the kind discussed by Dieter Freundlieb,[14] Culler appears content to cultivate those intertextual relations growing within the well-walled garden of prior literary discourse. Indeed, almost all intertextual theorists tend to work primarily on the relations between literary texts, as though the conventions of prior written discourse were the only conventions determining the production of texts.

As this article will presently suggest, this predominantly "literary" variant of intertextuality appears incapable of distinguishing the ways in which certain radical contemporary texts arise from or within the conventions of extra-literary discursive spaces, such as the fine arts, music, or new dimensions of technological creativity. Despite claims to embrace "everything," the practice and polemics of Culler and other intertextual theorists suggests that intertextuality simply denotes the study of those written texts—usually poems or novels— that makes best sense in terms of previous poetic and fictional practices. This conservative, over-literary mode of intertextuality is perhaps predicated upon one of Barthes's more misleading hypotheses: his wayward suggestion that ever since the epistemological break precipitated by Freudianism and Marxism, writing has undergone "no further break," so that "in a way it can be said that for the last hundred years we have been living in repetition" (156).

This cosy centennial concept inexplicably overlooks the innumerable conceptual and technological "breaks" inaugurated by the successive waves of modernist and postmodernist culture. Far from displaying "repetition," it is arguable that the twentieth century is notable above all as an era of explosive cultural crisis and of incessant cultural renewal. In this respect, Laurent Jenny's "La Stratégie de la forme" convincingly postulates that contemporary intertextual creativity (which he associates with the French novelists Claude Simon and Michel Butor), might be characterized in terms of the attempt "to identify those static syntagms (mythologies) ossified within phrases, to distance oneself from their

banality by exaggerating them, and finally to release the signifier from its scle-
rosis in order to reinstate it within a new system of signification" ("*mettre en
lumière les syntagmes figés [les 'mythologies'] ankylosés dans les phrases, se dis-
tancier par rapport à leur banalité en les outrant et enfin dégager le signifiant de sa
gangue pour le relancer dans un nouveau procès de signification*") (279).

Barthes's suggestion that the twentieth century is an era of unbroken textual "repetition" is doubly disadvantageous. It not only distracts attention from
the peculiarly contemporary problem of explicating the innovations of radical
discourse, but (what is worse) encourages the conservative intertextual practitioner's tendency to privilege the very banalities of prior discourse that least
resemble radical discourse.

Laurent Jenny offers an interesting exception to the rule of conservative
intertextual practice, in so far as his reflections upon literary variants of collage
in "Sémiotique du collage intertextuel" advocate the comparison of literary and
pictorial practices (176). At the same time, Jenny acknowledges that literary and
visual images inhabit different semiotic systems (170), thereby hinting at the
way in which a literary text may be explicated in the context of extra-literary discursive conventions. Barthes similarly looks beyond the purity of "writing itself"
from time to time, as for example in his reflections upon the "grain" of the voice,
or in his comparison of "the (readerly) text" with "a (classical musical score" in
S/Z.[15] Culler rarely makes such excursions into extra-literary territories, though
The Pursuit of Signs momentarily contextualizes the evolution of criticism in
terms of the musical conventions of "what Schoenberg achieved in his
Erwartung: a chromatic plenitude" (47), and thus exemplifies the advantages of
employing references from contexts outside "writing itself."

By deliberately venturing beyond the over-literary intertextuality confined
within "writing itself," the intertextual critic may enter a more expansive field of
studies. Here radical contemporary textual experiments—or interextual experiments—may best be explicated by analogy with the extra-literary conventions
peculiar to artistic, musical and technological discursive spaces, rather than in
terms of the literary conventions informing the literary discourse within which
conservative theory and practice locates intertextual relations.

Returning to Barthes's theories and practice, it might be argued that the
beauty of Barthes's breadth of vision arises from its capacity to evade the counterproductive caution of theorists such as Culler. Barthes certainly postulates
that all texts are explicitly or implicitly *déjà vu* and *déjà lu,* and "come from

codes which are known" (159); and yet he also speculates that certain verbal phenomena, such as the "grain" of the performer's voice, inhabit an uncharted discursive space outside of any "law of culture" and "rules of interpretation." In
other words, having announced the death of the author, Barthes's explorations
of creativity outside the restricted intertextual grid from which Culler would
derive his analytical "expectations" all but bring him to rehabilitate the author
in terms of the listener's relationship with the body of the authorial performer.
Having made rules, Barthes has the happy knack of locating their breaking-
points by complementing his literary studies with the implications of his studies of extra-literary creativity, thereby productively transgressing the Barthesian
theory that—in Culler's formulation—requires that "A text can be read only in
relation to other texts," being a product of "writing itself" (38).

Precisely by looking beyond "writing itself" to the performance of the song
and of instrumental music, Barthes generates reflections which, by analogy and
extension, might well prompt new strategies for explicating authorial readings
of writing itself and for analyzing such recent creative practices as performance
poetry and sound poetry.[16] In much the same way, Barthes's research notes
upon "The Third Meaning" of Sergei Eisenstein's film stills are pregnant with
insights applicable both to "writing itself" and to recent technological experiments with language, despite the fact that these insights derive from forbidden
fruit, or more precisely, from the contemplation of authorial subject-matter
(which Barthes repeatedly identifies in terms of "Eisensteinian meaning" [56],
"Eisensteinian realism" [57], and other equally telling concepts), drawn from a
hybrid discursive space outside "writing itself."

It is difficult to define precisely what Barthes understands by the "third
meanings" of Sergei Einstein's film stills, since this kind of meaning (like the
"grain" of the voice) exists "outside (articulated) language," so that it "disturbs,
sterilizes ... metalanguage (criticism)" (61). It inhabits "that region where articulated language is no longer more than approximative and where another language begins" (65), and is therefore something which "will not succeed in
existing, in entering the critic's metalanguage" (61). Put another way, the third
or "obtuse" meaning is "not situated structurally, a semantologist would not
agree as to its objective existence" (60); "but then," as Barthes immediately
reflects, "what is an objective reading?" (60).

Reading these notes one discovers what Samuel Beckett has felicitously
evoked as "a great mind in the throes";[17] the revelation of one of the great

contemporary manufacturers of "objective" critical metalanguages wrestling with the subjective impact of a film still which evokes ambiguous gestures that somehow elude his most precocious systems—which "my intellection cannot succeed in absorbing" (54). Thus, while in 1971 "From Work to Text" confidently affirms that the written text is composed of "citations which ... are anonymous, untraceable, and yet *already read*" (160), these notes from 1970 identify a mode of technological creativity in which the components of a photographic image— or visual "citations"—appear anonymous, untraceable, and moreover unreadable in so far as their image "outplays meaning—subverts not the content but the whole practice of meaning" (62). At best, Barthes confesses, "My reading remains suspended ... between definition and approximation" (61).

Confronted by something that (according to his metalinguistical preconceptions) should not be there—something which "appears to extend outside culture, knowledge, information" (55)—Barthes is as it were in the position of a latter-day Christopher Columbus setting eyes for the first time upon discursive continent he would rather not have discovered. Despite Ludwig Wittgenstein's affirmation to the contrary, Barthes appears to become aware that the limits of his critical language do not coincide with the limits of his world: a dilemma indeed. One might well compare Barthes's position with that of such epitomes of postmodern subjectivity as Jean-Paul Sartre's Roquentin, or Beckett's Watt. Like Barthes, Watt is tormented by the discovery of something which he cannot define and which therefore should not be there—the discovery that "nothing had happened, that a thing that was nothing had happened."[18]

Barthes's immediate response to this dilemma (which at first sight bids well to topple "pure" Barthesian theory into "impure" Beckettian angst) is, in his own words, "derisory." Since the third meanings emerging from Eisenstein's film stills are outside culture, and, moreover, "Indifferent to moral or aesthetic categories," Barthes argues that they are best conceptualized as being part of "the family of pun, buffoonery, useless expenditure," and are thus "on the side of the carnival" (55). Barthes's rhetoric is curiously puritanical here. One senses that having remained innocent and ignorant of these troublesome third meanings, he would like at least to remain innocent of espousing their cause (if not ignorant of their existence) by delegating them to the insignificant conceptual territory of the "useless" and the "carnival"—a limbo which presumably exists in the lower depths of that kind of textual hierarchy he dismisses elsewhere as "a crude honours list" (156).

Yet as Barthes observes in the early pages of *S/Z*, there is no such being as the "innocent subject": rather, the reader is "already . . . a plurality of other texts, of codes which are infinite" (10). The disturbing discovery of the film still's third meaning merely extends the infinity of codes—or approximate codes—with which Barthes is familiar, demonstrating perhaps that the subject's "I," the occupants of intertextual discursive spaces, and the conventions underlying these discursive spaces are all in a constant state of flux and renewal. The citations that make up a text are clearly not all "*already read*" as Barthes suggests in "From Work to Text." Rather, certain citations are necessarily recent since, like Eisenstein's film stills, they derive from twentieth-century technology, and like the stills discussed by Barthes, still await comprehensive decoding.

Abandoning his initial derisory response, Barthes formulates two very interesting counter-arguments to his earlier suggestion, in "The Death of the Author," that "the writer can only imitate a gesture that is always anterior, never original" (146). Firstly, having conceded that the impact of Eisenstein's stills may arise from what Baudelaire spoke of as "*the emphatic truth of gesture in the important moments of life*" (56; emphasis in original), having located this gestural impact within such details as "the excessive curve of the eyelids" or "the upward circumflex of the faded eyebrows" (57), Barthes toys with the possibility that such third meanings may be produced by both cinematic and non-cinematic authors, speculating: "Obtuse meanings are to be found not everywhere . . . but *somewhere*: in other *authors* of films (perhaps). In a certain manner of reading 'life' and so 'reality' itself" (60; emphasis in original). Barthes extends this speculation by suggesting that, unlike the writers he discusses in "The Death of the Author" (whose meanings are never original because they may "only imitate a gesture that is always anterior" [146]), the various authors who generate third meanings may well claim to be original in so far as their work "does not copy anything" (61), and is thus so excruciatingly difficult to read, describe and contextualize. After musing briefly upon the limited categories in the kind of "objective reading" obstinately resisted by the third meaning, Barthes interestingly identifies it with "an *accent*" or "the very form of an emergence, of a fold . . . marking the heavy layer of informations and significations." This "accent" denotes "A new—rare—practice affirmed against a majority practice" (62).

Since Barthes's notes do not elaborate this concept of the accent, it remains more useful as a heuristic image rather than as a precise concept contributing to an objective definition. Nevertheless, Barthes is in excellent company, since he unwittingly duplicates—or quotes without inverted commas—the very image employed by Marcel Proust to indicate that textual quality which, although objectively undefinable, signals the existence of a "new—rare—practice." Meditating upon the originality of the writer Bergotte, and virtually identifying a "grain of the text," Proust's narrator muses:

> This accent is not designated in the text, nothing indicates that it is there and yet it emerges of its own accord in the phrases, they cannot be read aloud in any other way, it is at once that which is most ephemeral and yet most profound in a writer's work, and it is this that bears witness to the quality of his personality . . .

> Cet accent n'est pas noté dans le texte, rien ne l'y indique et pourtant il s'ajoute de lui-même aux phrases, on ne peut pas les dire autrement, il est ce qu'il y avait de plus éphémère et pourtant de plus profond chez l'écrivain, et c'est cela qui portera témoignage sur sa nature . . .[19]

Considered collectively, Barthes's successive comments upon the various authors who might create new and rare modes of third meanings characterised by some kind of accent add up to form the first of the counter-arguments that we have associated with this essay. Instead of confirming Barthes's early suggestion in "The Death of the Author" that the writer may merely mix and remix prior discourse into works without originality, this argument suggests that both cinematic and non-cinematic authors may create original works.

The second counterargument in this essay implies that new, original works may be created not only by authors but also by their media—by new technology producing creative effects without counterpart in the intertextual happy hunting ground of prior discourse. Like third meanings, these technological innovations are not simply anti-theoretical, and therefore buffoonery or symptoms of "the carnival"; nor indeed are they literally outside culture; rather, they are *ante*-theoretical, or outside the predictably limited present terminology of those who would define culture. In Barthes's formulation, such innovations may be "born technically, occasionally even aesthetically," but have "still to be born theoretically" (67). Barthes refers here to the film, but his remarks apply equally illuminatingly to other similar technological modes of creativity, such as sound poetry, radio drama and various modes of literary and musical performance which use live and recorded language and sound.[20] It seems reasonable to assume that certain authors exploring these recent genres might similarly activate new modes of "third meaning" within puzzlingly original works.

It is of course difficult to defend the claim that a work is absolutely original; indeed, if this were the case, it seems unlikely that such a work would make any sense at all. Discussing extreme experiments that approximate to this curious condition, Burroughs comments: "I've done writing that I thought was interesting, experimentally, but simply not readable," adding, "I think *Finnegans Wake* rather represents a trap into which experimental writing can fall when it becomes purely experimental. I would go so far with any given experiment and then come back. . . . It's simply if you go too far in one direction, you can never get back, and you're out there in complete isolation."[21] In this respect, Burroughs confirms Claudio Guillén's lucid definition of "the new work" as being "both a deviant from the norm . . . and a process of communication referring to the norm."[22]

Nevertheless, despite the fact that most intertextual practitioners would probably locate both this process of deviation and these "norms" within written discourse, it seems possible to distinguish two distinct modes of "original" work. The first of these would obviously be the "original" work composed within the parameters of written discourse and both deviating from its norms and referring back to them. A second and more complex mode of "original" creativity would be the radical work which not only deviates from the conventions of written discourse and then refers back to them, but which also refers forward to the conventions of discursive spaces beyond written discourse, be these the prior conventions of painting or music, or the potential "theoretically unborn" conventions of new modes of technological creativity. The complexity of this twofold originality offers revealing challenges to the assumptions of orthodox intertextuality. For example, despite the fact that Culler's *The Pursuit of Signs* advocates a poetics that is "less interested in the occupants of that intertextual space which makes a work intelligible" than in "the conventions which underlie that discursive activity or space" (118), such radical creativity virtually obliges the critic to scrutinize individual works before aspiring to chart more general conventions, since they may be the only available representation of their new discursive practice. How, then, does one come to terms with rare examples of new creativity, particularly new forms of technological creativity? How does one place such works within the most elementary conceptual context?

Culler's reflections upon the somewhat less daunting project of analyzing the different interpretative operations applied to conventional texts provide a useful preliminary warning. He remarks that "since facts of interpretation constitute a point of departure and the data to be explained, a semiotic discussion will simply be judged irrelevant if it starts from a blatantly unrepresentative range of interpretations" (51).

In much the same way, it seems evident that any attempt to read, describe and analyze new forms of technological creativity modulating "writing itself" requires that the new work be contextualized and explained within a relevant and representative range of references. Yet how can this relevant and representative range of references be identified, if a new work is itself to all intents and purposes the solitary evidence of, and the solitary occupant of, a new discursive space?

At this point a conservative intertextual approach focusing almost exclusively upon the "references" of prior written discourse seems likely to break down, since its data would prove "blatantly unrepresentative" and incapable of explicating the new. Yet it might be argued that the creative strategy of experimental artists and writers such as Brion Gysin and William S. Burroughs provides some indication of the way in which the critic may extricate themself from this intertextual impasse. Moreover, attention to the specific theories of Gysin and Burroughs suggests that the creative speculations of the avant-garde may also helpfully complement—and at times, even partially anticipate—the analytical speculations of experimental theorists like Barthes.

For example, in 1968, Barthes's "The Death of the Author" cautioned that "the writer can only imitate a gesture that is always anterior, ever original. His only power is to mix writings. . . . Did he wish to *express himself*, he ought at least to know that the inner "thing" he thinks to "translate" is itself only a ready-formed dictionary, its words only explainable through other words. . ." (146). Ten years earlier, Gysin's "Statement on the Cut-Up Method and Permutated Poems" had already declared: "Words have a vitality of their own and you or anybody can make them gush into action. The permutated poems set the words spinning off on their own. . . . The poets are supposed to liberate the words. . . . Who told poets they were supposed to think? Poets have no words "of their very own." Writers don't own their words. Since when do words belong to anybody?"[23] The general rationale leading to Gysin's conclusion that "poets don't own words," and that language should be permutated and cut up, is perhaps still more interesting than these particular conclusions.[24] For arguably its premises exemplify a creative variant of the theoretical approach most likely to facilitate the explication of radically new works of literature.

Gysin outlines this approach in the opening paragraph to his statement on the cut-up method and permutated poems, revealing that his experiments were motivated primarily by the wish to manipulate words with the same facility with which visual materials are manipulated by the modernist artist. Commencing with one of the key statements in contemporary cultural criticism, this paragraph declared: "Writing is fifty years behind painting. I propose to apply the painter's technique to writing; things as simple and immediate as collage or montage. Cut right through the pages of any book or newsprint . . . lengthwise, for example, and shuffle the columns of text. Put them together at hazard and read the newly constituted message." The crucial concept here is Gysin's wish to bring writing up to date with painting, or to put it another way, his wish to animate the discursive space of writing with some of the conventions underlying the discursive space of experimental painting.

This aspiration first challenges Barthes's theory of textual production, which maintains that a text is a mixture of "words only explainable through other words" (146), and thus makes no provision for texts predicated upon artistic conventions or painterly techniques that are neither reducible to the conventions of prior literary discourse, nor explainable in terms of other words. Secondly, and reciprocally, Gysin's poetics challenges Barthes's theory of textual explication, since his work is best explained not so much in terms of a merely verbal or literary mode of intertextuality, as in the extra-verbal, extra-literary context of artworks which employ collage and montage techniques.

To argue that written texts, such as Gysin's poems, are explainable only in terms of "other words" in the literary context of "writing-itself" is surely to assume that writers are peculiarly innocent of extra-literary creativity. This assumption would make little sense at the best of times, but it makes no sense at all in the context of a poet like Gysin, who is not only a poet but also a painter, and moreover, a painter who writes poems according to the plastic conventions of prior artworks, rather than according to the literary conventions of prior "wordworks" in which conservative intertextual theory locates the foundations of all literary creativity. Accordingly, the intertextual critic should surely look to a more open mode of intertextuality in order to work within conceptual parameters commensurate not only with literary codes but also with such extra-literary codes as the collage and montage conventions underlying Gysin's poetry.

This stipulation may be unduly modest, predicated as it is upon such early-twentieth-century artistic conventions. For as William S. Burroughs intimates in the following passage from his novel *Nova Express*, the conventions underlying the now venerable and even rather quaint pre-technological manifestations of collage and montage (such as the pioneering works of the Cubist, Futurist, and Dadaist artists), are considerably less sophisticated than the conventions underlying their radical technological counterparts within the contemporary, postmodern discursive space of *intermedia*.[26] This discrepancy finds foul-mouthed formulation when the irrepressible "Mr Winkhorst" of "Lazarus & Co" triumphantly remonstrates: "'Sure, sure, but you see now why we had to laugh till we pissed watching those dumb rubes playing around with photomontage— Like charging a regiment of tanks with a defective slingshot.'"[27] Like many of the verbal outbursts in his fiction, this odd tirade dramatizes Burroughs's preoccupation with the ways in which variously sophisticated recorded words and images might be exploited as weapons, or means of social control. In this respect, photomontage is but a "slingshot" in comparison with the potency of the electronic mass media. The substance of this memorable simile is readily applicable to conventional, predominantly literary modes of intertextuality, which would somehow explain all textual innovation in terms of "pure" prior literary discourse. Lacking literary terms to conceptualize such basic extraliterary concepts as the verbal equivalent of photomontage, this conservative intertextual approach is worse than a "defective slingshot" when confronting the "tanks" of recent technological experimentation.[28]

It might be argued that Barthes's speculations upon the "grain" of the performer's voice and upon the "third meaning" of Eisenstein's film stills represent a wider, more satisfactory intertextual approach, insofar as they investigate extraliterary discourses, and implicitly illuminate analogous issues within radical literary discourses. Significantly, though, this illumination is only implicit. Unlike Gysin and Burroughs, Barthes neither seems particularly conversant with the collage narratives, visual poems, sound poems and multimedia performances that characterize the postmodern literary avant-garde, nor manifests any systematic desire to relate his general theories of "writing itself" to these radical practices. Indeed, reading Barthes, Kristeva, and Culler, it rapidly becomes apparent that the conservative quality of what Culler's *The Pursuit of Signs* succinctly defines as their "facts of interpretation"—their "point of departure" and their "data to be explained" (51)—necessarily restricts what one might term the "point of arrival" of their intertextual activities. By intentionally or accidentally remaining innocent of avant-garde discursive practices since the mid-fifties, their intertextual strategies become curiously obsolete before the extra-textual energies of the radical multimedia "text." This does not imply that the infinitely less rigorous speculations of Gysin and Burroughs offer any substitute for the complexity of orthodox intertextual theory. But it seems clear that Gysin's and Burroughs's experience of recent avant-garde discursive practices allows them to commence their speculations from an advantageously extra-literary "point of departure," focusing upon exemplarily contemporaneous "data to be explained." The "innocent" intertextual critic might benefit considerably from what Culler's *Structuralist Poetics* might term the "additional experience" (95) of Gysin and Burroughs.

As Laurent Jenny comments in "La Stratégie de la forme," definitions of intertextuality become most problematic during "periods of *intertextual crisis*" ("*Les périodes de* crises intertextuelles") that follow the introduction of new media; a notion that Jenny derives from Marshall McLuhan, whose argument—paraphrased by Jenny—locates the origins of these crises "not in the history of the creative subject but in the evolution of the media" ("*non dans l'histoire du sujet créateur mais dans l'évolution des média*" [259]). The last three decades can be seen as just such a period of crisis, and the work of avant-garde writers like Gysin and Burroughs is especially valuable in terms of the ways in which it exemplifies and pinpoints the quality of this crisis. As I have already remarked, Gysin's proposals to permutate and cut up language according to the discursive conventions of early-twentieth-century artistic experiments annunciated the predominantly conceptual intertextual crisis that came about when poets and painters systematically explored and appropriated each other's methods and materials in the late fifties, the sixties, and the seventies. (This conceptual crisis is anticipated, of course, by the experiments of the Futurist and Dadaist poets and artists.) It was certainly accelerated by the availability of new printing techniques permitting the inexpensive reproduction of graphic, typographic and photographic materials, but not all of these conceptual borrowings depended upon this new technology for their realization. The fact that such experiments have received negligible attention (or none at all) from most intertextual theorists typifies the way in which a preoccupation with "prior discourse" has led contemporary intertextuality to neglect contemporaneous discourse.[29]

More recently, Gysin has amusingly and perspicaciously alluded to the parallel and unambiguously technological intertextual crisis of sound poetry, or what he terms "machine poetry": that is, experiments with tape-recorded words and sounds that similarly date from the late fifties, when inexpensive tape-recorders first became widely available. Defining his own aspirations, and deploring the conservative creativity of his acquaintances, Gysin ruefully reminisces:

> I understand poetry really mostly as it is called in French *poésie sonore,* and what I would preferably have called "machine poetry." ... I don't mean getting up there and saying it once off, or declaiming it, or even performing it the way people do nowadays, but actually putting it through the changes that one can produce by tape-recording and all of the technology, or the even just *minimal* technology that one has in one's hands in the last few years ... and all the rest is really a terrible waste of time, I think. I'm sorry ... sorry for all the poets who don't think that ... some of them very charming friends ... but I don't know what they're doing, I really don't ... I just don't know ... seems to me that they're doing nothing. (49)

Making much the same criticism of his contemporaries, Burroughs has commented: "Most serious writers refuse to make themselves available to the things that technology is doing. I've never been able to understand this sort of fear. Many of them are afraid of tape-recorders and the idea of using any mechanical means for literary purposes seems to them some sort of a sacrilege."[30] Unlike such "serious" writers, and unlike most "serious" intertextual theorists, Burroughs has deliberately made himself available to "the things that technology is doing," and the things that technology may be made to do. While Burroughs's essays in *Electronic Revolution* discuss the destructive potential of the tape-recorder in terms of the ways in which "prerecorded cut/up tapes played back in the streets" may be used as "a revolutionary weapon" to "*spread rumors,*" "*discredit opponents,*" "*produce and escalate riots,*" and "*scramble* and *nullify associational lines put down by mass media,*"[31] Burroughs's interviews in *The Job* and his essays in other publications offer splendidly succinct analyses of the tape-recorder's creative potential. For example, just as Barthes's conclusion to "The Third Meaning" carefully defines the way in which "The still, by instituting a reading that is at once instantaneous and vertical, scorns logical time" (68), Burroughs's response to a question in *The Job* regarding the advantages of the tape-recorder cogently analyses the difference between written and tape-recorded variants of simultaneity: "Of course you can do all sorts of things on tape-recorders which can't be done anywhere else—effects of simultaneity, echoes, speed-ups, slow-downs, playing three tracks at once, and so forth. There are all sorts of things you can do on a tape-recorder that cannot possibly be indicated on a printed page. The concept of simultaneity cannot be indicated on a printed page except very crudely through the use of columns, and even then the reader must follow one column at a time." (13) More recently, Burroughs has alluded to the potential of "elaborate sound equipment" surpassing the tape-recorder, affirming that: "By using ever-expanding technical facilities, sound poetry can create effects that have never been produced before, thus opening a new frontier for poets."[32]

It should be obvious at this point that Gysin's and Burroughs's interviews and theoretical writings offer extremely valuable adjuncts to the insights of theorists such as Barthes. But as I have previously hinted, Gysin and Burroughs seem even more important in terms of the way in which their creative and theoretical strategies indicate how critics might resolve the seemingly impossible problem of explicating radical literary works without counterparts in prior literary discourse—the problem I have termed the "intertextual impasse." This strategy is perhaps best defined as an "intercontextual" approach to creative and theoretical problem.[33] For experimental writers like Burroughs and Gysin, this approach involves either the adoption of radical discursive conventions from an alternative, extra-literary genre, such as art, or the exploration of a new technological possibility resulting from what Jenny defines as an "intertextual crisis." In both cases, the writer abandons the conventions and the context of familiar, literary discourse, and moves into the unfamiliar and new context of discursive practices which, in Barthes's terms, may still not yet be "born theoretically" (67). For the theorist and analyst, an intercontextual approach involves the process of systematically looking beyond the contexts of previous literary discourse, and of explicating radically new literary work by analogy with other and similarly radical works from an extra-literary context. Although some aspects of radical works may be analyzable within the various intertextual systems of theorists such as Culler, Michael Riffaterre, Jenny, Harold Bloom, and Ann Jefferson, these systems—which are all designed to explicate such conventional genres as the poem or the novel—seem unlikely to account for the innovatory quality of such works.[34] Quite simply, radical works require radical contextualization.

The intercontextual approach is primarily concerned, therefore, with the problem of explicating radical, actual creativity (as opposed to prior creativity). As has been suggested, it is possible to identify two kinds of intercontextual problems. The first of these, exemplified by Gysin's appropriation of collage and montage techniques from the fine arts, concerns work in which discursive conventions from an extra-literary discursive space are used within a literary discursive space. The advantages of intercontextualizing this kind of problem become particularly clear if one considers the case of concrete poetry, an international movement with practitioners in Europe, North and South America, Australia and Japan. The conservative intertextual analyst, pledged to explain literary discourse in the context of prior literary discourse, might dwell for years upon the complex literary "citations" linking these five cultures without ever identifying the central convention in concrete poetry—a convention adopted from the "concrete art" of Swiss painters like Max Bill and their international counterparts. To relate concrete poetry simply to "writing itself," and to such prior writings as the poems of George Herbert or Ezra Pound, is to overlook the far more significant extra-literary conventions of European and Brazilian concrete art.[35]

The second and perhaps still more challenging intercontextual problem concerns works which do not borrow conventions from what one might think of as prior extra-literary discourse (as in the case of Gysin's cut-ups and the work of the concrete poet), but which participate with extra-literary works in the exploration of some new discursive space made available by those technological innovations that Jenny associates with the "intertextual crisis." This kind of problem can be partially exemplified with reference to the varied works of William S. Burroughs. Burroughs is an ideal subject for conventional intertextual studies in so far as some of his novels, such as *Nova Express,* cut up his manuscripts with texts by his favorite authors, and thus constitute what Burroughs himself terms "a composite of many writers living and dead."[36] He is also an author who has both written about and worked with the new technology, experimenting with tape-recorded works, with performances involving live actions and projections, and with collaborative films which fuse the discoveries made in his written cut-ups, his taped work and his performances.[37]

A conventional intertextual approach such as Jenny attempts in his article "La Stratégie de la forme" rapidly constructs a very misleading account of Burroughs. To be fair, the article includes several revealing generalizations, but Jenny confuses these insights by attempting to justify them in terms of Burroughs's prior writing. Diagnosing Burroughs's work as a clear case of "Intertextualmania" ("*La manie intertextuelle*" [281]), Jenny also very interestingly alludes to "the audiovisual medium that determines the work of William S. Burroughs" ("*le médium audiovisual qui détermine l'oeuvre de William Burroughs*" [259]). Unfortunately Jenny's observation functions thematically rather than intercontextually. Instead of tracing the way in which Burroughs has employed audiovisual media not only as a theme in his fiction and essays but also as the means of production of his tapes, performances and films, Jenny establishes an over-reductive connection between speculations in *Electronic Revolution* and Burroughs's oeuvre as a whole, arguing that Burroughs's primary achievement is his formulation of an anarchic writing which offers an antidote to the stupefying discourses of the mass media. Over-reacting to the claim in *Electronic Revolution* that prerecorded cut-ups might serve to "nullify associational lines put down by mass media" (126), Jenny's analysis of Burroughs's use of intertextuality concludes:

> It's a matter of rapidly throwing together various cut-up "techniques" in order to respond to the omnipresence of transmitters feeding us with their dead discourses (mass media, publicity etc.). It's a question of unchaining codes— not the subject any more—so that something will burst out, will escape: words beneath words, personal obsessions. Another kind of word is born which escapes from the totalitarianism of the media but retains their power, and turns against its old masters.

> *Il s'agit de bricoler en hâte des "techniques" de mise en pièces pour répondre à l'omniprésence des émetteurs qui nous nourrissent de leur discours mort (mass media, publicité etc.). Il faut faire délirer les codes—non plus les sujets—et quelque chose se déchirera, se libérera: mots sous les mots, obsessions personnelles. Une autre parole naît qui échappe au totalitarisme des media mais garde leur pouvoir, et se retourne contre ses anciens maîtres.* (281)

At best, this conclusion suggests that Burroughs exemplifies our first mode of intercontextuality, in so far as his writings may be said to adopt the conventions of the mass media (albeit in order to sabotage them). At worst, Jenny's account transforms Burroughs into some kind of T. S. Eliot, shoring fragmentary language against contemporary ruin. Overall, it seems to reiterate the "carnival" approach to the radical text, caricaturing Burroughs's writing as delinquent discourse, kicking against the pricks of majority practice.

In a sense, Burroughs's work is often doing just this. Yet to conclude one's analysis of Burroughs at this point is merely to confirm Andy Warhol's maxim that "People do tend to avoid new realities; they'd rather just add details to the old ones."[38] Burroughs does not simply add negative "details" or negative variants to old discursive practices; he does not just formulate anti-discourses predicated upon and preying upon the familiar written discourses of linear fiction and the familiar technological discourses of the mass media. Rather, his achievement is surely to have discovered the "new reality" of the unfamiliar "hybrid" technological discursive possibilities with which he has modulated language in his various experiment with tape and film. Jenny's error then, is to contextualize Burroughs's work in terms of his familiar and earlier writings, a process that Jean Ricardou terms "restricted intertextuality" ("*intertextualité restrainte*" [the relation of a text to other texts by the same writer]) as opposed to "generalized intertextuality" ("*intertextualité générale*" [the relation of a text to works by other writers]).[39] Had Jenny employed a more rigorous mode of what one might term "restricted intercontextuality," he might have made more profitable connections between Burroughs's work with both written and technological discourses. Had Jenny placed Burroughs within the context of "generalized intercontextuality," his conclusions might have been even more fruitful.

For as an archetypally intercontextual explorer—a writer fascinated by what he terms "effects that have never been produced before"[40]—Burroughs necessitates contextualization among comparable innovators. And in the absence of obvious literary peers, these points of comparison are often best located in extra-literary discursive spaces, such as the one occupied by the German composer Karlheinz Stockhausen, who has similarly advocated "sounds and sound relationships ... that lead us to believe that we have *never heard them before*."[41] One might multiply examples of this aspiration towards hitherto unrealized effects. The advantage of contextualizing Burroughs among fellow researchers such as Stockhausen is that he may then be defined and evaluated more precisely in terms of his particular use of the new media explored simultaneously by other contemporaries, instead of being clumsily typecast as just another tiresome "carnival" artiste, and deemed inconsequential because incompatible with the literary expectations generated by prior literary discourse.

Despite Jonathan Culler's surprising hostility in *The Pursuit of Signs* to comparative studies (especially as practiced by Harold Bloom), a comparative approach is obviously fundamental to this intercontextual perspective. First, the comparison of radical works from both literary and extra-literary discursive spaces permits radical literary works to be identified in two main categories: those which are predicated upon discursive conventions appropriated from the prior discourse of some extra-literary discursive space (such as the collage technique first elaborated in the fine arts), and those which explore concurrently with extra-literary occupants a new, technological discursive space, born of some intertextual crisis (such as the recorded works precipitated by the availability of the tape-recorder). Secondly, the process of gradually comparing different works predicated upon extra-literary discursive conventions, or exploring new, technological, extra-literary discursive spaces, eventually permits evaluation of both the quality and originality of these individual works, and the creative potential of these new discursive practices. This hypothesis may seem singularly unfashionable, particularly since the concept of originality has been decried by theorists like Barthes and poets like Gysin, who have respectively insisted that originality is impossible since the writer may only mix pre-existing words, and that there is thus no such thing as "'the very own words' of anyone . . . living or dead."[42]

Nevertheless, as we have already suggested, Barthes's consideration and inevitable comparison of different occupants of the new technological discursive space of the cinema revealingly prompts his undisguised admiration for what he takes to be the originality of Eisenstein's film stills. Accordingly, Barthes employs the adjective "Eisensteinian" throughout "The Third Meaning," and in addition labels at least one verbal formulation "SME's own word" (53). It would appear, then, that having replaced the myth of the author with the myth of scientific objectivity, Barthes finally refutes this second myth by asking, "but then what is an objective reading?" (60), and by suggesting that new discursive spaces such as the cinema not only precipitate original creativity such as Eisenstein's film stills, but also permit the original theoretical activity exemplified by Eisenstein's new terminology.

In much the same way, Brion Gysin's consideration and inevitable comparison of different occupants of the new discursive space of the "cut-up" has led him to concede that startling originality may well arise even within a textual convention intended to treat words anonymously, "like mere material" (184). Judging Burroughs to be the supreme master of cut-ups (just as Barthes suggests that Eisenstein exhibits a rare mastery of the cinema), Gysin attributes the success of Burroughs's cut-ups to the fact that they were applied to his own unusually original material. According to Gysin, "He covered tons of paper with his words and made them his very own words. . . . Used by another writer who was attempting cut-ups, one single word of Burroughs's vocabulary would run a stain right through the fabric of their prose. . . . One single high-powered Burroughs word could ruin a whole barrel of good everyday words, run the literary rot right through them. One sniff of that prose and you'd say, "Why, that's a Burroughs." (187, 191)

Like Burroughs and Barthes, Gysin has a gift for provocative overstatement. The implication of these remarks seems to be that Burroughs's texts generate something approximating to the "accents" discussed by Barthes and Proust, thereby remaining potent even within a mechanical, cut-up structure. In other words, if Barthes and Gysin assassinate the author when considering texts hypothetically—as mere materials—in order to delineate the conventions of literary competence, they also resurrect the author when they compare different texts—or different literary performances—and discover traces of authorial "accent" in a writer's own words.

The tension between these responses to the author is salutary, for it suggests that far from being "trivial" or "useless," as one might naively suppose the radical text to be, intercontextual creativity is more than likely to precipitate manifestations of what "The Third Meaning" terms the "rare" and the "new" (62), and thereby present fascinating challenges to our habitual assumptions about the production and explication of texts. For some critics, appropriate points of departure for the analysis of texts arising from contemporary intertextual crises will be found only by venturing beyond that conservative intertextuality, situated within the confines of the written text, to problematic intercontextual relations that make sense only in the wider context of the "sum" of old, new and nascent discursive practices and performances. This emphasis upon manifestations of the "rare" and the "new"—which emerge only in performances located beyond the parameters of literary competence—is of course at odds with Culler's defence, in *The Pursuit of Signs,* of an intertextual approach which "courts banality" in being "committed to studying meanings already known or attested within a culture in the hope of formulating the conventions that members of that culture are following" (99).

Yet there is something discomfortingly paradoxical in Culler's modest claim that he would merely "attempt to describe 'literary competence,'" (50), and that within his approach "notions of . . . a superreader ought to be avoided" (51), since in the very process of trouncing such intertextual rivals as Riffaterre for liking "nothing better than outdoing previous readers" (93) and thereby aspiring to be "superreaders," Culler's own critical performance is itself patently "outdoing" Riffaterre and company, and profiling Culler as a "superreader" or "supercritic."

It should be evident, then, that while certain texts and certain critical writings both court and evince the banality of mere "competence," other texts and other critical writings similarly court and evince the rare and the new, in performances "outdoing" the conventions of mere competence, and thereby validating the notion of the "super-writer" or the "super-reader." To deny the existence of such levels of extra-competent super-performance in one's theories, while exemplifying them in one's practice, is a curious delusion, liable to prompt the incompetent and embarrassed silence manifested by no less a rare and new super-reader than Barthes himself, when charged with his authorial—or superauthorial—status by John Weightman. Weightman relates, "In the early days I once asked him how it was, if he did not exist as a subjectivity, that I could recognise his style in everything he said or wrote. His reply was a pitying, ironical smile: trust a crass Englishman to pay a compliment in the form of a sceptical question!"[43]

Burroughs appears to make the same kind of sceptical criticism of this obsession with objectivity in the following passage from *The Naked Lunch*, characteristically intermingling his fascination with riots, his knowledge of obscure medical terminology, and his literary theories: "A battalion of rampant bores prowls the streets and hotel lobbies in search of victims. An intellectual avant-gardist—"Of course the only writing worth considering now is to be found in scientific reports and periodicals"—has given someone a bulbocapnine injection and is preparing to read him a bulletin" (38). Like Weightman, Burroughs intimates that avant-garde intellectuals such as Barthes and Culler are surely mistaken if they consider that everything may be reduced to scientific reports and bulletins. Yet the myth of objectivity appears to have convinced intertextual theorists that the objective concepts of the scriptor, the "banal" act of textual competence, and the anonymous reader whom Barthes would have "without history, biography, psychology" (148) have somehow displaced and replaced the subjectivity of the author, the "original" textual performance, and the super-reader.

If there is obviously a place for the text and the critic that would court "pure" objective banality, it is equally evident that the conceptual and technological intertextual crises of the last three decades have opened up radically new intercontextual creative possibilities which necessitate radically new intercontextual theoretical strategies. Writing to Alan Ansen, in the late fifties, Burroughs memorably formulated his case for "outdoing" the banalities of prior fictional discourse, confessing to feel "complete dissatisfaction with everything I have done in writing.... Unless writing has the danger and immediacy, the urgency of bullfighting, it is nowhere to my way of thinking.... I am tired of sitting behind the lines with an imperfect recording device receiving inaccurate bulletins.... I must reach the Front."[44] Intertextual theory and practice should similarly look beyond the banalities of prior literary discourse and prior literary expectations in order to assess the immediate implications of the intercontextual "Front."

postmodernity, métaphore manquée, and the myth of the trans-avant-garde }

THE ERAS OF MODERNISM AND OF POST-modernism are eras of conceptual, existential, and technological transition. Both in the years between the 1880s and the 1930s, and the years between the 1930s and the 1980s, cultural critics have been embarrassed by the proliferation of the new; by new ways of conceiving cultural reality, new ways of evaluating existence, and new ways of mechanizing cultural reality.[1]

These periods of "intertextual crisis" afflict both the creator and the critic alike.[2] As László Moholy-Nagy intimates in *Vision in Motion* (1947), the dilemma of modernist culture derives from the difficulties of working within the "new dimension" of "a new science and a new technology which could be used for the realization of all-embracing relationships." According to Moholy-Nagy, "Contemporary man threw himself into the experience of these new relationships. But saturated with old ideologies, he approached the new dimension with obsolete practices and failed to translate newly gained experience into emotional language and cultural reality."[3]

Jean Baudrillard has more recently suggested that contemporary modes of "old ideologies" and "obsolete practices" similarly obfuscate the quality of those cultural practices precipitated by the "new science" and "new technology" of our own times, observing: "Wanting to apply our old criteria ... we no doubt misapprehend what may be the occurrence, in this sensory sphere, of something new, ecstatic and obscene." These lines from Baudrillard's 1983 essay "The Ecstasy of Communication" refer to his hypothesis that the postmodern mass media sometimes generate a disturbingly euphoric impact, or what he terms the "obscene delerium of communication" or "negative ecstacy."[4]

This hypothesis is noteworthy, because in many of his other writings, such as "The Precession of Simulacra," of 1978, Baudrillard argues that the mass media neutralize reality by "substituting signs of the real for the real itself."[5] Accordingly, the mass media become what Baudrillard colorfully characterizes as "murderers of the real" ("Simulacra," 10), and the late twentieth century becomes an era in which "truth, reference and objective causes have ceased to exist" ("Simulacra," 6), and in which "the whole system becomes *weightless*, it is no longer anything but a gigantic simulacrum—not unreal, but a simulacrum, never again exchanging itself for what is real, but exchanging in itself, in an uninterrupted circuit without reference or circumference." ("Simulacra," 10-11; emphasis mine).

Baudrillard explains the process by which the imagery of the mass media becomes "weightless" by charting four phases in the neutralization of the image. According to this schema,

—it is the reflection of a basic reality
—it masks and perverts a basic reality
—it masks the absence of a basic reality
—it bears no relation to any reality whatever:
    it is its own pure simulacrum. ("Simulacra," 11)

As Ross Gibson has observed, this chronology begs comparison with Renato Poggioli's more positive analysis of avant-garde strategies in terms of the cycle of "Activism," "Antagonism, Nihilism," and "Agonism," and the subsequent resurgence of "Activism." As Gibson remarks, "Poggioli's format bends to circularity on the belief that although outmoded referents or systems of the real are constantly rejected and discredited in the dynamics of history, there is always an active, constructive impetus concomitant to agonism so long as life continues."[6]

Poggioli's chronology remains very much an analysis of the *macrostructure* of the avant-garde, that is, it only delineates the most general strategies of the avant-garde. This overview is usefully complemented by the more specific analysis that the French composer Michel Chion makes of the *microstructure* of *individual* avant-garde movements. According to Chion, each movement falls into four main phases: the "zero" or elementary, polemical phase, in which new materials and techniques are tested without any particular purpose in mind; the "imitative" phase, in which new materials and techniques are employed conservatively, in accordance with the conventions of established discourses; the "purist" phase, in which new materials and techniques are employed strictly in their own terms; and the final "hybrid" phase, in which all of these possibilities are consciously and confidently intermingled.[7]

Michel Chion's scheme may be further modified in its turn. First, the "zero" phase of avant-garde creativity may be subdivided in terms of two different kinds of impulses: the "primitive" (or the attempt to adopt earlier, pre-technological models) and the "futurist" (or the attempt to work with new and emergent technological possibilities). Second, if one conceives of any cultural period in terms of three general discursive area—that of "historical banalities" (or works reflecting the general concerns of any era in a conservative, uncomplicated manner); that of "mainstream experiments" (or those works variously extending and contorting the general conventions exemplified by "historical banalities"); and that of "avant-garde experiments" (or those works which not merely extend or contort accepted conventions but which recklessly experiment with new, unfamiliar discursive possibilities, be this by resurrecting "primitive" models or by exploring "futurist" technological possibilities)—then it may be possible to identify certain overlaps between the most extreme "mainstream" experiments of an era and the "hybrid" experiments of this era's avant-garde. For example, one might postulate that postmodern creativity witnesses a certain overlap between the most daring technological experiments of a "mainstream" writer like Samuel Beckett (such as *Krapp's Last Tape*) and the more conservative "hybrid" experiments of avant-garde creators such as the sound poet Henri Chopin, the composer Robert Ashley, and the installation artist Edward Kienholz.[8]

Placed in diagrammatic summary, then, postmodern culture might be conceived of in three contemporaneous and occasionally overlapping discursive areas: that of "historical banalities," such as the work of popular writers like Ian Fleming and the popular or commercial mass media; that of "mainstream" experiments such as the novels and films of writings like Samuel Beckett, William S. Burroughs, Alain Robbe-Grillet, and Marguerite Duras; and that of

"avant-garde" experiments, such as the multimedia creativity of still more experimental poets, writers, composers and artists. It is, of course, difficult to exemplify
this latter category because it is not generally known by the majority of readers,
spectators, listeners, and critics. Nevertheless, one might follow Chion's schema,
or our revised version of Chion's schema, and suggest that among contemporary
avant-garde creators, a *primitive* "zero" impulse appears to be present in the work
of poets such as Jerome Rothenberg, while a *futurist* "zero" impulse might be
exemplified by the early "machine poems" of Brion Gysin. Similarly, an "imitative" tendency might be discerned among collaborations between poets and
composers, such as François Dufrêne's work with the composer Pierre Henry.
"Purist" avant-garde works might include the "audiopoèmes" of Henri Chopin;
while "hybrid" works might number the various performances and multimedia
installations by Chopin and other sound poets, by composers like Robert Ashley,
and by artists like Edward Keinholz. At times these hybrid avant-garde creations
overlap with the most extreme experiments by mainstream postmodernists such
as Beckett and Burroughs. The following schema emerges:

Historical Banalities	Mainstream Experiments	Avant-Garde Experiments
Ian Fleming Commercial Mass Media	Beckett, Burroughs, Robbe-Grillet, Duras	Primitive (Rothenberg) *zero* Futurist (Gysin) *imitative* (Dufrêne) *purist* (Chopin)
	Overlap of extreme mainstream works with most accessible *hybrid* avant-garde works	*hybrid* (Performances and multimedia installa- tions by Chopin, Ashley and Kienholz)

As the following pages will suggest, Baudrillard and such disparate cultural
theorists as Roland Barthes and Achille Bonito Oliva consistently misread the complexity of postmodern cultural practices by predicating their theories upon only a
partial sampling of the various modes of postmodern creativity outlined above.

More often than not, their theories emphasize examples of historical banalities, "mainstream experiments," and such sections of avant-garde creativity as
its primitive "zero" phase and its "imitative" phase (because these tendencies

lend themselves most easily to derision in terms of their excessively "rigorous" or "nihilistic" qualities). In other words, there is an alarming tendency for cultural theorists to exaggerate the significance of familiar, historically "banal" discourses; to reduce mainstream and avant-garde experiments to the categories of familiar, prior discourse; and to overlook the unfamiliar, creative potential of the futurist, purist, and hybrid phases of contemporary avant-garde creativity. As Baudrillard's writings indicate, this reductive perspective rapidly persuades the critic that the postmodern era is a period of stasis and stultification.

Baudrillard's analyses of the mass-media eventually argue that postmodern technology inevitably generates—or *degenerates* into—"models of a real without origin or reality: a hyperreal" ("Simulacra," 2). Thus, according to Baudrillard's essay on "The Implosion of Meaning in the Media and the Implosion of the Social in the Masses" (1980); "*Meaning ... becomes impossible*" and it is therefore "*futile to dream of a revolution through either form or content, since both the medium and the real now form a single inscrutable nebula.*"[9] Put another way, in one of Baudrillard's key images, the mass media's "*bombardment of signs*" invariably "*dissolves mean*ing" and worse still, appears to "dissolve" its audience, which mutates into "an atomized, nuclearized, molecularized" blob of "fluid, mute masses" ("Implosion" 140; emphasis mine). At this point in Baudrillard's meditations, cultural analysis itself begins to mutate into something exceedingly close to science fiction.

Fanciful as it may be, Baudrillard's theory calls a number of similar formulations to mind when employing such figures as its allusion to the mass media's "bombardment of signs," and to this extent, Baudrillard's speculations fall into a long line of apocalyptic analyses of cultural change. At their most pessimistic, these analyses argue that "bombardment" by new "signs" signals the demise of all meaning, the impossibility of progress, and the collapse of cultural cohesion. At their most optimistic, in writings such as Moholy-Nagy's *Vision in Motion*, analyses of the emergence of new signs suggest that these unfamiliar discourses signal the advent of new modes of meaning and new ways of formulating reality.

Pessimistic—or conservative—variants of this bombardment thesis may be traced back to Max Nordau's *Degeneration*, a volume first published in 1895, in which Nordau fiercely condemned the "degenerate" symbolists and impressionists. Claiming that these pioneers of modernism simply produced symptoms of "the vertigo and whirl of our frenzied life," Nordau dismissed their works as the "consequences of states of fatigue and exhaustion" and as the manifestations of "degeneration and hysteria" peculiar to "weak-minded or mentally-unbalanced persons."[10]

These conclusions stem from Nordau's thesis that certain degenerates could not survive the "constant state of nervous excitement" (*Degeneration*, 35) peculiar to modernization and "the perpetual noises, and the various sights in the streets of a large town" (*Degeneration*, 39). Turning his attention from the complexity of the metropolis to the mass media of modernization, Nordau muses upon the way in which the "humblest village inhabitant" is bombarded by information "if he do but read his paper" and consequently "takes part . . . by a continuous and receptive curiosity, in the thousand events which take place in all the parts of the globe, and interests himself simultaneously in the issue of a revolution in Chile, in a bush-war in East Africa, a massacre in North China, a famine in Russia, a street-row in Spain, and an international exhibition in North America." (*Degeneration*, 39).

Nordau associates both the shock of the new and what one might term the "shock of the *news*" with the ways in which the noises and sights of urban life and the "constant expectations of the newspaper" continually cost our brains "wear and tear" (*Degeneration*, 39) and ultimately destroy "the equilibrium of thousands of brains which lacked staying power" (*Degeneration*, 37). With the advantages of hindsight it is easy to criticize Nordau's exaggerated accounts of the trauma of modernization and his dubious diagnosis of such ailments as "railway-spine" and "railway-brain" (*Degeneration*, 41). Offering a far more positive "bombardment" thesis, Futurists such as F. T. Marinetti and Luigi Russolo welcomed the simultaneous sensations of the modern city and, as Marinetti's "Synthesist Theatre" manifesto of 1915 testifies, aspired towards new technological modes of creativity commensurate with the ways in which "reality . . . bombards us with . . . fragments of inter-connected events."[11]

While Marinetti and Russolo lacked appropriate technology, the postmodern mass media, the "mainstream" creators of postmodernity, and the postmodern avant-garde all potentially possess means of realizing the Futurists' wildest aspirations. Indeed, as should be abundantly evident, it is precisely the availability of postmodern technology which differentiates its cultural practices from those of modernism. Ironically, the surprisingly circumscribed perspective of Baudrillard's most influential writings give little indication of the positive potential of postmodern creativity. Comparison of Baudrillard's conclusions with those of rather more lucid postmodern writers, such as William S. Burroughs, proves particularly revealing.

Like Baudrillard's theories, Burroughs's writings unexpectedly fluctuate between flights of fictional fancy and perceptive insights into the neutralizing nature of the mass media. Somewhat as Baudrillard preposterously postulates that Los Angeles is "nothing more than an immense script and a perpetual motion picture" ("Simulacra," 26), Burroughs cynically quips: "The sky is thin as paper. The whole place could go up in ten minutes. That's the charm of Los Angeles."[12] As we have remarked, Baudrillard's more sober speculations consider the ways in which the mass media's "bombardment of signs" ("Implosion," 140) dissolve all meaning. Burroughs similarly observes: "If you're absolutely bombarded with images from passing trucks and cars and televisions and newspapers, you become blunted and this makes a permanent haze in front of your eyes, you can't see anything."[13] Again, just as Baudrillard's essay on "The Orders of Simulacra" asserts that "the role of the message" in the "modern media" is "no longer information, but . . . control" ("Simulacra," 119), Burroughs's interviews of 1969 elaborate the implications of an era in which "image and word are the instruments of control used by the press" (*The Job*, 51).

Despite these and other parallels, Baudrillard's and Burroughs's theories rapidly part company. For while Baudrillard usually emphatically associates "bombardment" by the mass media, and the mass media's "interrogation by converging light/sound/ultra-sound waves" ("Implosion," 140), with the dissolution of all meaning and with the permanent disruption of any "revolution through either form or content" ("Implosion," 142), Burroughs argues that radical creativity may well emulate and eclipse the impact of the mass media. Thus, while Burroughs concedes that "the novelistic form is probably outmoded," he also surmises that writing itself may "compete with television and photo magazines" once writers "develop more precise techniques producing the same effect on the reader as a lurid action photo" (*The Job*, 11). (As later chapters will indicate, Baudrillard's most recent writings increasingly share Burroughs's confidence in the positive energies of photographic media.)

One might define this aspiration in terms of Burroughs's confidence in modes of *conceptual* revolution, that is, his belief that innovations in one discourse (in this instance, television and photography) may be replicated within another discourse (in this instance, writing). In much the same way, Burroughs has advocated experiments with cut-up and montage techniques derived from painting in order to close the "gap" between writing and painting and thereby open "a whole new dimension to writing" (*The Job*, 12).

At the same time, Burroughs has also conceived of, and at times worked with, different kinds of *technological* revolution, such as recording tape and film.[14] As the very title of *Electronic Revolution* (1971) suggests, the essays in this treatise look beyond the strategies which Burroughs dismisses as "19th century tactics" and consider ways of "bringing the revolution into the 20th century which includes, above all, the mass media."[15] Burroughs argues, for instance, that "You could cause a riot easily. All you have to do is take the tape recorders with riot material already recorded . . . When you start playing it back, you're going to have more scuffles . . . a recorded whistle will bring cops, a recorded gunshot when they have their guns out . . . well . . . it's as simple as that." Discussing the implications of technology for more creative enterprises, Burroughs has in turn speculated that "ever-expanding technical facilities . . . can create effects that have never been produced before, thus opening a new frontier for poets."[16]

Although Burroughs admits that his own technological experiments have proved "rather inconclusive" (*The Job*, 16) and adds that nowadays he does not even possess a tape-recorder,[17] Burroughs's writings, unlike those of Baudrillard, insist that *conceptual* and *technological* experiments may "break down the principal instruments of control, which are word and image, and to some extent . . . nullify them" (*The Job*, 19).

In other words, whereas Baudrillard's discussions of multi-mediated simulation exaggerate the trauma of the "bombardment" by the postmodern mass media (just as Max Nordau exaggerates the impact of the modernist mass media), Burroughs rather more helpfully intimates that the most negative energies of the postmodern mass media may to some extent be neutralized in their turn and that, far from transforming whole populations into what Baudrillard calls "fluid, mute masses" ("Implosion," 140), these mass media only influence a fraction of their audience. Cautiously evaluating the "bombardment" of newsprint, Burroughs observes: "Newspapers are looking for statistical effects, not expecting to get every individual—if they get something like thirty or twenty per cent they're doing well."[18]

At their most fanciful, Burroughs's theories culminate in his speculation that language itself might be refined into a deadly weapon. Adumbrating this thesis in an interview of 1972, Burroughs malevolently mused, "If I really knew how to write, I could write something that someone would read and it would kill them. . . . any effect you want could be produced if you were precise enough in your knowledge or technique."[19] To date, there appear no reasons why this speculation should be taken literally. The interesting point here, however, is not so much the sinister or disruptive quality of Burroughs's project as his refreshing emphasis upon the evocative quality of language, and his equally salutary enthusiasm for various kinds of innovatory "knowledge or technique." In this respect, Burroughs seems admirably sensitive to the three defining characteristics of postmodern culture: its *existential shifts*, its *conceptual shifts,* and its *technological shifts.*

If one accepts that modernism might be periodized from the 1880s, when Symbolism and Impressionism heralded the avalanche of subsequent modernist "isms" (such as Cubism, Expressionism, Futurism, Dadaism, Suprematism, Constructivism, and Surrealism), to the early 1930s, when the first writings of Jean-Paul Sartre, Raymond Queneau, and Samuel Beckett revealed the emergence of postmodern modes of creativity (such as the "new novel," the "anti-novel," the Theater of the Absurd, magic realism, beat poetry, concrete poetry, abstract expressionism, pop art, op art, happenings, minimal art, conceptual art, and so on, right up to the trans-avant-garde), then one might very generally distinguish the terms of postmodernity from the temper of modernity in terms of a fairly prevalent *existential shift.*

Despite such exceptions as the work of Edvard Munch or George Grosz, the prevailing temper of modernism seems to be one of confidence and wonder, be this the mysterious wonder of Paul Gauguin, the sensual wonder of Pierre Auguste Renoir, or the more abstract wonder of artists like Jean (Hans) Arp or Kasimir Malevish. By contrast, it is not difficult to detect a prevailing sense of pessimism and disenchantment in much early and mid-trajectory postmodern art, be this the solitary isolation of Alberto Giacometti's figures, the solipsistic writhings of Francis Bacon's figures, or the more mysterious, apocalyptic landscapes and figures of trans-avant-garde painters such as Enzo Cucchi.

The same distinction recurs when we consider modernist and postmodernist literature. Early postmodern writers usually tend to subvert and negate the optimism of modernism. Whereas a rainy day or cloudy seascape could delight modernist artists like James Abbot McNeil Whistler and modernist writers like James Joyce and Marcel Proust, pioneer postmodernists such as Beckett and Burroughs transform the harmonies of modernist discourse into their own peculiarly solipsic and apocalyptic evocations of incoherence and desolation. This transition from metaphorical unity to the kind of disunity that one might associate with the failed metaphor, or the *métaphore manquée,* is memorably exemplified by Beckett's and Burroughs's respective variations upon the justly celebrated concluding paragraph to Joyce's story "The Dead."

At the end of "The Dead," Joyce's hero, Gabriel Conroy, looks out onto gently falling snow as he reassesses his existence during a moment of cosmic harmony in which he attains both private revelation and a certain solidarity with "all the living and the dead." Joyce's story concludes: "A few light taps upon the pane made him turn to the window. It had begun to snow again. He watched sleepily the flakes, silver and dark, falling obliquely against the lamplight . . . It was falling on the dark central place, on the treeless hills, falling softly upon the Bog of Allen and, farther westward, softly falling into the dark mutinous Shannon waves . . . His soul swooned slowly as he heard the snow falling faintly through the universe and faintly falling, like the descent of their last end, upon all the living and the dead."[20] Here, then, an ecstacy of alliteration and permutation interlinks Joyce's softly swooning hero with past and present, the living and the dead, and, indeed, the entirety of Ireland.

Proust similarly associates such spectacles with a certain rather pregnant sense of consolation in an early essay entitled "Clouds" of 1885 or 1886, in which the artist-as-a-misty-eyed-young-man expostulates: "Oh beautiful clouds, thank you for all the comfort that you have given to those who are unhappy. For your approach fills them with that melancholy reverie, with that poetic sadness, which alone may palliate our cruellest sufferings."[21] In their different ways, both Joyce's and Proust's heroes find themselves comforted and, indeed, uplifted by scattered showers or distant clouds. Generating a sense of cosmic harmony, or a sense of "poetic sadness," these natural phenomena fill the modernist hero with wonder before the metaphorical unity of all things, and leave this species more or less quite literally "singing in the rain."

By contrast, most early postmodern fiction seems distinguished by its paucity of metaphorical harmony and by the prevalence of its evocations of incoherence, chaos, and disintegration. To this extent, Baudrillard quite properly describes the early postmodern situation as that of "the schizo . . . living in the greatest confusion" ("Ecstacy," 133), just as Fredric Jameson associates the postmodern temper with the "schizophrenic . . . experience of isolated, disconnected, discontinuous material signifiers which fail to link up into a coherent sequence."[22]

For example, toward the end of his first novel, *Dream of Fair to Middling Women* (1932), Beckett elaborately parodies the last paragraph of Joyce's "The

Dead," reducing modernist harmonies to his own highly solipsistic brand of postmodernist banalities and cynicism. Shortly before the end of this novel, its hero, Belacqua, sits down in the rain, upon the pavement, before his final exit "in a panic of discomfort," and contemplates the surrounding vista.[23] Initially, Beckett seems to imitate Joyce's lines. Belacqua notices that "The wind had fallen ... and the rain fell in a uniform untroubled manner. It fell upon the bay, the champaign-land and the mountains, and notably upon the central bog it fell with a rather desolate uniformity" (*Dream*, 239).

Having set the scene in a Joycean manner, Beckett promptly "unsets" it in a thoroughly postmodern and Beckettian manner by remorselessly trivializing this incident. Belacqua neither swoons with profound self-knowledge like Joyce's hero nor attains the kind of poetic palliation that the Proustian protagonist receives beneath cloudy skies. Instead, Belacqua deplores the way in which his imagination makes metaphorical mischief by confusing clouds with the Welsh Hills. Proust usually welcomes such confusions, cherishing "those optical illusions which make up our first impressions,"[24] and his principal hero, Marcel, floats through *A la recherche du temps perdu* in an endless haze of metaphorical musings. Belacqua, by contrast, has little patience for such perceptual fancies and cynically comments: "What would Ireland be, though, without this rain of hers. Rain is part of her charm, the impression one enjoys before landscape in Ireland ... of seeing it through a veil of tears ... to what source can this benefit be ascribed if not to our "*incontinent skies?*" (*Dream*, 239–40; emphasis mine). This irreverent reference to Ireland's "incontinent skies" precipitates the narrator's brutal dismissal of metaphorical confusions, as he grimly concludes: "Standing on the Big Sugarloaf, it may be objected ... the Welsh Hills are frequently plainly to be discerned. Don't cod yourselves. Those are clouds that you see, or your own nostalgia" (*Dream*, 240).

As William S. Burroughs has observed, Beckett's writings tend to evoke "inward" experience (and, one might add, "inward" confusions), whereas Burroughs's own writings tend to explore "what's out there" (or modes of social, or "outward," *confusions*).[25] This distinction becomes particularly apparent if one considers the way in which Burroughs's *Dead Fingers Talk* (1963) transforms Joycean harmonies into an apocalyptic vision of urban chaos, as one of its characters hears and sees "Empty streets and from radios in empty houses a twanging sound of sirens that rose and fell vibrating the windows—The air was full of luminous grey flakes falling softly on crumpled cloth bodies—The street led to an open square—He could see people running now suddenly collapse on to a heap of clothes—The grey flakes were falling heavier, falling through all the buildings of the city."[26] By the end of this episode, Burroughs depicts the disintegration of existence as a whole, describing "Panic through streets of image—dead nitrous streets of an old film set—Paper moon and muslin trees in the black silver sky great rents as the cover of the world rained down in luminous film flakes" (*Dead Fingers*, 172).

By now it should be clear, then, that one definition of the temper of early postmodern fiction might spring from the distinctive dichotomy between the *optimistic*, all-encompassing, predominantly *metaphorical* vision of modernist writers such as Joyce and Proust and the *pessimistic*, all-fragmenting, predominantly *antimetaphorical* vision of early postmodernists such as Beckett and Burroughs. In addition to this *existential shift* between modernism and postmodernism, one might also identify a second and, at times, overlapping series of *conceptual shifts* between the poetics of modernism and postmodernism.

These conceptual shifts generally simplify, amplify, or systematize the formal innovations of modernism. For example, the slashed canvasses of the Italian artist Lucio Fontana might be said to simplify the impressionist or expressionist brush stroke into one dramatic, quintessential gesture. Similarly, the dazzling black and white undulating lines of Bridget Riley's op art seems to synthesize the kinetic illusion that Futurist artists attempted to illustrate in paintings such as Balla's famous *Leash in Motion* of 1912. At the other extreme, the monumental minimal sculptures of Richard Serra, such as *One Ton Prop* (1969), might be said to amplify Malevich's famous *Basic Suprematist Element: The Square* (1913) into huge, three-dimensional proportions. In much the same way, Robert Rauschenberg's canvasses and collages appear to amplify the innovations of modernists like Kurt Schwitters. In this respect, postmodernism becomes modernism writ large. In both cases, the innovatory *concepts* of modernism find refinement, elaboration, and fulfillment in the works of postmodernism.

As we have suggested, this kind of conceptual shift may also culminate in the systematization of the modernist gesture: a process by which tentative aspiration attains methodical consolidation. The Russian artist Ivan Puni's *Relief with Dish* (1915) might be said to find postmodern systematization in the "snare" pictures of Daniel Spoerri. Similarly, the Dadaist Walter Serner's "Poem" of 1917, which in fact consisted of the performance or action of approaching an empty armchair, bowing deeply, and placing a bunch of flowers upon it, appears to anticipate the way in which the Fluxus group systematically elaborated this kind of gestural, performance art in their happenings and events throughout the sixties. If it is true, as the veteran Dadaists Hans Richter and Raoul Hausmann argue,[27] that Puni's relief and Serner's performance carried more substantial political and poetical impact than their contemporary variations, then this too exemplifies the existential shift between the relatively serious and confident experiments of modernism and the more frivolous, world-weary, and cynical initial rituals of postmodernism.

The most positive momentum in both early and late postmodern culture may also be defined in terms of a third general category: that of the *technological shift* or the process by which modernist aspirations find realization, and perhaps elaboration, via postmodern technology. Walter Benjamin nicely annunciates this process when pondering the way in which avant-garde art "aspires to effects which could only be fully obtained with a changed technical standard, that is to say, in a new art form."[28] Benjamin exemplifies this shift by suggesting that the Dadaists' pictorial and literary experiments sought "effects which the public today seeks in the film" ("The Work of Art," 239). One might additionally exemplify this kind of technological shift with reference to the ways in which the kinetic constructions of postmodernists like Jean Tinguely and Nicolas Schöffer respectively transform such modernist "blueprints" as Francis Picabia's drawings and Marcel Duchamp's kinetic experiments (for example, *Bicycle Wheel* of 1913 and his rotating glass plates of 1920) into tangible modes of "machine art."

Avant-garde postmodern literature may in turn be defined by equally affirmative conceptual and technological shifts. As I have argued elsewhere, the work of the concrete poets variously refines, amplifies, and systematizes the Dadaists' and Futurists' experiments with spatial—as opposed to linear—typography, and have similarly adapted certain conceptual paradigms from modernist art, in order to bring postmodern literature "up to date," as it were, with Modernist and postmodernist painting.[29] Very generally, concrete poetry might be considered an attempt to organize language with the same geometrical rigor and coherence with which modernists like Malevich and postmodernists like Max Bill have manipulated form and color. At the other extreme, Burroughs's cut-ups might be defined as attempts to bring literature "up to date" with the more haphazard experiments of modernism. In this respect, as Burroughs himself admits, his cut-ups systematize the early experiments with aleatory composition of modernists like Tristan Tzara (*Paris Review,* 24).

In addition to these *conceptual shifts,* by means of which postmodernist writing variously appropriates and elaborates the aspirations of the literary and artistic avant-gardes of modernism, avant-garde postmodern writing also evinces a number of *technological shifts.* Concrete poets like Ian Hamilton Finlay have worked with new media such as neon lighting, while sound poets, text-sound composers, and experimental novelists like Burroughs have all worked with tape-recorded language and sounds, producing *sonomontages—* or the kind of "radio art" anticipated by the manifestos of such modernist avant-gardists as Marinetti.

It is tempting, perhaps, to overlook the crucial technological creativity of postmodernism—or to misinterpret postmodern technology as a source of stasis, superficiality, and so on, as Baudrillard argues in "On Nihilism" (1981) when postulating that "post-modernity . . . is the immense process of the destruction of meaning."[30] Reducing history to an ever more nihilistic scenario, Baudrillard contrasts postmodernity with its forebear, modernity, which he defines as "the radical destruction of appearances" ("On Nihilism," 10), and seems to anticipate a future without history, in which "The Year 2000 Will Not Take Place."[31]

The problem with this analysis is, of course, that it only considers one side of the dialectic between destruction and construction, between degeneration and generation, and between dissolution and innovation. As Baudrillard more persuasively postulates, when discussing the "negative ecstasy" ("Ecstacy," 132) generated by mass media such as radio, postmodern technology simultaneously inaugurates both the neutralization and the acceleration of cultural practices. As Roland Barthes and Jean-François Lyotard perceptively stipulate in two of their more persuasive paragraphs, the innovations and accelerations of postmodern cultural practices are especially baffling because they transcend the taxonomy of prior theoretical discourse. In Barthes's terms, postmodernity (which he does not really mention as such) is that which precedes theory insofar as it may be "born technically, occasionally even aesthetically," well before it is "born theoretically."[32] Creative essence, then, precedes analytical existence.

Put in Lyotard's terms, *creativity precedes theoretical legislation.* To this extent, the cultural theorist must necessarily suspend theoretical disbelief and *neutralize* all the sacred cows, clichés, and categories of prior cultural and critical discourse in order to apprehend the innovations of postmodernity in their own unfamiliar terms. For as Lyotard observes, "A postmodern artist or writer is in the position of a philosopher: the text he writes, the work he produces are not in principle governed by pre-established rules, and they cannot be judged according to a determining judgement, by applying familiar categories to the text or to the work. . . . the artist and the writer, then, are working without rules in order to formulate *the rules of what will have been done.*"[33]

The weaknesses of much postmodern cultural theory arise precisely from its author' reluctance to suspend, and perhaps sacrifice, their "pre-established rules." Somewhat as Shakespeare's Macduff protests "All my pretty ones?/Did you say all?," cultural critics seem extremely reluctant to sacrifice *all* their pretty preestablished suppositions. In consequence, postmodern critical theory all too frequently caricatures postmodern cultural practices in terms of simplistic existential and conceptual shifts, and all but ignores the positive implications of the crucial technological shifts which, perhaps more than any other factor, determine the specificity of postmodern creativity.

As we have suggested, this process of over-simplification becomes particularly explicit if one considers the surprisingly similar ways in which Achille Bonito Oliva and Roland Barthes discuss their favorite aspects of postmodern culture. It is perhaps most instructive to begin by examining the ways in which Oliva defends the neo-Expressionist painting that he christens the "trans-avant-garde" in his volume entitled *Trans-avantgarde International.*[34] As becomes apparent, Oliva's polemic repeatedly exhibits the same kinds of prejudices and preconceptions that similarly, though somewhat less obviously, inhibit the insights of Roland Barthes's early theoretical writings in *Critical Essays* and *Image-Music-Text.* Arguably, Barthes's later speculations, in *Camera Lucida,* make amends for these initial misconceptions.

Picking up the prevalent refrain that the postmodern era is "a generalized situation of catastrophe" in which "the very idea of progress has entered into a crisis situation" (48), and affirming Baudrillard's theory that ours is an age which witnesses "the dissolution of TV into life, the dissolution of life into TV" ("Simulacra," 55), Oliva argues that the postmodern mass media inaugurate an epoch of "indifference" in which such events as the "tragedy of Vietnam" have found themselves "played out . . . before the indifference of the eyes of America as a pure, spectacular image which lost dramatic depth and was flattened on the screen as pure appearance and disappearance" (147).

This observation leads, in turn, to Oliva's claim that the painterly gestures of trans-avant-garde painting are alone capable of "restoring to the image the semantic depth that appears to have been cancelled by mass civilization" (148). This claim is certainly stirring. Ironically, Oliva repeatedly contradicts it in the main sections of his argument and, as becomes evident, insists that trans-avant-garde painting, like the images of the mass media, is an art of "uninhibited superficiality" in which the image is "relieved of any weight it may have borne" (68). In other words, like Baudrillard, Achille Bonito Oliva finally subscribes to the fancy that the postmodern era is one in which "the whole system becomes weightless" ("Simulacra," 10).

Oliva prepares the way to this conclusion by asserting (rather than in any way demonstrating) that, as Baudrillard also argues, it is "futile to dream of a revolution through either form or content" ("Implosion," 142). In Oliva's formulation, the aforementioned "generalized situation of catastrophe" (48) peculiar to our time "has caused the historical optimism of the avant-garde—the idea of progress inherent in its experimentation with new techniques and new materials—to collapse"(8). Accordingly, Oliva rejects the whole idea of evaluating art in terms of revolution or progress, arguing that, "If art no longer sustains the myth of experimenting with new techniques and new materials, if its advancement and its currentness do not depend on the use of procedures connected with the avant-garde tradition, obviously it is no longer possible to judge it on the basis of such parameters" (82).

Oliva's argument hinges on a significant "if," and upon his eccentric indifference toward what he variously derides as the "myth" (82), the "superstitions" (46), the "euphoric idea" (40), and the "snug harbor" (48), of experimentation. Despite the fact that exhibitions such as Frank Popper's *Electra: Electricity and Electronics in 20th Century Art* (Musée d'Art Moderne de la Ville de Paris, 1983) testify to the potential of "new techniques and new materials,"[35] Oliva effortlessly rejects "the tyranny of newness" (84) and what he calls "the technological fetish" (81) in favor of what we might term the "tyranny of prior discourse" and the "pre-technological fetish."

Much of Oliva's hostility to avant-garde and technological art derives from his understandable impatience with "the impersonality" (6) of the art of the seventies (which he rather narrowly associates with minimal and conceptual art). In its place, Oliva advocates the revived subjectivity of "manual skill" and "a pleasure of execution which brings the tradition of painting back into art" (6). According to Oliva's argument, trans-avant-garde painting accomplishes these aims by "overcoming the pure experimentalism of techniques and new materials" (74) and by substituting a sort of "precarious eroticism" (64), along with "the pleasure of representing imperceptible notions" (32), for the minimalists' and the conceptualists' tendency "to diminish and annul every trace of subjectivity" (31). Rejecting the "puritanical rigor" (31) and the "geometric rigor" of what he loosely terms "past art experiences," Oliva advocates an art of "Oppulence" (34); an art of "eclectic association" (76); an art that "combines hot and cold, concrete and abstract, day and night, in a timeless and pervasive intertexture" (22); and an art which also obligingly permits the recovery of "the genius loci," or "the anthropological roots of the cultural territory inhabited by the artist" (76).

Paradoxically, the substance of Oliva's thesis insists that this supposedly erotic, eclectic, anthropologically specific, and semantically deep art is primarily an art of whimsical *surface*. It is an art of the "bewildered image" (16), of the "gentle constellation" (58), and of the "soft object"; an art, then, which like some lightly-boiled Humpty Dumpty sits indecisively "between invention and convention" (20), "between comic and tragic" (50), and "between turbulence and serenity, drama and comedy, myth and everyday occurrence, tragedy and irony" (66). As Oliva's "betweens" accumulate, one becomes aware that his theory of trans-avant-garde painting conceives not so much of a *fusion* of the comic and tragic, and so on, as a *diffusion* of these qualities: a middle way which at best generates a certain hedonistic "intensity" as it "lets the image ride without asking where it comes from or where it is going, following drifts of pleasure which also re-establish the primacy of the intensity of the work over that of the technique" (66).

Oliva specifies that this unreflective, uncritical mode of "bewildered," "gentle," and "soft" art avoids and evades and, indeed, neutralizes all depth and all profundity by "displaying . . . *flexible laterality*": a quality that Oliva defines as the process of "translating the historic depth of the recovered languages into *a disenchanted and uninhibited superficiality*" (68; emphasis mine). Bringing everything to the surface or to "the skin" (62) of painting, the art of the transavant-garde not only *diffuses* the comic and the tragic, by insinuating itself above and between them, but as the following lines suggest also appears to *defuse* their explosive content. For, as Oliva specifies, the generation of "uninhibited superficiality" means "putting drama, myth and tragedy in such a condition that they do nothing more than afford an occasion for an image that is *relieved of any weight that it may have born*" (68; emphasis mine).

By way of rider, Oliva adds that the weightless images arising from this uninhibited superficiality" are to some extent "quick and illusive as the electronic images of television" (68). If the images of trans-avant-garde painting differ at all from those of television, then it is because "Trans-avantgarde painting slows down this speed in the viscosity of painted matter, and thereby introduces a protracted time, a duration which echoes art's eternal desire for immortality" (68). In other words, trans-avant-garde painting effects a *conceptual shift* by containing and restraining television within its own painterly terms, "shifting it from the speed of the television image to the viscous slowness of the production time of painting" (147–18). The problem with this account of the trans-avant-garde, which, as we have seen, claims that trans-avant-garde painting "is now the only avant-garde possible" (48), is that it drastically oversimplifies the complexity of postmodern creativity. Oliva's hypotheses travesty each of the "shifts" with which we have attempted to define postmodernity. First, while asserting that the past decades represent an era of "catastrophe," Oliva contends that trans-avant-garde art is weightless, superficial, and quite *un*tragic (a debatable point at the best of times) and makes no mention of the peculiarly pervasive pessimism that seems to give earlier postmodern literature (such as the writings of Beckett and Burroughs) and painting (such as the canvases of Bacon and Giacometti) its gloomy quality. Thus, despite his repeated allusions to the "widespread catastrophe" (60) of recent times, Oliva consistently overlooks the *existential shifts* differentiating the temper of early postmodernism from modernism.

Second, Oliva offers a slightly more satisfactory account of the *conceptual shifts* peculiar to postmodernity, citing the ways in which certain artists have appropriated aspects of earlier, "anthropological roots" (76), along with aspects of the "television image" (147–48). Paradoxically, though, Oliva conflates this "eclectic association" (76) of previous painterly styles, and this painterly appropriation and transformation of technological discourses, with the singular feat of "proceeding . . . through *all* the territories of culture" and "*all* those styles which had previously given rise to debate among the avant-garde movements" (54), and thereby "absorbing and masticating . . . *all* the conquests of the avant-garde" (77–78).

While trans-avant-garde painting may perhaps absorb many of the stylistic conquests of the avant-garde, it patently cannot absorb all aspects of postmodern culture within its pre-technological, painterly terms, any more than traditional analytical categories can wholly absorb new cultural practices within past criteria. Oliva's third and most misleading error derives from his indifference toward the creative potential of technological media and his concomitant insistence upon the "collapse" (8) of the technological avant-garde.

At best, Oliva's hypotheses offer a healthy antidote to the equally misleading misreadings of postmodern creativity collected in Roland Barthes's early essays. Whereas Barthes's theories celebrate the supposedly *objective* superficiality of Alain Robbe-Grillet's fiction, Oliva's observations systematically celebrate the antithetical *subjective* superficiality of trans-avant-garde painting. In this respect, both Barthes and Oliva construct, or invent, delusory variations of an idyllic art of *surface* that apparently "synthesizes" all prior modes of discourse, evades all traces of tragedy, and illustrates the impossibility of any kind of progress, revolution, or originality.

According to Barthes's essay "The Death of the Author" (1968), all writing may, in principle, be explicated in terms of the codes and conventions of prior discourse, without reference to their author's subjectivity. In Barthes's terms (or remixings), the writer may only "mix writings," and writings may only be understood "through other words, and so on indefinitely" (*Image-Music-Text*, 146). In much the same way, Barthes's "Introduction to the Structural Analysis of Narratives" (1966) argues that "what happens'" in narrative is "language alone" and the fluctuations of narrative "logic" (*Image-Music-Text*, 124), rather than anything referentially or deeply tragic or erotic. Accordingly, it makes little sense to attempt to interpret anything beneath this "logic," since "In the multiplicity of writing, everything is, to be disentangled, nothing deciphered; the structure can be followed . . . but *there is nothing beneath;* the space of writing is to be ranged over, not pierced" (*Image-Music Text*, 147; emphasis mine).

Not surprisingly, Barthes enthusiastically acclaimed the "new" novels of Alain Robbe-Grillet. The answer to a structuralist critic's prayer, these novels appear to offer a simple, objective mode of narrative without the least trace of anything subjective or tragic. Thus, according to Barthes's essay entitled "Objective Literature" (1954), Robbe-Grillet's fiction "*has no alibi, no density and no depth: it remains on the surface of the object* and inspects it impartially . . . it is the exact opposite of poetic writing. Here the word does not explode, nor explore . . . language here is not the rape of an abyss, but *the rapture of a surface.*"[36]

One can see Barthes's point, or at least one can see Barthes's point up to a certain point. Much of Robbe-Grillet's fiction appears to do little more than record the most superficial and the most mathematical aspects of reality. For example, when describing a pier in *The Voyeur*, Robbe-Grillet's narrator relates: "The pier, which seemed longer than it actually was as an effect of perspective, extended from both sides of this base line in a cluster of parallels describing, with a precision accentuated even more sharply by the morning light, a series of elongated planes alternately horizontal and vertical."[37]

In a sense this is *Cubist* writing, and, in a sense, Barthes's early theories are Cubist theories. In both instances, writer and theorist appear most concerned to break reality into its tangible, logical, and most neutral components. Put another way, Barthes and Robbe-Grillet seem preoccupied with the very antithesis of the superficial "Opulence" (34) that we might characterize as the *Expressionist* subject matter and discourse of Achille Bonito Oliva and the artists of the trans-avant-garde. In Barthes's terms, Robbe-Grillet "removes any possibility of metaphor" and "cuts" his objects off "that network of analogical forms or states which has always passed for the poet's privileged terrain" (*Critical Essays*, 17).

Somewhat as Oliva claims that subjective surfaces of trans-avant-garde painting synthesize and derive from "all . . . styles" and "*all the territories of culture*" (54; emphasis mine), Barthes argues that all writing interweaves "a tissue of quotations drawn from *the innumerable centres of culture*," and is therefore "never original" (*Image-Music-Text*, 146; emphasis mine). Moreover, just as Oliva claims that trans-avant-garde painting also absorbs the filmic qualities of the "television image" (147–18), Barthes likewise argues that Robbe-Grillet's narratives interweave both prior discourses and "a mental complexity derived from the contemporary arts and sciences such as the new physics and the cinema" (*Critical Essays*, 23). Like Oliva, Barthes has his cake and eats it: he claims that his object is at once as old as the hills, and as up to date as the mass media. Musing upon Robbe-Grillet's tedious distillation of the kind of writing that Proust dismissed as "the miserable statement of line and surface,"[38] Barthes finally persuades himself that "we recognise here the same revolution which the cinema has worked upon our visual reflexes" (*Critical Essays*, 18).

This assertion is at once excessively generous and astonishingly inaccurate. Like Achille Bonito Oliva, Barthes reduces postmodernity to its conceptual shifts and ignores the specificity of its *technological* shifts. Arguably, the "same revolution" which the cinema effects may only be found within the *technologically* revolutionary works of postmodern art and postmodern literature, such as the installations of Edward Keinholz or the multimedia compositions of sound

poets like Henri Chopin and composers like Robert Ashley. But of such technological creativity Barthes and Oliva say nothing, or next to nothing.

In a sense, trans-avant-garde painting and the "purely optical" quality that
Barthes attributes to Robbe-Grillet's prose (*Critical Essays*, 21) simply proffer the
pre-technological shadow of postmodernism's technological innovations. The
trans-avant-garde's neo-Expressionist canvasses and Robbe-Grillet's neo-Cubist
narratives typify the ways in which predominantly modernist modes of painting and writing have attempted to imitate the innovations of postmodern technology without ever actually employing these innovations, somewhat as high
chic fashions might imitate the hue of paramilitary camouflage without ever
encountering the cry of live ammunition. As such, trans-avant-garde painting
and the "new novel" offer striking examples of postmodern *simulcra*. In both
cases, the artist or novelist offers their audience the *reflection* of mass media discourses. More disturbingly still, both Achille Bonito Oliva's writings and Roland
Barthes's writings appear content to equate postmodernity in general with such
simulacra, without ever coming to terms with the more perplexing, but more
substantial, innovations of the postmodern avant-garde's technological and
partially technological creativity.

As we have seen, Oliva rather crudely dismisses the avant-garde, or at least
the technological avant-garde, by equating it with the excessive "rigor" of "experimental rules" (44) and with the neutralizing effects of mass civilization. In addition to this, Oliva also asserts that the present era of "catastrophe" makes the
"superstitions of experimentation" (46) redundant, ridiculous, and irredeemably
irrelevant. Oliva's hypotheses hinder rather than help, because they stubbornly
ignore the *subjective impulse* in avant-garde creativity, the *positive potential* of the
mass media, and the *reality* of postmodern technological experimentation.

At his most cautious, Barthes similarly asserts that substantial avant-
gardes cannot possibly exist, since both the avant-garde in general and the climate of the twentieth century in particular appear incompatible with artistic
innovation. According to his essay "Whose theater? Whose *Avant-Garde*?"
(1956), the avant-garde is both ineffective and nihilistic, since it "rarely pursues
its career as a prodigal son all the way" (*Critical Essays*, 68), and since it not only
"wants to die" but also "wants everything to die with it" (*Critical Essays*, 69).
And, according to Barthes's essay "From Work to Text" (1971), avant-garde
innovation appears inconceivable since the last hundred years are, by
Barthesian definition, an era of "*repetition*" in which "history . . . allows us

merely to slide, to vary, to exceed, to repudiate" (*Image-Music-Text,* 156; emphasis mine), but never to innovate.

To be fair, Barthes's early essays do occasionally question these theses when addressing extra-literary modes of creativity. For example, Barthes's musings upon Eisenstein's film stills, in "The Third Meaning," lead him to define the "filmic" as "that which in the film cannot be described" and which "neither the simple photograph nor figurative painting can assume" ("The Third Meaning," 64, 66). More recently, in *Camera Lucida* (1980), Barthes has identified the equally indefinable dimension of "*punctum,*" or an aspect of the photograph which "holds me" and seems to "prick me," though "I cannot say why."[39] Barthes defines this kind of detail as being "certain" but "unlocatable," since "it does not find its sign" among the familiar conventions, codes, and categories of "knowledge" and "culture" (*Camera Lucida,* 51). In this respect, "*punctum*" appears to transcend or "disturb" the realm of "*studium*" (or those familiar discourses that are "always coded" and which are therefore always decodable and definable) (*Camera Lucida,* 27, 51).

At this point, Barthes's argument seems on the point of inventing a whole theory of "*punctum*" and, indeed, a whole theory of those technologically generated modes of "*punctum*" which testify most clearly to the existence of new realms of "certain" but temporarily "unlocatable" modes of postmodern creativity. It is to this kind of "certain" but "unlocatable" mode of technological discourse that Baudrillard refers, when fleetingly acknowledging that the mass media generate something "new, ecstatic and obscene" ("Ecstacy," 132).

Of course, there is no reason why these most striking elements of technological creativity should automatically be qualified as "obscene." Nor should they necessarily be tarred by the brush of the Baudrillardian concept of "ecstasy," which refers to complacent or indolent "fascination" or a condition in which "one is no longer in a state to judge" and one "no longer has the potential to reflect."[40] Rather, as Lyotard suggests, these effects anticipate "the rules of what will have been done" ("Answering the Question," 341). Or, in Renato Poggioli's classic formulation, these effects are not "*anti*-theoretical" but "*ante*-theoretical."[41] The task of the postmodern cultual theorists is surely not simply to pronounce such effects indefinable, as Baudrillard does when dubbing them "ecstatic and obscene," but rather to formulate new categories in order to define their innovatory cultural reality.

Barthes's *Camera Lucida* prepares the ground for this enterprise. As the pages of this book locate the technological "*punctum*" of the photograph, Barthes signals his escape from such early postmodern theoretical myths as the assumptions that creativity may be reduced to a "logic" or "surface"; that progress in the arts is impossible; that avant-gardes are hopelessly nihilistic; and that pretechnological discourses may somehow or other assimilate and articulate the qualities of technological creativity. At one blow, Barthes's identification of technological "*punctum*" deflates both his own earlier theories (with their fascination for Robbe-Grillet's supposedly perfectly objective "surfaces"), and Achille Bonito Oliva's subsequent theories (with their fascination for the trans-avantgarde's supposedly perfectly subjective "surfaces"), by indicating that technological innovations *may* take place; that technological innovations are *not* always explicable in terms of familiar, pretechnological codes and categories; and that new technological works *are* sufficiently evocative to raise the existential questions that Barthes associates with "true metaphysics" (*Camera Lucida*, 85).

At this point, the structuralist myth of omnipresent "prior discourse" and trans-avant-garde myth of the "collapse" of experimental art are finally deflated. So too are the cults of the "surface" and of the "weightless." While it is tempting to assert that the late twentieth century is an apocalyptic age in which all cultural practices have become superficial, weightless, static, vacuously objective, vacuously subjective, or vacuously obscene, it eventually becomes evident that postmodern culture may well sometimes be all of these things, especially when considered in terms of its commercial mass media, or in terms of its most misanthropic early experimental gestures, but that it may also function more profoundly, more "weightily," and more radically when subsequently exploring the complex creative potential of its ever-evolving technology. Considered comprehensively, in terms of both its banalities and its innovations, postmodernism becomes definable as a substantial alternative to modernism and as the substantial consequence of its own distinctive existential, conceptual, and technological "shifts." To neglect these shifts is to neglect the most significant cultural mutations of our time.

baudrillard's *amérique* and the "abyss of modernity" 4

NOTHING COULD BE MORE NATURAL than to confuse the names of the French symbolist poet Charles Baudelaire and the French poststructuralist poet Jean Baudrillard. Both writers explore realms of sensual or conceptual extremes: in Baudelaire's case, the charms of "perfumes cool as the flesh of children . . . And others, corrupt, rich and triumphant"[1]; in Baudrillard's case, the partially poetic, partially parodic hypotheses—fueled by "provocative logic"[2]—which find their most provocative form in his ponderings upon American culture, entitled *Amérique*.[3]

How ironic then that *Amérique,* one of the most amusing examples of this century's fin-de-siècle magic realism should appear within the Trojan horse (or under the lamb's clothing) of Baudrillardian sociological speculation, a genre more likely to be cataloged and shelved under "theory" than *belles lettres.* Nevertheless, in a decade where fiction has virtually burst at its bindings under the pressure of self-reflective, self-critical, self-analytical and self-deconstructive hot air, Baudrillard's travels in *Amérique* offer a refreshing alternative to 'theoretical' fiction—something one might define, perhaps, as "fictional" theory.

Like Jonathan Swift's chronology of Gulliver's voyage to the land of the Houyhnhnms, the essays in *Amérique* record its narrator's love-hate relationship with their destination, with the difference that whereas Gulliver rather enviously (and slightly resentfully) contrasts the supreme rationality of the Houyhnhnm species with the Yahoo-like traits of his English countrymen, Baudrillard rather resentfully (and slightly enviously) contrasts the relaxed modernity of the American Yahoo with the staid, Houyhnhmn-like rationality and restraint of the European— and more particularly, French—intellectual tradition.

At the climax of *Amérique*, Baudrillard elaborates his general conclusion with characteristic bathos and bravado. America, apparently, is "Vulgar but *easy*" (187); a culture characterized by "the absence, and moreover the irrelevance of metaphysics and the imaginary" (166); a culture in which "its inhabitants can neither analyze nor conceptualize" (167); and thus an "anticulture" or "anti-utopia" (194) offering what Baudrillard hails as "the ideal embodiment (*idéaltype*) of the end of our culture" (195). Somewhat as Baudelaire's "Invitation to the Voyage" envisages utopian land-scapes, where "all is order and beauty. Luxuriance, calm and opulence,"[4] *Amérique* applauds its anti-utopian subject as the site of "unreason, deterritorization, the inde-terminacy of the subject and of language, the neutralization of all values, the death of culture" (194).

According to Baudrillard, the seemingly irreversible dissolution of these cate-gories constitutes the precondition of America's "easy" (his English) vulgarity. This is a cultural condition that he subsequently redefines with terms like "*inculture*" *and* "*métavulgarité*" (203), and which he still more tellingly distinguishes as "radical modernity" (160)—a mentality that the European sensibility seems incapable of sharing, savoring, or indeed understanding.

Like those middle-aged misfits who proverbially find themselves "too old to rock 'n' roll, too young to die," Baudrillard, speaking for the European intelligentsia, announces that this kind of modernity is permanently out of reach to those formed or deformed by European culture; those living "at the center, but at the center of the Old World" (161). Briefly, "modernity, as the original rupture with a certain history, will never be ours" (160). Or, put another way, "America is itself in a state of rapture and of radical modernity: it is therefore here that modernity is original, and nowhere else. We can only imitate it . . . we can never really be modern . . . in the strict sense of the term, and we can never have the same liberty—not that formal liberty which we take for granted, but that concrete, flexible, functional, active liberty which we see operating in the American institution, and in the head of each citizen." (160–61).

Elaborating this simplistic distinction between European cultural traditions and America's "radical modernity", Baudrillard similarly speculates: "When I see Americans, especially intellectuals, gazing with nostalgia towards Europe, its history, its metaphysics, its cuisine, its past, I sense this is a poor exchange. History and marxism are like fine wines and food: they don't travel well across the ocean, despite desperate efforts to acclimatize them. It is poetic justice that we Europeans have never really been able to assimilate modernity, which also resists travelling across the ocean, but in the other direction. There are certain products which do not tolerate import-export. Too bad for us, too bad for them." (157–58).

Interviewed in *Art Press* about *Amérique,* Baudrillard freely admits that this book "should not be read as a realist text", but rather as an example of "my sort of fictionizing", a process that he defines in terms of his impulse to draft "scenarios" which "*play out* the end of things" and "offer a complete parody" of their subject matter.[5] In this respect, his conclusion in the lines above wittily and wilfully exaggerates the incompatibility between European and American culture. The very prevalence of Baudrillardian hypotheses in American critical writings testifies to the extent to which that most lightweight of cultural commerce, the theoretical rag trade, flourishes between New York and Paris.

One could also point to other, more substantial examples of trans-Atlantic exchange, particularly in the fields of technocreativity: in literature, the impact in Paris of Americans such as William S. Burroughs and Brion Gysin (expatriates whose research alongside and with the French members of the *Poésie-Action* group precipitated modes of performance poetry and sound poetry combining live, prerecorded and technologically orchestrated sound and image); in art, the equally technological experiments of Americans such as Frank Malina (whose work alongside other expatriate and French artists in Paris precipitated new modes of kinetic art combining mechanical, magnetic, electromechanical and electronic systems).[6]

Baudrillard neither refers to such technological trans-Atlantic creativity nor appears even to acknowledge or appreciate its existence. In this respect, his parodic "fictionizing" is far less "complete" than he might imagine. What Baudrillard "plays out" are the coordinates of predominantly banal and boring cultural clichés, such as the tired old complaint that contemporary architecture eliminates metropolitan identity and transforms erstwhile individual cities into indistinguishable mazes of flat, neutral glass. Or that other apocalyptic favourite, the myth that the mass media neutralize reality, somewhat as video "killed" the radio star.

Of course, there is more to *Amérique* than this. Baudrillard repeatedly pinpoints the paradoxes of contemporary American values, and for good measure counterpoints these criticisms with rhapsodic allusion to the urban jungle's primitive counterpart: a peculiarly idealized concept of the harsh, cruel, merciless Californian deserts. Denouncing New York as a crazy, anarchic, inhuman limbo epitomizing all the cultural catastrophes he ever dared dream of from the comfort of his Parisian desk, and at the same time marveling before both its captivating energy and ferocity as well as the still more seductive ferocity and inhumanity of the American desert, Baudrillard's vision of American culture vacillates between images of unrestrained urban chaos—depicted somewhat in the manner of George Grosz's 1917 *Funeral Procession* (*Dedicated to Oskar Panizza*)—and evocations of the harsh, surreal beauty of the deserts portrayed by Yves Tanguy or Salvador Dali.

In this respect, *Amérique* hovers between two poles: its relatively contemporary satire of specific slices and segments of the Big Apple, and its nostalgically surreal meditations upon the Baudrillardian antidote to this madhouse: the selfsame desert serving as destination for such archetypical cynics as Molière's *Misanthrope*. Like many European writers and intellectuals, Baudrillard seems trapped between his distaste for the cultural, social and political anti-climax in Europe after the fizzle of May '68, and his reluctant fascination for the equally distasteful vivacity of American technoculture. In Baudrillardian terms, European intellectuals are both intimidated by "the abominable weight of our culture" (186) and tormented by the impossibly vulgar American dream: an ideal that Baudrillard, appropriating the apocalyptic rhetoric of Barthes, associates with all the advantages and disadvantages of "the zero degree of culture" signaling the end of the European tradition and the beginning of American modernity.

Bewailing the European intellectual's incapacity to savor this ambiguous idea, Baudrillard insists: "We will never catch up with them, and we can never attain this candour. We can merely imitate or parody them fifty years in arrears—without success, moreover. We lack the spirit and the audacity of what could be termed the zero degree of a culture, the power of the lack of culture" (155–56). From this it seems to follow that, "We will always remain nostalgic utopians torn by this ideal, but finally repelled by its realisation" (156). Summarizing the dilemma of the European intellectual (or at least what he takes to be the European dilemma), Baudrillard describes his response to American modernity as "a mixture of fascination and resentment" (193), explaining: "We are still burdened by the cult of difference, and thus handicapped with regard to radical modernity, which rests on indifference. We become modern and indifferent halfheartedly, whence the lack of flair of our modernity and the absence of any modernist spirit in our undertakings. We have nothing of the *evil demon* of modernity, that which drives innovation to excess, and thereby rediscovers a kind of fantastic freedom" (193).

Baudrillard's fatalistic summary of this supposed crisis of culture typifies the lament of a number of equally apocalyptic Europeans. The East German playwright Heiner Müller (best known, perhaps, for his recent collaborations with Robert Wilson[7]) evokes much the same dilemma in his play *Hamletmachine*, a text insisting that there is something terminally rotten in contemporary Europe. As Müller specifies, "*Hamletmachine* isn't . . . simply a description of people missing the occasions and chances of history. . . . It is about the results of missed occasions, about history as a story of chances lost. That is more than plain disappointment, it is the description of the petrification of hope."[8] Like Baudrillard, Müller suggests that the European sensibility may at best assimilate and accept American cultural alternatives with a certain half-heartedness or resentment. His latter-day Hamlet is "The man between the ages who knows that the old age is obsolete, yet the new age has barbarian features he simply cannot stomach."[9]

To cite one further example of this crisis—admittedly, a slightly more muted example—Umberto Eco's essays in *Travels in Hyperreality* repeatedly argue that contemporary experience is now mediated by mass media which "cannot be criticised with the traditional criticism", and which, "instinctively, high school kids know . . . better than some seventy-year-old pedagogue."[10] With this in mind, Eco hints that "All the professors of theory of communications, trained by the texts of twenty years ago (this includes me), should be pensioned off" (149)—notionally resigning, as it were, before the shock of the new mass media age. Elsewhere, Eco once again acknowledges the impact of media culture and the enviable facility with which its younger viewers have absorbed the codes and conventions of this alternative to what Müller calls "the old age." Yet as the following lines indicate, Eco, like Müller's Hamlet, finally kicks against the pricks of innovation, calling somewhat indirectly upon "moralists" to condemn the "barbarian features" of the media.

Eco's observations begin, generously enough, with the avowal: "It is the visual work (cinema, videotape, mural, comic strip, photograph) that is now a part of our memory. Which ... seems to confirm a hypothesis already ventured, namely that the younger generations have absorbed as elements of their behaviour a series of elements filtered through the mass media (and coming, in some cases, from the most impenetrable areas of our century's artistic experimentation)" (213–14). Having wistfully and somewhat admiringly postulated that "younger generations have mysteriously mastered consequences of some of the "most impenetrable" artistic experiments of our era, Eco adds: "To tell the truth, it isn't even necessary to talk about new generations: if you are barely middle-aged, you will have learned personally the extent to which experience (love, fear, or hope) is filtered through 'already seen' images"; before still more ambiguously musing, "I leave it to moralists to deplore this way of living by intermediate communication: We must bear in mind mankind has never done anything else ..." (214).

I think it is worth quoting this meditation at some length if only to indicate the mixed reactions that Eco appears to experience before the mass media. While he recognizes their importance and their omnipresence, and while he bows in awe before those younger contemporaries whose effortless absorption of the shocks of the new identifies them as splendid examples of that species which Eco's Futurist forebears defined as "*the primitives of a completely renovated sensitiveness*,"[11] Eco's ethical uncertainty regarding such "indeterminate communication" seems to trigger off his appeal to unspecified "moralists" to deplore the innovatory discourses absorbed, accepted and legitimated by the "renovated sensitiveness" of these "primitives."

In his turn, Baudrillard often tends to recoil before manifestations of the new media. Quite frequently in *Amérique* he appears to condemn the mass media for their vacuity. But on other occasions, he celebrates this same vacuity in terms of "the fascination of nonsense" (240) and the discovery that one can delight in the liquidation of all culture and can exalt in the consecration of indifference (241). Both of these options neglect the positive potential of the mass-media, caricaturing them as being either negatively or positively vacuous, but never anything other than vacuous. Whereas John Cage comes to terms with technological culture by means of a "techno-logic" asserting that "our souls are conveniently electronic (omni-attentive),"[12] and therefore capable of attending to and comprehending electronic culture,

Baudrillard's *Amérique* argues that mass media culture renders the soul omni-inattentive.

Discussing the Roxy, for example, Baudrillard observes that this amalgam of carefully orchestrated lighting, strobe effects and flickering dancers offers "the same effects as a screen" (73). Accordingly, it typifies the "perpetual video" effect that he both deplores for "its intensity on the surface and its insignificance in depth" and welcomes as "the special effect of our time" (74).

While a diet of endless soap opera, disco lights, or indeed Baudrillardian over-statement may persuade the unwary reader that ours is a culture of intensely superficial mediated reality, and of little significant profundity, Cage is surely far more persuasive when he argues that machines "can tend toward our stupefaction or our enlivenment."[13] It is this crucial force for *enlivenment* that Baudrillard tends to ignore in *Amérique*, or else reduces to ironic paradox. By contrast, Cage's writings eagerly await "the technology to come,"[14] and assert the necessity of progress in the arts and in the media, reasoning, "Without the avant-garde, which I think is flexibility of the mind and freedom from institutions, theories and laws, you won't have invention and obviously, from a practical point of view … society needs invention."[15]

While Baudrillard appears happy to invent evermore fantastic formulae for contemporary crises, his main focus is clearly on traces of *stupefaction* in technological society. On occasion, the writings of Cage and Baudrillard address the same general symptoms of American society—a new machine, or a machine that appears to malfunction. But whereas Cage exploits such anecdotes to point towards new ways of thinking about art and of making art, Baudrillard, often with an equally poetic turn of thought, transforms his subject matter into evidence of the terminal decline of the American sensibility.

Recounting one of his favorite anecdotes in order to illustrate the advantages of creatively interweaving electronic and "live" performance, Cage reminisces: "I remember once when I was giving a performance with David Tudor—of what we called 'live' electronic music. There was one machine that was under my control which was not plugged in. But it worked anyway! … It worked as though it was plugged in. And I said, 'Isn't that strange?' to David. He said, 'No. It's because it's so close to the others that are plugged in.' So that is was vibrating sympathetically! Isn't that amazing!"[16]

Cage's *Indeterminacy* (1959) abounds with similar accounts of how machines of one kind or another lurch into modes of malfunctioning

mechanical poetry in motion. For Baudrillard, such spectacles are at best surreal icons of technological paradox and superficiality. Peering into ghostly
motels and meditating upon the eccentricities of Las Vegas, *Amérique* treats
the reader to such maxims as: "nothing is more mysterious than a television
left on in an empty room" (100), or "nothing is more beautiful than air-con-
ditioning in the heat, or speeding through a natural setting, or electric lighting on in the middle of the day" (133).

This is the discourse of the nineteenth-century dandy—of Baudelaire,
Oscar Wilde or Karl-Joris Huysmans, and all those preferring what the latter's
Des Esseintes defines as "ingenious trickery . . . clever simulation, "imaginary
pleasures."[17] Yet, in a sense nothing is less mysterious than such paradoxes. After
such apocalyptic jesters, there can be no more jokes about or allusions to the
mysterious beauty of paradoxical objects. Small wonder, perhaps, that
Baudrillard self-consciously appropriates one of his most cherished images of
American culture from Alfred Jarry's novel *Le Surmâle* (1902). Recycling Jarry's
wit for late-twentieth-century readers, Baudrillard suggests that Reagan's
American "continues to function like a body moving by acquired velocity . . . like
an unconscious man held upright by the power of balance. Or, more amusingly, like the cyclists in Jarry's *Surmâle*, who have died of exhaustion pedaling
across the wastes of Siberia but continue to propel the Great Machine, having
converted their cadaveric rigor into driving force" (228–29).

Not content with summarizing Jarry, Baudrillard erupts: "What a superb
fiction: the dead are perhaps capable of accelerating and propelling the
machine even better than the living, *because they have no more problems*"
(229; emphasis in the original). This aside, pivoting upon the word "perhaps," superimposes Baudrillard's contemporary vision of the yuppified living dead, born of the late 1960s and early 1970s, onto Jarry's "superb fiction,"
bringing it up to date in terms of his own special mode of "fictionizing."[18]
Disenchanted with the consequences of what he nostalgically calls "the orgy
of the 1960s and 70s" (220), and yet bemused by the generation engendered
in this era, Baudrillard introduces this "new race" (220) as the antiseptic
"Clean and perfect" (his English) offspring of "business" and "showbiz"
(219), namely, "A generation born of the 1960s and 70s unencumbered by any
nostalgia, bad conscience, or even subconscious awareness of those crazy
years. Purged of every last trace of marginality as if by cosmetic surgery—new
faces, new nails, neurons polished and armed with software" (219).

One recognizes the symptoms. Dystopian fictions from Yevgeny Ivanovich Zamyatin's *We* (1920) to Aldous Huxley's *Brave New World* (1932), George Orwell's *Nineteen Eighty-four* (1949) and Kurt Vonnegut's *Player Piano* (1952) have contrasted nostalgic "primitive" mentalities with the futuristic functionality of those purged of such sensibility by cerebral or ideological "surgery." Even Charles Dickens hits out at the overly polished neurones of Bitzer, the prototype punk-haired structuralist brat who "looked as though, if he were cut, he would bleed white."[19] Where Baudrillard differs from Huxley and company, however, is in his diagnosis of these symptoms. Whereas these writers conscientiously contrast the limitations of new, "Clean and perfect" generations with other, older, more imperfect but more humane, modes of existence, Baudrillard appears equally enthusiastic about both the pallid, indifferent yuppies of the 1980s and their "primitive" antithesis: "the tribes, gangs, mafias" (41) of New York.

Pondering upon the noble savagery of New York street culture, Baudrillard pauses to admire the way in which the break-dancer "freezes his movement in a derisory gesture," presenting a deliberately laconic, antiheroic "ironic and indolent pose of death" (43). Elsewhere, Baudrillard virtually suggests that Hispanics are the sole survivors of Los Angeles insofar as they alone appear to be in their element on its streets: "In this centrifugal metropolis, once you leave your car you are a delinquent; once you start walking you are a menace to law and order, like stray dogs on the highway. Only the third world have the right to walk. It is their privilege in a way, like that of occupying deserted inner city areas" (115).

Heiner Müller likewise romanticizes cultural minorities. Applauding "The murals painted by minority groups and the proletarian art of the subway, anonymously created with the stolen paint," he glowingly concludes: "Here the underprivileged reach out of their misery and encroach upon the *realm of freedom* which lies beyond privileges."[20]

In his turn, Umberto Eco seems to invent an apocalyptic New York, "filled with immigrants ... drained of its old inhabitants," and fast "approaching the point where nearly all its inhabitants will be non-white" (77). Like Baudrillard, Eco argues that the "generation of the 1980s" seems to be returning to the conservatism of the "average crew-cut executive," rather than espousing the alternative values of the 1960s and 70s inspired by "Herman Hesse, the zodiac, alchemy, the thoughts of Mao, marijuana, and urban guerrilla techniques" (76). But like Müller and Baudrillard, Eco hints that a remnant of primitive resistance remains: "this phenomenon," he notes, "concerns the upper middle class, not the kids we see break-dancing" (76).

As I have suggested, such enthusiasm for the break-dancing and graffiti-scrawling metropolitan noble savage seems naive in the extreme. Over a century ago, George Eliot wittily questioned the merits of the rustic idyll, deliberating: "The selfish instincts are not subdued by the sight of buttercups, nor is integrity in the least established by that classic rural occupation, sheep-washing. To make men moral, something more is requisite than to turn them out to grass."[21]

One might well add that something more is requisite to counter the threats of urban decay and yuppie conservatism than to turn kids on with grass, to encourage graffiti art or break-dancing, or to trust that cultural apathy may be subdued by the sight of subway coaches sprayed buttercup, gold, silver, or whatever. For Heiner Müller, mannerist dance and arcs of color "created with stolen paints" may offer comforting paradigms for the "universal discourse" that "omits nothing and excludes no one," and perhaps constitutes the sole alternative to the imminent "silence of entropy."[22] Nevertheless, such rituals seem peculiarly romantic and surprisingly nostalgic solutions, rather than offering the greater challenge of exploring and elaborating more contemporary, and indeed more *futuristic,* creativity predicated upon specific evolving technologies (as opposed to imprecise recipes for a classless, all-inclusive "universal discourse").

Ironically, Baudrillard has little time for positive, or new modes of techno-logical, discourse. Persuaded that American culture is a confusing amalgam of "space, speed, cinema, technology" (200), his meditations culminate in the rel-atively myopic conclusion that America simultaneously reveals "the miracle of realized utopia,"[23] and, at the other extreme, the "*mythical* banality" (189) and superficiality of the apocalyptic dystopia that he enthusiastically diagnoses "not only in technological development but in the surpassing of technologies in the excessive play of technology, not only in modernity but in the exaggeration of modern forms . . . not only in banality but in the apocalyptic forms of banality, not only in everyday reality but the hyperreality of this existence which, in every respect presents all the characteristics of fiction" (189).

Pushing poetic and fictional license to its limit, Baudrillard concludes that America's fictional mode of existence "anticipates the imaginary by realizing it," and that it is "the surpassing of the imaginary in reality" (190). For Baudrillard, America is stranger than fiction, and more imaginary than the wildest imagination. At this juncture one might ask precisely *whose* fictions, and *whose* imaginations, seem to be eclipsed by American reality in this way. If America eclipses any particular sense of the imaginary or of the fictional, then this is the imaginative and fictive quality of Baudrillard's earlier writings. It is perhaps for this reason that he insists the European mind, particularly minds akin to his own, can never really be *modern*.

Yet however industriously Baudrillard may attempt to scandalize or seduce his public by inventing increasingly imaginary fictions, such hypotheses seem fated to be eclipsed by still stranger everyday American hyperreality. While Baudrillard once cheerfully conceded—in response to Sylvère Lotringer's suggestion that his theories function by "Cultivating paradox in order to revulse theory"[24]—"I greatly enjoy provoking that revulsion," *Amérique* suggests that the wildest European dreams now seem singularly tame when viewed from American shores. Cutting his losses as it were, Baudrillard's more recent interviews acknowledge this paradox, while also accrediting his previous (fictional) theories with a certain prophetic flair. Discussing his work with Jacques Henric and Guy Scarpetta, Baudrillard explains: "All of the themes that I first examined in my previous books suddenly appeared, in America, stretching before me in concrete form. In a way, then, I finally left theory behind me and at the same time rediscovered all the questions and the enigmas that I had first posited conceptually."[25]

To some extent, then, Baudrillard has nothing very new to say about America, save to exaggerate the degree to which American life confirms his earlier speculations. At its most amusing level, *Amérique* offers memorable vignettes of New York—such as the observation that New Yorkers, though having "nothing in common" still sense that "magic feeling of closeness" that Baudrillard attributes to the "ecstasy of promiscuity" (35). Here as elsewhere, his rhetoric erupts in an "ecstasy" of hyperbole, or hyper-hyperbole. Baudrillard marvels before the spectacle of "modern demolition," likening it to "the fireworks of our childhood" (39); defines New York as an "anti-Ark" where everybody is alone, where the couple is virtually outdated, and where only "tribes, gangs, mafias . . . can survive" (41); concedes that the mentally ill should indeed be released from hospitals, since "It is hard to see why such a crazy city should keep its crazies hidden away" (42); and views the New York marathon as an apocalyptic spectacle in which "everyone seeks death, death from exhaustion" (43). Finally, Baudrillard asserts that while "We in Europe possess the art of thinking over, analyzing, and reflecting upon things," New York's "explosive truths" (50) appear to resist all thought, analysis, and reflection. He concludes: "No one is capable of analyzing [this society], least of all American intellectuals locked up in their campuses, totally estranged from that fabulous, concrete mythology going on around them" (50–51).

Predictably, Baudrillard presents himself as an exception to this rule. Caricaturing himself as some sort of cerebral Batman or Superman, "jumping with feline agility from one airport to another" and serving as "Aeronautic missionary.... Talking on the silence of the masses and on the end of history" (31), Baudrillard gradually hints that quite unlike other European and American intellectuals, he *does* in fact understand America–or at least, a certain essential aspect of America.

At this point, Baudrillard's meditations set foot on familiar literary territory: the highways, deserts, and shanty towns celebrated by innumerable writers, poets, and pop singers. Somewhat as Jack Kerouac, William S. Burroughs, Vladimir Nabokov, Allen Ginsberg, Ed Dorn, Chuck Berry and Bob Dylan have all evoked some aspect of their travels "on the road" or across "Route 66" and so forth, Baudrillard in turn announces, "My hunting grounds are the deserts, the mountains, the freeways, Los Angeles. The safeways, the ghost towns or the downtowns—not academic conferences. The deserts, their deserts, I know them better than they do ... and I get more from the desert on the concrete, social life of America than I would ever get from official or intellectual sociality" (125–26).

Alternatively, reconsidered in an early-nineteenth-century context, these lines also seem related in tone to such romantic idylls as William Wordsworth's allusion to his poetic hunting grounds,

> Whose dwelling is the light of setting suns,
> And the round ocean and the living air,
> And the blue sky, and in the mind of man.[26]

Or again, placed in a later, fin-de-siècle, symbolist context, Baudrillard's claim to understand "their deserts ... better than they do" reminds one of Baudelaire's suggestion that the poet may decode nature's "forest of symbols," whereas, according to G.-Albert Aurier, "the imbecile human flock, duped by the appearances that lead them to the denial of essential ideas, will pass forever blind."[27] Compounding his disdain for the "imbecile human flock", Baudrillard adds: "While they spend their time in libraries, I spend mine in the desert and on the road. While they derive their material from the history of ideas, I take mine from actual events, from the action on the streets or from sites of natural beauty" (125).

Perhaps Baudrillard might have added that his concept of "natural" beauty also derives from the history of literature from Symbolists like Baudelaire and from proto-Surrealists such as the author of *Les Chants de Maldoror*.[28] Announcing his intention to "depict the delights of cruelty" in this "cold and grave chant," Maldoror taunts the reader with memories of rending a child and drinking his blood; of admiring the ferocity with which a huge female shark savages her rivals in order to gorge upon the "eggless omlet" made up of survivors from a ship wreck; of plunging into the sea and wounding the shark with his knife, while murmuring "here is someone more evil than I," and of abandoning himself to a "long, chaste and hideous coupling" with this "first love." Baudrillard's meditations upon the California desert display surprising counterparts to Maldoror's sadistic musings.

This preoccupation with the deserts of California seems to stem from Baudrillard's assertion that he can learn more about America from its highways, byways, and deserts, and from the secondary and slightly paradoxical suggestion that such spots epitomize the superficiality to be found within its metropolitan "anticulture" (194) or "lack of culture" (201). The "natural," it seems, appeals to him precisely in terms of its co-present, equivalent, *unnatural* superficiality. While the architecture of the Hotel Bonaventure can prompt such awestruck comments as: "Purely illusionist architecture, pure spatio-temporal gadgetry, is this still architecture?" Ludic and hallucinatory, is this postmodern architecture? (118), Baudrillard's reflections upon American deserts insist that they too combine hallucinatory fusions of the pure and the artificial.

Self-consciously relating this curious aesthetic to that of Baudelaire, Baudrillard observes: "For we moderns and ultramoderns, as for Baudelaire, who knew that the secret of true modernity lies in artifice, the only natural spectacles that impress are those which simultaneously betray the most striking depth *and the absolute simulation of this depth*" (139); (emphasis in the original).

For this reason, Baudrillard applauds "the exceptional scenery of the deserts in the West," on the grounds that "they combine the most ancestral hieroglyph, the most dazzling light, and the most complete superficiality" (140).

Baudrillard's vision differs from that of Baudelaire, however, in terms of the peculiarly menacing and sadistic quality of his artificial paradises. While

Baudelaire's poem "Invitation to the Voyage" conjures the sensual delights of an island where the poet and his beloved may live together under tropical sunsets, in an idyll of "Luxuriance, calm and opulence,"[29] Baudrillard associates the American deserts with a "surreality" and a "magical presence, having nothing to do with nature" (13) which one might well think of as the zero degree of "Luxuriance . . . and opulence." So far as Baudrillard is concerned, the desert is an unearthly, apocalyptic zone, "beyond the squalid phase of decomposition, the humid phase of the body, the organic phase of nature." Deserts, then, are "sublime forms distanced from all society, all sentimentality, all sexuality" (142–42).

It therefore follows that one has no need of a companion in the desert. "Speech, even company, is always too much," and here "The caress has no meaning," unless (like the embrace of Maldoror with the enormous female shark), "the woman herself is desert-like, has a spontaneous and superficial animality, in which the carnal combines with aridity and discrimination" (142). At this point, Baudrillard's partially disincarnated carnal idyll concurrently corresponds both to such surrealist ideals as Paul Éluard's fantasy of a woman whose presence "does not let me sleep," but rather makes ". . . the sun evaporate/ And me laugh cry and laugh/ Speak when I have nothing to say,"[30] and to such Symbolist icons as Fernand Khnoppf's premonition of similarly erotic animality in his painting *Art or The Carexsses (1896)*.

Baudrillard's musings upon the merits of this kind fin-de-siècle femme fatale amusingly and confusingly steer his argument away from the twentieth century, with its a American metropolitan superpersons such as Miss America, and toward such late nineteenth-century fantasies as Jean Delville's *Idol of Perversity (1891)*. Sinking ever deeper into decadent fictional depths, Baudrillard adds that the American desert deserves an "extremely cruel religion" and "sacrifices equal to the surrounding cataclysmic natural order" (14). By coincidence, William S. Burroughs's novel, *The Western Lands,* meditates upon the mythological cruelty of another such desert religion, that of the ancient Egyptian "Shining Ones," remarking that those who would be living Gods required "superhuman" inhumanity. As Burroughs's narrator explains: "Consider the Pharaohs: their presence was Godlike. They performed superhuman feats of strength and dexterity. . . . They became Gods, and to be a God means meting out at times terrible sanctions: cutting the hands off a thief or the lips off a perjurer. Now imagine some academic, bad-Catholic individual as God. He simply can't bear to cause any suffering at all. So what happens? Nothing."[31]

Burroughs exemplifies his favored alternative to the ineffective, humanis-
tic, "bad-Catholic" intellectual in such vignettes of cheerful brutality as the fleeting episode where one of his protagonists, Kim Carsons, "thanking Allah for eyes
to see and hands to push", ponders: "'Only fools do those villains pity who are
punished, before they have done their mischief' ... as he shoves a horrid rednecked oaf out of the lifeboat. The sharks cut his screams to a bearable pitch and
period" (223). One senses something here of Maldoror's good-humored enthusiasm for his favorite shark-amour. Like Lautréamont, Burroughs counters
"horrid rednecked" mediocrity with "the delights of cruelty," in a consciously
ambivalent text.

Baudrillard's theoretical counterparts to such Burroughsian incidents seem
far more sinister. Having established that the desert requires cataclysmic sacrifices comparable, perhaps, to the sadistic retribution that Burroughs associates
with the Pharoahs, Baudrillard's descriptions of Death Valley's fusion of "Fire,
heat, light, all the elements of sacrifice" lead him to make the astonishing proposal that "One should always bring something to sacrifice in the desert, and
offer it as a victim. A woman. If something has to disappear there, something
equal in beauty to the desert, why not a woman?" (132).

It is difficult to know what to make of such studiedly sexist speculation.
Slipping away from his comparison of Europe and America in the late twentieth century into a nostalgic nineteenth-century time warp where Symbolist,
Surrealist, and Sadian values intermingle and overturn, Baudrillard's partially
focused ponderings upon New York spiral imperceptibly into anachronistic
erotic hyperspace—into realms of sentimental cruelty and cliché far-removed
from the "radical modernity" (193) of America. Against his better judgment
perhaps, Baudrillard's reports from the continent of the future drift back into
the escapist dreams of the preceding *fin-de-siècle*, such as Des Esseintes's similar attempt to combine and confuse "natural profundity" with its "absolute simulation"(139) by gathering natural flowers that would look like fakes."[32]

To be sure, Baudrillard's hypothetical project is quite the reverse of this
anachronistic, escapist pastime. Rather than planning to follow in the path of
Huysmans, Baudelaire, Lautréamont, Jarry, Wilde or any other of the mid-to-late
nineteenth-century apocalyptics which his mid-to-late twentieth-century apocalyptic musings call to mind, Baudrillard defends and defines his research in terms
of his wish to pursue "some new situation to its very limits" so as to break into
"hyperspace and trans-infinity", and thereby peer beyond "the end of things."[33]

Yet rather than really projecting his hypotheses and his exegeses *beyond* "the end of things," or even into the present, Baudrillard's epistle from America compulsively reduces the present to paradigms of the European past, or to what Baudrillard disparagingly terms "the bourgeois dream of the nineteenth century" (146). If it is indeed the case, as Baudrillard claims, that Santa Barbara is his "predestined" objective ("I was here in my imagination long before travelling to it" [143]), it rapidly becomes evident that the terms of his imagination are way out of synchronization with their subject. A mixture of film titles—Baudrillard successively finds counterparts to the "universe" of *Blade Runner* (77), *Planet of the Apes* (96), *Alien* (98), *American Graffiti* (130) and "the camera of John Ford" (139), to mention but a few of such references—and of revived late nineteenth-century discourse (such as his explicit references to Baudelaire and Jarry, and his implicit replication of the turn of paradox, phrase or thought of Lautréamont, Wilde, or Huysmans)—the rhetoric of *Amérique* ironically confirms Baudrillard's eccentric contention that Europe and America are utterly divided by the "abyss of modernity.... One is born modern, but one cannot become so" (146).

Here, as almost everywhere else, Baudrillard exaggerates his case. Innumerable artists have successfully crossed the Atlantean "abyss of modernity" in both directions. Suffice it to suggest that for all its wit, its insights, poetry and its imagination, *Amérique* frequently misses its mark. Baudrillard's barbs wing their way not so much from the heights of visionary hyperspace as from the revisionary realm of *fin-de-siècle* sniper-space, reflecting on and deflecting away from their subject matter as factual or semifactual observation transmutes into oneiric overstatement. In this respect, Baudrillard's self-indulgent "fictions" charm and disarm both their reader and their writer as one senses one's critical sensibility gradually disintegrating and evaporating in the wake of his beguiling generalizations.

Over and above (or under and beneath) Baudrillard's intoxicating rhetoric one senses a certain maudlin disappointment, akin perhaps to the "great pain" that Burroughs associates with "certain players" in *Nova Express,* who understand their dilemma only too well, to the point of being unable to extricate themselves from this pain save through "a round of exquisite festivals." As Burroughs' narrator explains, "You understand the mind works with *une rapidité incroyable* but the movements are very slow—So a player may see on the board great joy or a terrible fate see also the move to take or avoid see also that he can not make the move in time—This gives rise of course to great pain which they must always conceal in a round of exquisite festivals—"[34]

Like these unfortunate "players," Baudrillard appears painfully aware that he is trapped within a contradictory game, glimpsing the paradoxical "great joy" and "terrible fate" of America, yet finding himself to be incapable of personally making the move" to radical modernity—a dilemma prompting his nostalgic "festivals" or fictions praising the cruelty and superficiality of the American desert. One can understand Baudrillard's disappointment before his sense of the impossibility of ever becoming "radically modern," but one wonders why his discussion of the paradoxes of American culture emphasise their mutually neutralizing contradictions, rather than what Cage might term their potential for "enlivenment."[35] In all likelihood, Cage would probably deny the very existence of such contradictions and refer instead to his notion of "a harmony to which many are unaccustomed."[36] Indeed, the postmodern American sensibility begs definition in terms of its tendency to juxtapose paradoxical materials in the confident belief that they will cohere in predictable, if indefinable ways. Unlike the Surrealist aesthetic, with its distinction between the mundane and the marvelous, this American aesthetic simply seems to assert that there are neglected, unexpected, but ultimately ordinary, everyday modes of coherence awaiting rediscovery, be these Cage's chance compositions, Burroughs's cut-ups, or the autistic rituals inspiring the theatre of Robert Wilson.

Alluding to this "pragmatic" mode of "paradoxical" consciousness in one of the most perspicacious paragraphs of *Amérique*, Baudrillard comments: "We live in a state of negativity and contradiction, whereas they live in a state of paradox (since the idea of a realized utopia is paradoxical). And the quality of the American way of life comes for the most part from this pragmatic and paradoxical attitude, whereas ours is characterized by the subtlety of its critical spirit" (16–57). Baudrillard is surely correct here. The essence of many of the most interesting modes of postmodern American creativity is their open-minded fusion of contradictory discourses. As William Carlos Williams once remarked, American creativity seems inseparable from "a mixing of categories, a fault in logic that is unimaginable in a person of orderly mind."[37]

For all its willful fun and games, *Amérique* seems to be the product of precisely the same kind of excessively "orderly mind" that Voltaire ridiculed in *Candide,* in the character of his irrepressibility optimistic philosopher, Dr Pangloss. Just as Pangloss seems blind, deaf and dumb to the sufferings of his companions as he doggedly demonstrates "the rightness of all things,"[38]

Baudrillard—the Pangloss, perhaps, of apocalyptic postmodern pessimism—
appears to gloss over the specific felicities of contemporary culture in his efforts
to demonstrate that America has no culture and is variously "neither a dream
nor a reality, but a hyperreality" (57), "a gigantic hologram" (59), "the living offspring of cinema" (111), "heir to the deserts" (126), "realized utopia" (152), or
indeed "a desert" itself (198).

There are good reasons for hailing *Amérique* as the work of a considerable
poet. But, one way or another, Baudrillard's poetical flourishes transform the
"now" into the discourse of the "then," equating American in the mid-1980s
with the theoretical discourse in which he claims to have predicted his discoveries, "in Paris" (17). More specifically, his apocalyptic terminology either
deflates the lively paradoxes of American techno-culture into the deadly contradictions distilled by the European intelligentsia's terminally "orderly mind,"
or inflates the terms of such paradoxes out of all recognition by describing them
in the nostalgic, semi-Symbolist, and semi-Surrealist rhetoric beloved by the
old-style semi-bohemians of the Parisian literati.

To be sure, Baudrillard's splendidly poetical and fictional speculations
offer a welcome explosion in the wake of structuralism's more neutral notations, just as the "spaghetti-Expressionism" of artists such as Enzo Cucchi offers
timely alternatives to the arid geometry of hard-core minimalist art. Having
wandered through whole galleries of work by such minimal masters as Donald
Judd, Carl Andre and Sol LeWitt, one cannot help applauding curatorial decisions to fill subsequent galleries with the primitive iconography and mythological fantasies of Cucchi and other virtuosi of the trans-avant-garde.[39]
Despite one's admiration for the rigorous draughtmanship and documentation
constituting the work of Sol LeWitt, there comes a time when one feels still
more momentary sympathy for works such as Enzo Cucchi's *Wounded
Painting*, with its anguished, anthropomorphized pages. Likewise, having
endured the hyper-objectivity of early Barthesian edicts, it is refreshing to
savour the ever-escalating eccentricity of Baudrillard's imaginative impreca-
tions. Small wonder, then, that Baudrillard might be acclaimed as the most
popular of contemporary theoreticians.

Nevertheless, as Baudrillard himself now admits, his labors seem a little
forced, given that most of the values pilloried in *Amérique* and in its precursors
were already discredited (or at least defamed) some half century ago, during the
era he fondly recalls as the "high point of disappearance . . . situated between

Nietzsche and the 1920s and 30s."[40] Born too late to savor the real thing, the contemporary reader may well feel seduced—initially—by Baudrillard's simulation, or revival, of the "Nietzsche-effect."

But as the great "Dadasophe" Raoul Hausmann wisely remarked, "a general climactic situation cannot be repeated" and consequently revivals or "'Renaissances' are, for the most part, sad and without issue."[41] Baudrillard admits as much when he concedes that "we no longer even have the work of mourning to go through; all that remains is a state of melancholia."[42] All that remains *where?* Once again, the limits of Baudrillard's rhetoric restrict the limits of his world.

The fatal weakness in Baudrillard's seductive melancholia (and indeed, in any number of similarly apocalyptic misreadings of postmodernity), is its compulsive neglect of the substance of contemporary culture and its insistence upon the correspondence between everyday reality and apocalyptic terminology; a delusion that becomes doubly delusory when this terminology derives from outdated muses and metaphors. Persuaded, for whatever reasons or nonreasons, that American cities are hyperreal mirages both like and equal to the exoticism, eroticism and superficiality of the desert, and are therefore best definable in terms of virtually interchangeable mythologies concerning the "desert effect" or the "video effect" that seem to pervade all aspects of contemporary culture, Baudrillard's deliberations consistently overlook the actuality of contemporary culture, whether European, American, or from any other continent for that matter.

What seems plain, if one looks beyond the trivia of the highways and the byways distracting Baudrillard's attention, is the quantity of positive technocreativity on both sides of the trans-Atlantic "abyss." Put another way, for all the superficial evidence to the contrary, there is not (or at least, need not be) any "abyss of modernity" between technologically advanced contemporary cultures. Both sides of the Atlantic abound in substantial innovative creativity, such as the video installations that Nam June Paik and Marie-Jo Lafontaine contributed to the 1987 Documenta.[43] That Paik should be a Korean artist residing variously in Germany and America, or that Lafontaine should be a Belgian artist exhibited in an array of European countries, is perhaps beside the point. More significant than their national identity is their international cultural identity, as pioneers of the relatively new multimedia discursive space of multimonitor video installations.

Paik's contribution to the 1987 Documenta was a quintessentially trans-Atlantic composition—a multiscreened video orchestration of a performance by the late Joseph Beuys, which, far from neutralizing Beuys's performance, transported its register and its impact into radically new realms of sonic and iconic energy, way beyond the familiar conventions of live, monodimensional, real-time performance, within the technospace of the 1980s and 90s that many of the other artists in this exhibition were exploring, and are continuing to explore, all over the world. If, as William S. Burroughs once remarked, "Anyone who can pick up a frying pan owns death,"[44] then reciprocally it might well be argued that any artist who can pick up a video camera owns life—in the sense that, for all its initial imperfections and annoyances, the technoart of the multimedia artist still seems very much what Samuel Beckett calls "an untilled field,"[45] precipitating surprisingly fresh, innovative creativity.

At this juncture, it is helpful to turn once again to the writings of Burroughs, and more particularly to the passage in *Nova Express* where Burroughs, prophetically foreshadowing the present plague of tired apocalyptic writings, alludes to a "stale movie" screened by the ubiquitous "Mr Bradley Mr Martin." Triumphantly reporting the fate of this unfortunate film, Burroughs's narrator introduces it in terms of a pseudohistorical reference to one of his own publications: "In 1960 with the publication of *Minutes to Go*, Martin's stale movie was greeted by an unprecedented chorus of boos and a concerted walkout—'We seen this five times already and not standing still for another twilight of your tired Gods'" (13).

It is now 1988, some quarter century or more after 1960; and yet, so far as one can tell, Baudrillard's successive writings have treated their readers to depiction after depiction of the "twilight" of assorted trans-Atlantic "tired Gods" without ever suffering from any such "concerted walkout." One wonders why. That this should be the case is surely a tribute to both Baudrillard's mastery and refinement of revived *fin-de-siècle*, "twilight" rhetoric, and to his audience's insatiable appetite for apocalyptic entertainment: a remarkable achievement in both instances.

But when Baudrillard's *Amérique* is considered in terms of its capacity to offer cultural analysis commensurate with the contemporaneity of its subject matter, this volume's anachronistic apocalyptic rhetoric begs a harsher verdict. As Burroughs reminds us in *Nova Express*, there is nothing more absurd than the vain attempt to master the present with obsolete munitions—a *very* fatal strategy, "*Like charging a regiment of tanks with a defective slingshot.*"[46]

jameson's complaint

video art and the intertextual "time–wall"

5

> *All right, B. J. cut. From now on we run a good clean show. A show you can take your kids and your grandmother to see it. Just good clean magic for all the family.*

As William S. Burroughs intimates in the lines above from "St Louis Return," cinema and video seldom simply offer innocuous "good clean magic for all the family."[1] Like any other genre, video displays an array of effects, ranging from the good, the bad, and the ugly to the downright nasty. Unlike older genres, video also challenges our cultural expectations. First, as Walter Benjamin might have argued, it realizes modernism's vague aspirations toward "effects which could only be obtained by a changed technical standard."[2] Video *is* this sort of changed technical standard. Second, as a specifically postmodern practice interacting with other genres, video precipitates an increasingly prevalent multimedia sensibility.

Arguably, the most compelling examples of distinctively *post*modern creativity emerge within video art and its multimedia corollaries. Any understanding of contemporary art necessitates the critical examination of video's taped authorial works and its more impersonal installations, and of new modes of multimedia performance combining live and technological performance, or reconceptualizing traditional theater in terms of video's special qualities and effects.

Ironically, as Umberto Eco points out in his articles on the new media, those "trained by the texts of twenty years ago" often seem quite helpless before multimedia art. By contrast, younger generations born within the welter of the new media "instinctively . . . know these things better than some seventy-year-old pedagogue," having "absorbed as elements of their behaviour a series of elements filtered through the mass media (and coming, in some cases, from the most impenetrable areas of our century's artistic experimentation)."[3]

At its most positive extreme, postmodern creativity exhibits identical virtues. Absorbing and internalizing the lessons of modernism's most impenetrable experimentation, and at the same time mastering the more "impenetrable" advances in late-twentieth-century technology, postmodern video artists such as Nam June Paik and postmodern multimedia artists such as Robert Wilson create the quintessentially late-twentieth-century art that conservative critics such as Charles Jencks have incredulously characterized as that "strange even paradoxical thing": an art "more modern than Modern," and "more avant-garde" than the modernist avant-garde.[4]

At its most misleading extreme, the postmodern cultural theory of critics such as Jencks and Fredric Jameson dismisses contemporary technological creativity in far more negative terms. Postmodern culture, it seems, coincides with the mythological "deaths" of authoriality, originality, spirituality, monumentality, beauty, profundity—everything, in fact, except apocalyptic cliché. According to Jencks, for example, postmodern culture subverts the ideals of the modernist tradition in a "series of self-cancelling steps"; reduces art and music to the "all white canvas" and "absolute silence"; and transforms its public into "lobotomized mass-media illiterates."[5]

Jencks's concept of the mass-media illiterate has an unexpected double-edge. On the one hand, it obviously refers to those nurtured on televised kitsch, incapable of reading anything more challenging than comic book captions. But as recent discussions of postmodern video art suggest, the same formulation also applies to theorists nurtured on the printed page: those who vaguely sense the significance of video art, but who find themselves incapable of deliberating upon it in anything other than derisive terminology. Jean Baudrillard, for example, hails video as "the special effect of our time," but in the next breath rather ambiguously applauds and deplores video for its "intensity on the surface" and its "insignificance in depth."[6] More recently, Baudrillard has evoked video as "a foreign domain" in which he wants "to remain a foreigner."[7]

In much the same way, Fredric Jameson emphasizes the significance of video, and half-heartedly acknowledges that video artists such as Nam June Paik have "identified a whole range of things to do and then moved in to colonize this new space."[8] Thereafter, Jameson alludes rather uncertainly to Paik's "quintessentially postmodern dispositions," and adds the scathing afterthought, "only the most misguided museum visitor would look for 'art' in the content of the video images themselves."[9]

Surely the reverse obtains. Only the most misguided or the most cynical viewer would suppose that Paik's work consists solely of discursive self-referentiality. Briefly, Jameson's deliberations upon postmodern video art, and upon postmodern culture in general, project their own conceptual confusion upon such subject matter. Jameson appears the victim of two afflictions: his tendency toward premature exasperation, and his more general disadvantage as one of the many contemporary intellectuals who appear trapped behind what one might think of as the intertextual "time–wall."

These complaints become most explicit in Jameson's article entitled "Reading without interpretation: Postmodernism and the Video-text,"[10] an essay continually informed by overliteral responses to Roland Barthes's provocative overstatement in "Death of the Author."[11] Parisian polemic has long perfected exaggeration and heuristic hyperbole into something of an art form; a tradition which culminates in Baudrillard's seductive "fictionalizing."[12] One thinks, for example, of the impossible, inflexible imperatives of Surrealists such as Luis Buñuel or André Breton. Declaring that "NOTHING" in his film *Un Chien andalou* "SYMBOLISES ANYTHING," Buñuel explains that this work's scenario evolved according to strict adherence to principles determining that "When an image or idea appeared the collaborators discarded it immediately if it was derived from remembrance, or from their cultural pattern or if, simply, it had a conscious association with another earlier idea. They accepted only those representations as valid which, though they moved them profoundly, had no possible explanation."[13]

As Buñuel indicates, his fidelity to the articles of Surrealism proved supremely impractical. Faced with the possibility that the supposedly subversive *Un Chien andalou* might become a public success, and confronted by

Breton's astonishing question "are you with the police or with us?" Buñuel suggested that we burn the negative on the *Place du Tetre* in Montmartre, something I would have done without hesitation had the group agreed to it."[14] Jameson's pursuit of Barthes's early "purist" ideals leads to much the same kind of self-destructive logic as that born of Buñuel's dedication to Breton's most austere edicts.

Buñuel's and Jameson's conclusions offer a pleasing asymmetry. While the former defend authorial insight and scorn cultural convention, the latter reassert Barthes's claim that texts contain no other content that a "performative" function. According to *The Death of the Author,* "The fact is . . . that writing can no longer designate an operation of notation, representation, 'depiction' . . . rather, it designates exactly what linguists . . . call a performative . . . in which the enunciation has no other content . . . than the act by which it is uttered" (145–46). Taken to its extreme, Barthes's argument proposes that "In the multiplicity of writing, everything is to be *disentangled,* nothing *deciphered,* the structure can be followed, 'run' (like the thread of a stocking), at every point and at every level, but there is nothing beneath" (147). Jameson takes this hypothesis very seriously. Recycling it some twenty years after its initial formulation, he applies it once again both to the "postmodern text" in general, and to video in particular (taking video to be a "privileged exemplar" of postmodernism's products), observing that they may be defined as "a structure or sign-flow which resists meaning, whose fundamental inner logic is the exclusion of themes . . . and which therefore systematically sets out to shortcircuit traditional interpretive temptations" (219). In much the same way, Baudrillard sweepingly dismisses the referential potential of the electronic media, arguing that the screen "only communicates images, not a particular time and place," so that, "In the end it makes everything circulate in one space, without depth, where all the objects must be able to follow one after the other without slowing down or stopping the circuit."[15]

One reads Jameson's account of video's "exclusion of themes" with considerable nostalgia. In almost identical terms, Barthes's early essay on the *nouveau roman* "Objective literature"(1954) insisted that Robbe-Grillet's novels were "not composed in depth"; did not "protect a heart" beneath their surface; and contained "no thematics."[16] Rather, they apparently "assassinate the classical object" in a "well-planned murder" that "cuts them off from . . . the poet's privileged terrain."[17] It is scarcely surprising that Robbe-Grillet subsequently disassociated his work from Barthes's oversimplistic exegesis.[18] Nor indeed is one startled by Barthes's shift of focus from "studium" (or anonymous, general codes), to "punctum" (or idiosyncratic, personal responses), in both his essays on photography in *Camera Lucida*,[19] and such diary entries as the following observations of 5 August 1977:

"Continuing *War and Peace*, I have a violent emotion, reading the death of old Prince Bolkonsky, his last words of tenderness to his daughter. Literature has an effect of truth much more violent for me than that of religion."[20]

Jameson perceives little "truth" and "violent emotion." Having declared video to be "a sign-flow which resists meaning," he makes the extraordinary suggestion that "Whatever a good, let alone a great videotext might be, it will be bad or flawed whenever . . . interpretation proves possible, whenever the text slackly opens up . . . places and areas of thematization" (219).

Jameson appears to generate this strange definition of video by combining Barthes's theories of intertextuality with a number of concepts and metaphors borrowed from the writings of Raymond Williams and Jean Baudrillard. His hypothesis that video becomes "flawed" whenever it permits thematic interpretation stems from Williams's suggestion that television evinces "a situation of total flow . . .streaming before us all day long without interruption" (202). Applying this concept of "total flow" to video, Jameson argues that video art should *only* exist and should *only* be apprehended as a vague, uninterrupted flow of superficial fragments. Accordingly, he concludes that "Video-viewing . . . involves immersion in the total flow of the thing itself, preferably a kind of random succession of three or four hours of tape at regular intervals . . . *What is quite out of the question is to look at a single 'video work' all by itself*" (208).[21]

The reasons for Jameson's hostility to the acknowledgement of the single work of video art rapidly become evident. So far as he is concerned postmodern culture demarcates—or ought to demarcate—a cultural revolution or terror eliminating all traces of original creativity. Rejecting both the rhetoric and the reality of cultural innovation, and refusing even to contemplate individual video works, Jameson warns the viewer that "to select—even as an 'example'— a single video text, and to discuss it in isolation, is fatally to regenerate the illusion of the masterpiece or the canonical text" (208).

This morbid fear of masterpieces coexists with Jameson's suspicion that the postmodern revolution may not yet have exterminated *all* traces of the modernist aesthetic. Rephrasing the warning italicized in the lines above, he still more misguidedly protests that "The discussion, the indispensable preliminary selection and isolation, of a single 'text' ... automatically transforms it back into a 'work,' turns the anonymous videomaker back into a named artist or 'auteur,' *opens the way for the return of all those features of an older modernist aesthetic which it was in the revolutionary nature of the newer medium to have precisely effaced and dispelled*" (209).[22]

There is no special reason why the new postmodern media should by its very "revolutionary nature" *efface* the modernist aesthetic. As John Cage remarks, "Machines ... can tend toward our stupefaction or our enlivenment."[23] Revolutionary aesthetics have always posited an oppositional relationship between the present and the past, but in Jameson's case, revolutionary practices are taken as evidence not only of the "effacement" of the past, but—by deft movements of retrospective redefinition—as proof that the past never really existed save in terms of present, revolutionary arguments. Thus, whereas the Russian Constructivist Alexei Gan, writing in 1922, entertained the distinction between modernist "industrial culture" and premodernist art, "indissolubly linked with theology, metaphysics and mysticism" which "arose naturally, developed naturally, and disappeared naturally,"[24] Jameson denies even this "natural" contrast. Apparently there never were, never are, and never could be any positive alternatives to what Jameson identifies as mediated culture informed by the "deep underlying materiality of all things" (199).

Jameson's hypotheses pivot upon the questionable assumption that the postmodern age coincides with "the extinction of the sacred and the 'spiritual'" (199). Dominated by Jameson's alternative to the deep underlying spirituality of all things—the deep underlying materiality of all things—the present appears to be a time when "there are no more masterpieces, no more great books," and "even the concept of good books has become problematical" (208). Adding what one might think of as retrospective insult to contemporary injury, Jameson adds that culture "always was material." From this it would appear to follow that "older forms or genres" and "older spiritual exercises and meditations ... were also in their different ways media products" (199). Viewed with Jamesonian hindsight, all cultural practices become redefined as "material" and as "mediated" products. *Everything,* it seems, is material, in its own way.

At this point, Jameson equates the material with the textual. Reaffirming Roland Barthes's argument that everything is intertextual, in its own way, he advises the reader: "Everything can now be a text ... while objects that were formerly 'works' can now be reread as immense ensembles or systems of texts of

various kinds, superimposed on each other by way of the various intertextuali-
ties, successions of fragments, or yet again, sheer process (henceforth called textual production or textualization)" (208).

Barthes, of course, argued that this sort of "textualization" could at least be
"followed" and "disentangled," if not "deciphered."[25] Unwilling, it seems, even to
credit postmodern video art with this kind of tangible coherence, Jameson turns
for inspiration to Baudrillard's apocalyptic assertion that "The mass-media are
anti-mediatory and . . . fabricate non-communication."[26] Reconceptualized in
such rhetoric, postmodern video's "non-communication" appears to evince a
"logic of rotating conjunction and disjunction" (221), resisting both thematic
analysis and sustained structural investigation. At best, the viewer simply perceives vacuous "good clean magic" or "a ceaseless rotation of elements such that
they change place at every moment, with the result that no single element can
occupy the position of 'interpretant' (or that of primary sign) for any length of
time" (218).

Taking up another of Baudrillard's provocative phrases—his suggestion that
the postmodern era witnesses "the dissolution of life into TV"—Jameson asserts
that video somehow "dissolves" both its viewer's and its author's sense of identity and subjectivity. Introducing this insight with reference to intuitions born of
his own dissolving subjectivity, he confides: "I have the feeling that mechanical
depersonalization (or decentering the subject) goes even further in the new
medium, where auteurs themselves are dissolved along with the spectator" (205).

This sweeping feeling derives from extremely general meditation, rather
than from selective study of specific examples of subject matter. The weakest
trends in postmodern culture—be these modes of video art or modes of poststructuralist theory—certainly drift into vacuous "rotating conjunction and disjunction," dissolving both their author's presence and their audience's patience.
It is to such "degraded" (210) material that Jameson turns his attention.

Apart from his sporadic asides to the "unimaginable informational garbage"
polluting the media works of the "new media society" (210), Jameson considers
only one specific video composition: "a twenty-nine minute 'work' entitled
AlienN A T I O N (1988), produced at the School of the Art Institute of
Chicago"(209), and only one specific multimedia performance: Laurie Anderson's
USA (which also contains the word "alienation"). Persuaded that neither work
deploys or distinguishes the implications of the former's "obliging title" particularly when compared with the rigor of Karl Marx's "Early manuscripts" (217),

Jameson dismisses the thematic potential of both video art and multimedia performance art in the supremely subjective speculation "one has the deeper feeling that 'texts' like *USA* or *AlienN A T I O N* ought not to have any 'meaning' at all, in that thematic sense" (217–218).

This is surely one of Jameson's most ill-considered speculations, especially when one reflects that he is claiming to discuss postmodern video "in its strongest and most original and most authentic form" (223). One scarcely expects the logic of video and multimedia performance to replicate that of Marx's "Early manuscripts." But one might well expect Jameson to substantiate his deeper feelings with more careful reference to these new arts. This is not to be. At best, he rather languidly delegates detailed research to the reader (despite his repeated prohibition of precisely this kind of impressionistic response), concluding: "This is something everyone is free to verify, by self-observation and a little closer attention to those moments in which we briefly feel that disillusionment I have described experiencing at the thematically explicit moments in *USA*" (218).

Jameson belatedly—and somewhat ineffectively—acknowledges the confusion and contradiction in his argument, when he concedes that he is the victim of the "hegemony of theories of textuality and textualization"; a set of presuppositions that he finally criticizes as a "vicious circle" or "double-bind" (221). Despite this insight, Jameson placidly acquiesces to the grip of what we might call these "critical vices," insofar as he observes "your entry ticket to the public sphere in which these matters are debated is an agreement, tacit or otherwise, with the basic presuppositions of a general problem-field" (221).

Jean-François Lyotard rather more convincingly posits that critics and artists should think and create more independently, by "working without rules in order to formulate the rules of what will have been done."[28] On occasion, Jameson likewise aspires to define video "afresh . . . without imported and extrapolated categories" (201). As he remarks to Anders Stephanson, his hypotheses approximate most closely to Lyotard's ideal when they work with allegories inventing what one might think of as fictional systems and landmarks in order to encompass "what will have been done": "In trying to theorize the systematic, I was using certain of these things as allegories. From this angle it makes no sense trying to look for individual trends, and individual artists are only interesting if one finds some moment where the system as a whole, or some limit of it, is being touched."[29]

Jameson's allegories display two fundamental weaknesses. First, they depend upon reductive intertextual theory. Second, they consistently neglect the crucial individual artists and trends that most clearly exemplify "what will have been done." As Jameson admits in his essay on "Postmodernism and Utopia"(1988), his overly systematic allegories and paradigms take no account of artists such as Hans Haacke, whose work he acclaims as "a kind of cultural production which is clearly postmodern and equally clearly political and oppositional—something that does not compute with the paradigm and does not seem to have been theoretically foreseen by it."[30]

As becomes increasingly evident, Jameson's accounts of postmodern video and postmodern multimedia performance leave far too much *unforeseen*—and far too much *unseen*. While Jameson modestly prefaces the following account of his responses to Rauschenberg's work with the confession "I don't know how great Rauschenberg is," his subsequent comments reveal the way in which his impatience before unfamiliar postmodern art leads him to dismiss it almost by very definition as inconsequential, submonumental, and so on. In this respect, one might respond that Jameson *always* seems to have known that Rauschenberg's work could never be "great," since by very Jamesonian definition, it resists prolonged examination and profound meditation, instantly becoming out of mind when out of sight. Rapidly transforming tentative confusion into dogmatic delusion, Jameson relates: "I saw a wonderful show of his in China, a glittering set of things which offered all kinds of postmodern experiences. But when they're over, they're over. The textual object is not, in other words, a work of art, a 'masterwork' like the Modernist monument was. You go into a Rauschenberg show and experience a process done in very expert and inventive ways; and when you leave, it's over."[31]

Jameson's argument seems trapped within its own momentum. Given the historical, technological, and aesthetic character of postmodernism, one would scarcely expect it to produce "masterworks" that were *literally* "like the Modernist monument." Nevertheless, it seems injudiciously impetuous to infer that postmodern culture is axiomatically submonumental simply because it—quite predictably—offers alternatives to modernism's monuments. The social, technological and aesthetic problems of our time are substantially different to those of the twenties, and it is to artistic responses to these recent problems—be they monumental or otherwise—that the cultural critic should turn.

As John G. Hanhardt remarks, the most interesting works of video art offer striking ripostes to the supposedly neutralizing impact of television and video. Commenting upon the work of Wolf Vostell and Nam June Paik, Hanhardt suggests that "The achievements of Paik and Vostell, both independently and collaboratively, were to strip television of its institutional meanings and expose its manipulation of images as a powerful co-optive force in capitalist society."[32]

In this respect, Paik and Vostell are notable for their subversive interactive aesthetic. In Hanhardt's terms, "By alerting us to how we look at television, Paik and Vostell proclaimed the possibility of changing this relationship from a passive to an active one."[33] Marita Sturken makes very much the same observation. Emphasizing the way in which "Paik combined the destruction of TV's popular image with clever interpretations of video's role in the communications future and a reinterpretation of the role of the viewer," Sturken adds, "Many of his TV sculptures are intended to involve the viewers and to question their passive role . . . by using their voices or images as visual material."[34]

Other works such as Paik's *Beuys' Voice*—quite literally, a monumental installation shown in different versions at Documenta 8, at Paik's Hayward retrospective *Video Works 1963–88* (where it deployed fifty-five television sets), at the 1990 Sydney Biennale and at the Fluxus segment of the 1990 Venice Biennale—employ the more personal, biographical materials that Jameson deems incompatible with video art. Based upon footage of one of Paik's last performances with Beuys, *Beuys' Voice* is at once an orchestration of the "grain" of Beuys' voice and a celebration of Paik's admiration and reverence for a late friend and collaborator.

At first, *Beuys' Voice* seems an extremely confusing work. Then, as the eye settles, one becomes aware of its two basic sections: a central set of screens displaying sections and sub-sections of footage of Beuys's performance, and two end sections, consisting of screens framing more rapid sequences of more abstract and distorted imagery. Paik remarks that his more recent piece, *Living with the Living Theater* (1989), similarly combines sequences of relatively legible, slow footage with more demanding, more accelerated imagery. Contemplating successive variants of *Beuys' Voice* in Kassel, London, Sydney, and Venice, one gradually becomes aware of the respective felicities of its different incarnations, and begins to evaluate and compare the "art" and content of Paik's video images (despite Jameson's injunction that only the most misguided viewer might attempt this exercise). Likewise, the more one sees of other artists' video installations, the easier it becomes to assess Paik's contributions to this genre.

Although it is certainly dwarfed by Paik's 1003 monitor installation *Tadaikson (The more The better)* (1988) in the Seoul Museum of Modern Art, there would appear good reasons for citing Paik's *Beuys' Voice* as an archetypal postmodern multimedia monument. Movingly combining a variety of more or less legible visual and sonic narratives, ranging from footage of Beuys to more abstract fragmentation, Paik dynamically demonstrates the surprisingly positive potential of the multiscreened video installation. All the same, it is a slow, laborious process, coming to terms with his unfamiliar endeavors. As Paik perspicaciously intimates in an early manifesto entitled "Afterlude to the Exposition of Experimental Television 1963, March, Galerie Parnass," his work demands considerable attention and contemplation; hence his final suggestion, "Anyway, if you see my TV, please, see it more than thirty minutes."[35]

New video requires at least partial contemplation in its own terms, rather than those of other more familiar prior discourse. As John Cage suggests, innovative art increases our awareness of the unknown, as much as of the known, revealing possibilities that one can only apprehend slowly, in time, rather than instantaneously, within the categories of the past. Whereas Jameson dismisses and deplores Rauschenberg's experiments with the aside "when you leave, it's over," Cage rather more generously ponders upon his discovery of Robert Ryman's white paintings: "The work of Ryman I was not familiar with, until I saw this retrospective show. And it was amazing to see what had happened to his dedication to white.... I came away from that exhibition with a renewed sense of joy, and even a joy close to a change of mind.... And the discoveries don't give you a sense of the loss of the ability to discover, but rather, an intensification of that."[36]

Jameson's analyses seem to lack this quality of renewed joy before significant discovery for the simple reason that they discredit this eventuality from the very beginning of their inquiries. As he points out in "Postmodernism and Utopia," and in his earlier essay "Postmodernism, or the Cultural Logic of Capitalism" (1984), such dogmatic assumptions invariably fail at the very point at which they seem most likely to succeed, because the critic "paints himself into a corner where his critical sensibility becomes "paralysed ... in the face of the model itself."[37]

Throughout his essay on video art Jameson's critical sensibility appears to be paralyzed by his assertion that postmodern culture coincides with the death of the author, the spectator and any kind of meaningful creativity. Having painted himself into a corner in which the concept of "mediated" appears synonymous with "exterminated," Jameson has no other option than to reiterate the tired complaint: "The autonomous work of art along with the old subject or ego— seems to have vanished, to have been volatized. Nowhere is this more materially demonstrable than within the 'texts' of experimental video" (208).

Jameson could not be more mistaken. Nowhere are the artist's and the spectator's subjectivity more relentlessly registered, resurrected and reaf- firmed than in postmodern video art, video installations and multimedia performance.

Firstly, as Cage and Paik suggest, the very process of employing the new technologies may function as a conceptual revelation for the artist. Discussing the tape recorder, Cage proposes that magnetic tape "introduces the unknown with such clarity that anyone has the opportunity of having his habits blown away like dust."[38] Paik likewise argues that experiments with television expose the artist to radical alternatives to the "one book with one- way direction" of "poor Joyce," and speculates that television collages and installations may well reveal glimpses of "Eternity," insofar as "The simulta- neous perception of the parallel flow of thirteen independent TV movements can perhaps realize this old dream of mystics."[39] As Cage and Paik indicate, the video artist's subject or ego may frequently be "volatized" very produc- tively by the new media in the very process of creating an installation or art- work. Secondly, at a subsequent performative or explorative level, the interactive relationships between the artist or the viewer and the completed installation or artwork similarly provoke states of heightened self-awareness before the camera.

As Rosalind Krauss reminds us, most video art produced on tape employs "the body of the artist-practitioners" as its "central instrument."[40] One thinks of Paik's Self Portrait (1970); of Vito Acconci's attempt to frustrate this process in Face-Off (1972); or of Robert Morris's multiple self-portraits in Exchange (1973).[41] The more one examines such video works the more obvious it becomes that it is postmodern intertextual theory—not post- modern multimedia art—that conspires to short-circuit "traditional inter- pretive temptations" (219).

Or as Mona da Vinci puts it, video is a medium "encouraging self-analysis."[42] Far from neutralizing authoriality and meaning, a tape such as Paik's *Nam June Paik, Edited for TV* (1976) begs definition as a highly personal contribution to explicit cultural debate. Wittily juxtaposing the image of Paik's frowning face with the caption "But then I thought: Actually 'zen' is boring too,"[43] this work almost certainly responds to the celebrated passage in *Silence*, in which John Cage defends the teachings of Zen, observing: "In Zen they say: If something is boring after two minutes, try it for four. If still boring, try it for eight, sixteen, thirty-two and so on. Eventually one discovers that it's not boring at all but very interesting."[44]

Paik's tape, then, seems best understood as a very personal dramatization of his riposte to another specific subjectivity: John Cage. In somewhat the same way, viewers examining video installations might be said to dramatize their analysis of the cameras, monitors, and mirrors making up such works as they walk within them, modifying their understanding as they modify images of their movements. To quote Krauss again, "the central instrument" of such video installations "has usually been the body of the responding viewer."[45] At the same time though, video installations also correspond more than any other kind of video art to Jameson's claim that the genre is primarily a self-referential practice, evoking "reproductive technology itself" (222).

Paradoxically perhaps, video installations activate and accelerate two quite different modes of perception. As Jameson postulates, they invite the impersonal analysis of their technological structure and construction. But as Krauss remarks, this analysis is itself born of the viewer's extremely personal experience of performing and observing successive physical gestures monitored and mediated by an installation. In this respect, the viewer's physical and cerebral participation are interlinked with unprecedented intimacy and immediacy. Contemplating a painting like René Magritte's *Reproduction Prohibited* (*Portrait of Mr. James*) (1937), one responds from without to an image of exterior perception: Magritte's paradoxical reiterated image of Mr. James's back, standing before, and reflected within, the mirror before him.[46] By contrast, installations such as Peter Campus's *Shadow Projection* (1974) reveal video's capacity to place the viewer within an inescapably interactive situation; in this instance, "doubling" evidence of self-awareness by superimposing images of both the spectator's back and the spectator's shadow.[47]

The same kind of intensified subjectivity emerges in another variant of video art: the multimedia performance, in which actions upon stage and actions upon screen intermingle. At its most amusing and most provocative, this quintessentially postmodern mode of performance culminates in works such as Paik's *TV Cello* and *TV Bra*. According to the artist, *TV Bra for Living Sculpture* (1969), a performance installation requiring Charlotte Moorman to play a cello connected to two screens ornamenting her breasts, exemplified a more "human use of technology," in the sense that it allows the performer to wear and to play video; a historic victory as it were for subjectivity over the electronic media.[48] Commenting upon the way in which "the performer caused images on the screen to change" in this work's companion piece, *Concerto for TV Cello and Videotapes* (1971), Gregory Battcock enthusiastically observed: "It was an theoretical masterpiece, because instead of 'being on television,' the televisions were, in fact, on Charlotte Moorman."[49]

Battcock's rhetoric offers a refreshing alternative to Jameson's gloomy generalizations. While the lines above delightedly acclaim Paik's *TV Cello* as a masterpiece, Jameson's fidelity to "purist" anti-authorial theory leads him to dismiss the very possibility of video artists or video masterpieces. Bewildered by the "hybrid" energies of video's "multiplicity of new forms," Jameson rather plaintively confides: "one is tempted to wonder whether any description or theory could ever encompass their variety" (203), before once again intoning his familiar litany of disbelief: "there are no videos, there can never be a video canon, even an auteur theory, of video . . . becomes very problematic indeed" (208–9).

Trapped by his own theoretical prejudices within an analytical double bind asserting that all postmodern "texts" are superficial submonumental disappointments that "all turn out to be 'the same' in a peculiarly unhelpful way" (222), Jameson attempts to evade his unhelpful anti-authorial assumptions by recourse to the authorial fiction that he proudly describes as "a kind of myth I have found useful in characterizing the nature of contemporary (postmodernist) cultural production" (222). According to this mythology, "the moment of modernism" witnesses the decline of "the referent, or the objective world, or reality," to "a feeble existence on the horizon like a shrunken star or red dwarf"(222).

In the wake of this precursor, postmodern culture demands definition as an era of total crisis, when "reference and reality disappear altogether." Elaborating this apocalyptic fiction, Jameson concludes: "we are left with that pure and random play of signifiers . . . which no longer produces monumental works of the modernist type, but ceaselessly reshuffles the fragments of preexistent texts, the

building blocks of older cultural and social production, in some new and heightened bricolage; metabooks which cannibalize other books, metatexts which col-
late bits of other texts" (223).

Interpreted in this way, the mediated reality of postmodernism appears to
represent the dead end of modernism; or a realm of ceaselessly recycled, submonumental fragments, bereft of all prior value. Viewed diagrammatically,
this reading of the transition from modernism to postmodernism (or the sad
story of cultural decline from the mid-twenties to the mid-fifties), might be
represented by the falling hypotenuse of an erstwhile lofty triangle:

modernism

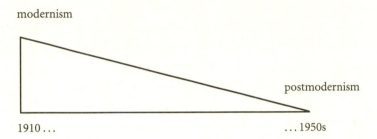

1910...   ...1950s

While one may have many reservations and doubts about many aspects of
postmodern creativity, it is absurd to dismiss present times as an era of post-
mortem culture, devoid of authorial or aesthetic life. Such anti-authorial and
anti-aesthetic speculation is still more misleading than the authorial and aesthetic mythologies it purports to correct. Viewed more carefully, the decline of
modernism—or the existential and aesthetic confusion of the thirties, forties,
and fifties leads not so much to the terminal dead end of creativity, as to the
painful transitional process separating modernism's demise from the rise of
postmodern creativity. Briefly, the three decades from the mid-fifties to the present are best understood as a period of intense cultural rejuvenation and innovation marked by the "live ends" of what one might think of as postmodern
technoculture.

For one reason or another, Jameson and many other theorists appear incapable of looking beyond the crises of the mid-twentieth century. Or put another way, in terms of a paradox outlined by the German writer Heiner Müller,
Jameson seems to be trapped behind a "time-wall", unable either to enter or even
envisage postmodernism's positive new discursive spaces. Introducing the concept of the"time-wall" with reference to the way in which this kind of obstruc-
tion may have protected Moscow in the last war, Heiner Müller comments: "I

was very impressed by the remark of a young man who was writing an essay on my work. He remembered that he never quite understood why the German Wehrmacht didn't succeed in entering Moscow during the Second World War. They just stood there. They couldn't go further. He didn't believe in geographic reasons. He didn't believe in ideological reasons. There simply was a time-wall. They were not on the same track."[50]

Heiner Müller's image of the "time-wall" proves particularly helpful. While one would not want to argue that entire nations or generations are trapped behind such barriers (as Baudrillard proposes, when suggesting that the "abyss of modernity" separates French intellectuals from America),[51] it would certainly seem to be the case that an overdose of intertextual dogma and of apocalyptic mythology prevents Jameson and his fellow thinkers from coming to terms with the rise of postmodernism. Charted diagrammatically, the transition between Modernism and the first three or four decades of postmodernism begs representation in terms of two equally monumental aesthetic eras separated by the crises and the "time-wall" peculiar to the early postmodern decades between the mid-thirties and mid-fifties.

Trapped behind the thirties-fifties "time-wall," Jameson compulsively contrasts the apparent inauthenticity of the "now" with the authenticity of modernism's "then." Veering close to self-parody, his most recent ponderings upon "the new painting" dismiss this development as: "Surrealism without the Unconscious . . . Chagall's folk iconography without Judaism or the peasants, Klee's stick drawings without Klee's peculiar personal project, schizophrenic art without schizophrenia, 'surrealism' without its manifesto or its avant garde."[52]

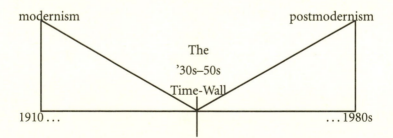

Jameson's cultural obituaries are surely premature. As the veteran Surrealist poet and novelist Louis Aragon rather unexpectedly proposes, crucial aspects of the Surrealist dream appear alive and well in that most recent of postmodern practices: the multimedia performance born of what one might think of as postmodernism's positive "mediatic" sensibility. Writing an open letter to André Breton about the first Paris production of Robert Wilson's *Deafman Glance,* Aragon recalls: "I never saw anything more beautiful in the world since I was born. Never has any play come anywhere near this one . . . Bob Wilson's piece which comes to us from Iowa, is not surrealism at all, however easy it is for people to call it that, but it is what we others, who fathered surrealism, what we dreamed it might become after us, beyond us."[53]

"*After us, beyond us*": in four brief words, Aragon pinpoints the essential difference between positive variants of postmodernism and modernism. Postmodernism is something that is not modernism; that comes after modernism; that is radically separated from modernism; but which realizes modernism's aspirations in terms of its own subsequent technology and sensibility. As I have suggested elsewhere, American postmodern creativity appears to assimilate and legitimate modernism's innovations and discoveries, employing and extending them in a matter-of-fact, unself-conscious way, rather than announcing them as some sort of excursion into the Surrealist realm of the "marvellous."[54] Not surprisingly then, Robert Wilson's multimedia performances resist definition in terms of familiar Surrealist categories. What one witnesses here is not so much neutralized Surrealism, or "Surrealism without the Unconscious," as Surrealism without friction in an age in which its mysteries are public knowledge, As William S. Burroughs remarks, "the unconscious was much more unconscious in Freud's day than in ours."[55] If automatic writing and collage composition were novelties in the twenties, this is no longer the case.

Robert Wilson's multimedia performances typify the ways in which video art precipitates some of the most interesting postmodern creativity of the eighties. Translating video's digital editing techniques and luscious color into dazzlingly rapid or excruciatingly prolonged fusions of familiar real-time theatre and multimediated *son et lumière,* Wilson's works for the stage offer a litmus test to the spectator's sensibility, frustrating prior expectations but also affording the delight of new, emergent conventions to those willing and able to look beyond the "time-wall" of habit. Not surprisingly, one's first experience of Wilson's work is very much a process of examining and defining it as self-referential "reproductive technology itself." (222). But thereafter, more positive post-Jamesonian categories come to mind.

The more closely one examines Wilson's work and the more times one attends a particular example of Wilson's work, the more evident it becomes that his multimedia theater is not *simply* a surprising "structure or sign-flow which resists meaning" (219), but rather a sign-flow which *generates* meaning, although not, perhaps, the kind of meaning to which one is accustomed. As Stefan Brecht reports, Wilson seems most interested to create conditions in which one senses "a non-verbal, arational communication taking place . . . by harmonious vibration."[56]

At times, this kind of "arational communication" emerges between the lines and the gestures of traditional theatrical performance. But at its most forceful, the impact of Wilson's imagination reaches us through the utterly postmodern state-of-the-art technology that Eco associates with "a series of elements filtered through the mass media."[57] Considered in terms of the unfashionable concept of the author, Wilson's vision might also be said to be filtered through his correspondingly postmodern state-of-the-art *sensibility,* born of and attuned to video's capacity to accelerate, decelerate, fragment, superimpose, juxtapose, and generally transmute sound, image, color and movement with unprecedented immediacy and precision.

Faced with such shifts in creative technology and sensibility, cultural critics tend to suspend or assert disbelief, entrusting themselves to new developments beyond the "time-wall" of familiar discourse, or distrusting and denouncing new unfamiliar practices. Writing to the *Village Voice* in 1966, John Cage memorably exemplified the former option, announcing: "Nowadays everything happens at once and our souls are conveniently electronic (omniattentive)."[58]

At the other extreme, Jameson argues that postmodern video art and multimedia performance "ought not to have any 'meaning'" (217), somewhat as Georg Lukács claims, that "modernism must deprive literature of a sense of perspective."[59]

Neither modernism, postmodernism—or whatever follows—"ought to" or "must" necessarily *neutralize* meaning or perspective. On the contrary, new practices appear new precisely because they *dramatize* relatively unconventional modes of representing and evaluating reality. (Conversely, such dramatizations only seem to neutralize meaning insofar as their new possibilities *precede* theoretical legitimization). In this respect anti-art is best understood as ante-art, adumbrating new conventions.[60]

As post-revolutionary Russian experiments demonstrate, innovative creativity does not so much extinguish old values and old debates as rekindle them in new contexts. Creating predominantly similar geometrical compositions,

Constructivists such as Alexei Gan associated "industrial culture" with the death and disappearance of "theology, metaphysics and mysticism," whereas Suprematists such as Kasimir Malevich entitled their work with such self-consciously metaphysical definitions as *Suprematist composition conveying the feeling of a mystic "wave" from outer space.*[61]

History repeats itself in the eighties. While Jameson argues that postmodern culture brings about "the extinction of the sacred and the 'spiritual'" (199), Robert Wilson discusses ways of conveying the sacred and the spiritual with technological symbolism. Referring to his projected production of Richard Wagner's *Parsifal,* Wilson speculates for example that "vertical beams of light" might evince a more authentic "religious attitude" than the "fake" and "sacrilegious detail" of "naturalistic acting."[62]

To discuss Wilson's art in this way is obviously to cite it as what Jameson would term all "privileged exemplar" (219) of postmodern creativity. Writing on emergent media, one necessarily gestures in the dark, attempting to identify the most significant examples of new, unfamiliar practices, in order to delineate their most varied traits. Jameson's meditations upon video art and upon multimedia performance select far too few examples, and focus upon weak examples which confirm rather than challenge his overly systematic and overly simplistic presuppositions.

Trapped behind the "time-wall" of Barthesian and Baudrillardian overstatement, Jameson's writings appear to function most profitably as "privileged exemplars" of the dangers of reacting overliterally to such "imported and extrapolated categories" (201). To be sure, authorial essentialism and the excesses of "traditional interpretive temptations" (219) may also prove counterproductive, but they do at least have the virtue of directing critical attention toward innovative creativity, rather than prompting arrogant denial of its existence and its authenticity. As Nam June Paik suggests "We must give up certain parts of intellectual vanity, and look at the good parts of so-called high-tech research."[63]

Adequate exegesis of postmodern video and multimedia performance requires the critic to forsake intertextual essentialism and apocalyptic cliché and to return to the rather more daunting tasks of *observing, analyzing, interpreting* and *evaluating* the new arts of the eighties and the nineties.

postmodernism and the multimedia sensibility

heiner müller's *hamletmachine* and the art of robert wilson

6

ROBERT WILSON'S ADAPTION—OR TRANS-mutation—of the German playwright Heiner Müller's *Hamletmachine* typifies both the relatively textual, monodimensional quality of Müller's postmodernity, and the more dynamic, multimedia vision of its producer. *Hamletmachine's* London season opened at the Almeida Theatre, a theater which could well have been renamed the "All-Media" for this occasion. Mixing almost every theatrical and extra-theatrical trick in the postmodern book, it combined classical declamation, parodic classical declamation, autistic anti-declamation, colloquial declamation, cry, whisper, laugh, whimper, tape-recorded screech and mutter, tape-recorded noise, mime, acrobatics, sculptural immobility, videoesque choreography, virtuoso lighting, projected slide imagery, black and white and colored film imagery, digitally deconstructed video image, and an array of musical sound tracks ranging from the nostalgic tango accompanying the cast's final bow, to the echoing tones of a piano piece by Lieber and Stoller (composers of Elvis Presley's "Hound Dog").

Wilson's comments to the London press regarding this "most mature and powerful" of his productions both pleased and teased.[1] On the one hand, Wilson insisted all his work is "political" and that "the words are important" in Müller's play.[2] On the other hand, he confessed, "I feel something's missing when everything's explained."[3] Defending his reluctance to treat Müller's text too closely, Wilson adds: "When we try to interpret the text, the meanings of the words are narrowed and so I try not to interpret them."[4] Not surprisingly, Wilson equates his theatre with an art of "variations and themes," and with the attempt "to build an agreed language with the audience and then . . . destroy it in order to rebuild."[5] As he explains, "I try to tell my actors not to try to understand what they're doing. They can have understandings and ideas about their parts, but if they try and fix a single understanding it will be a distortion."[6]

To some extent, one is familiar with this kind of unholy alliance between systematically constructed or deconstructed form and exasperatingly ambiguous content. Samuel Beckett, for example, tends to argue that it is "the shape" that matters in his work, while concurrently counterpointing such shape with the hauntingly ambiguous theatrical images, phrases or themes that he has associated with the mysterious capacity of his plays to "claw."[7] In this respect, Beckett's vision emerges between the lines of dramatic structure, evading form and evincing "mess."[8] Working rather differently with the orderly and the apparently disorderly, John Cage interweaves precision and imprecision, deriving "rules" from chance procedures, and composing scores permitting unscored, improvised performance. Unlike Beckett, Cage evades conventional form in order to reveal the advantages of "mess," or what he associates with "a harmony to which many are unaccustomed."[9] Rather than attempting to convey personal angst—as Beckett does—by exhibiting the tension between symmetrical form and unspeakable theme, Cage attempts to evoke the impersonal unity interlinking his incongruous materials, proposing that "all things, sounds, stories (and, by extension, beings), are related, and that this complexity is more evident when it is not over-simplified by an idea of relationship in one person's mind."[10]

Wilson's aesthetic seems to hover somewhere between Beckett's and Cage's antithetical explorations of form, ambiguity, chance, and rule. As Janny Donker remarks, Wilson has much in common with both Beckett and Cage in so far as "he refrains from handing his players any definite 'message' to be conveyed by their actions on stage."[11] Like Cage's music, Wilson's theater also appears concerned with modes of implicit harmony and cohesion interlinking divergent materials, and like Beckett's productions of his plays, Wilson's orchestrations of sound, word, image, gesture, and light demand impeccable timing and delivery.

"More than any other form of theatre, perhaps, Bob Wilson's work depends for its effect on accuracy of execution. If the space slackens, if movement betrays uncertainty, if an actor's voice lacks power, if the lights do not work exactly on schedule, if props or backdrops do not behave as they should there is no thrilling plot, no psychological drama to keep the audience's interest from falling."[12]

Wilson's *Hamletmachine* offers an exception to this rule, in so far as this play evinces the message and the drama of Müller's profound disenchantment with his times. As Müller specifies, this message and this drama are extremely bleak. Müller's "Hamlet" appears to be a post-apocalyptic rebel without a cause, doomed to exist, yet without the capacity for authentic existence. In Müller's terms, *Hamletmachine* evokes "The man between the ages who knows that the old age is obsolete, yet the new age has barbarian features he simply cannot stomach."[13] Trapped between two eras, the protagonists of *Hamletmachine* seem quintessential victims of the so-called postmodern crisis; survivors of historical, epistemological, and cultural catastrophes, and testimony, to paraphrase Müller, to the results of missed occasions and to history as a story of chances lost. As Müller notes, this sense of crisis "is more than plain disappointment, it is the description of the petrification of a hope."[14]

Intermingling Wilson's multimedia innovations and Müller's multi-textual symptoms of the contemporary wasteland, *Hamletmachine* appears an archetypal postmodern extravaganza, born successively of Müller's disillusion before "the petrification of hope" and of Wilson's antithetical enthusiasm before the exciting potential of extraliterary, multimedia performance.

Wilson's critics were divided regarding the success of his production of *Hamletmachine*. Stephanie Jordan, for example, argues that "this concise play . . . suits Wilson's imagination well," and that "the structures in which Müller's attitudes are presented . . . seem to have interested Wilson," since "he has assumed them in kind, from the multi-referential surface to the series of closed forms in which the play is constructed."[15] While it is true that Wilson respects the five sections, or "closed forms" to which Jordan refers, and also works with multi-referential surfaces like Müller, his theater differs from that of Müller in terms of its tendency to push multi-referentiality to quite staggering extremes.

At the same time, Wilson counterpoints this thematic ambiguity with strongly ritualistic structural repetitions quite at odds with the unpredictable momentum of Müller's original text. Wilson's production begins with a series of paradigmatic gestures, establishing the visual "score" against which the subsequent sections of his spectacle syncopate successive segments of Müller's text. With each successive section, Wilson's action moves round the stage through ninety degrees, offering a series of more or less cubist variations. Wilson explains: "I read Heiner's text first and then I tried to forget about it. I want it to work as a silent piece first of all, and then to put the text to the movements."[16] Reorchestrated in terms of these "movements," and reanimated by multimedia choreography, Müller might well complain that his text has been taken away, placed within a minimalist strait jacket, and then frightened out of its wits by maximal electric shock treatment.

Oversensitive to the minimalist rigor of Wilson's production, and under-sensitive to the innumerable verbal, gestural, and technological tricks and tics with which Wilson's cast reverberate, critics have condemned the way in which the "biliously rhapsodic" tenor of Müller's writing appears reduced to "rigidly mechanistic routine."[17] Complaining that Wilson's aesthetic "imposes its own classicism" upon Müller's "fragmented text," Michael Billington concluded, "I get the sense of a cold, puritan aestheticism at work that seems very different from the raw, jagged energy of Müller's text with its eclectic mixture of Shakespeare, Marx, Eliot and Pound."[18]

Müller's fragmented script certainly has a raw, jagged, eclectic energy. But so too does Wilson's still more eclectic, multimedia superfragmentation of Müller's script. What one witnesses in Wilson's production is hysteria at two speeds; a tense amalgam of punctiliously decelerated and punctiliously acceler-ated word and gesture. In this respect, Wilson's dramatic vision shares the ener-gy of the break-dancer's movements, and probably derives in part from the same precursor: the carefully edited and carefully exaggerated dance routines accompanying video-clip productions of pop records. Somewhat as sophisti-cated video-editing allows rock stars like Prince and Madonna to effect split-sec-ond, beat-to-beat transitions from costume to costume, or from pose to pout, anticipating real-time variations of such transitions in their subsequent perfor-mances, the same technological possibilities seem to inform the schizophrenic rapidity with which Wilson's protagonists slip from frozen solemnity to hyper-active hilarity in *Hamletmachine*. One detects little trace of this characteristically American, late postmodern gestural energy in Müller's more conventionally collaged play-script.

A heady mixture of absurdist dialogue and of beat generation mono-logue, Müller's *Hamletmachine* falls into five acts introduced by semi-surreal, semi-expressionist stage directions. The first act offers the cryptic specification "1. FAMILY SCRAPBOOK"; establishing, perhaps, the source or the context of the opening monologue.[19] Act 2 begins:

2. THE EUROPE OF WOMEN
Enormous room. Ophelia. Her heart is a clock.

The directions in the next act are even more mysterious, combining reference to the "university of the dead" with a series of abrupt images and actions evincing the violent velocity of expressionist playlets such as Oskar Kokoschka's *Murder the Hope of Women*. Introducing a scherzo that might well be dubbed "schizo," Müller stipulates the following action:

3. SCHERZO
The university of the dead. Whispering and muttering. From their gravestones (lecterns), the dead philosophers throw their books at Hamlet. Gallery (ballet of the dead women). The woman dangling from the rope. The woman with her arteries cut open, etc. . . . Hamlet views them with the attitude of a visitor in a museum (theatre). The dead women tear his clothes off his body. Out of an upended coffin, labelled HAMLET I, step Claudius and Ophelia, the latter dressed and made up like a whore. Striptease by Ophelia.

Act four, one discovers, takes place in — or depicts:

4. PEST IN BUDA/ BATTLEFIELD FOR GREENLAND
Space 2, as destroyed by Ophelia. An empty armour, an axe stuck in the helmet.

The fifth and final act of *Hamletmachine* appears within a still stranger space, to the accompaniment of still stranger ritual; a mixture of time and submerged disjecta that Müller describes as:

5. FIERCELY ENDURING / MILLENIUMS / IN THE GRUESOME ARMOUR
The deep sea. Ophelia in a wheel chair. Fish, debris, dead bodies and limbs drift by . . . While two men in white smocks wrap gauze around her and the wheelchair, from bottom to top.

For all their self-conscious mystery and imprecision, there is something quite unmysterious and precise about Müller's stage directions, just as there is something surprisingly unsurprising about the obscurity of the monologues and dialogues in *Hamletmachine*. In both instances one frequently confronts something very close to recycled, partially politicized surrealism. Indeed, as Peter Kemp remarks, Müller's imagery has a "quaint 1930s ring," and often appears "Rear-guard, not *avant-garde.*"[20]

Act 1 begins fairly coherently as a voice from—or of—the "family scrap-book" announces: "I was Hamlet," and act 2 appears more or less comprehensi-ble as Ophelia (and/or "chorus/Hamlet" announce[s]): "I am Ophelia." Act 3 begins rather more curiously. Ophelia's unusual question: "Do you want to eat my heart, Hamlet?" elicits the response "I want to be a woman," as the various "dead philosophers" and company go through their paces. It is in act four, how-ever, that Müller's play reaches its anachronistic apotheosis. Soliloquy and sce-nario undergo metamorphoses that Salvador Dali might applaud, while Müller's rhetoric runs through a medley of late modernist and early postmod-ern melodies, ranging from Eliotesque abstraction to Ginsbergian imprecation and Warholian self-negation.

Gathering half-hearted steam in an Eliotesque accent, Hamlet initially muses:

> The stove smoulders in wartime October
> A BAD COLD HE HAD OF IT JUST THE WORST TIME
> JUST THE WORST TIME OF THE YEAR FOR A REVOLUTION
> Through the suburbs cement in bloom walks
> Doctor Zhivago weeps
> For his wolves

A few lines later, when the "Hamlet-Player" emerges from his Hamlet cos-tume—and from Hamlet's parodic high modernist anti-narrative—he delivers the following self-parodic exercise in self-deprecating low postmodernist cliché:

> I am not Hamlet. I don't take part any more.
> My words have nothing more to say to me.
> My thoughts suck the blood out of the images.
> My drama doesn't happen anymore.

While the Hamlet-Player continues in this vein until he determines "I won't play along anymore," stagehands "*Unnoticed by the Hamlet-Player . . . place a refrigerator and three TV-sets on stage.*" Hereafter, the Hamlet-Player appears upstaged by this kitchen-sink technology, playing second fiddle to the televised image, as he comments:

The set is a monument. It shows a man who made history, enlarged a hundred times. The petrification of hope. His name is interchangeable, the hope has not been fulfilled . . .

A photograph in the program suggests that this monument depicts Stalin, and at this point in the script, *Hamletmachine* appears to make its most concrete political comment. Ironically, while he seems keen to trace the events following this monument's destruction, the Hamlet-Player cannot do so. His script "has been lost."

By way of compensation, this player offers a hodgepodge of B-grade protest poetry. Recycling Jean-Paul Sartre, Allen Ginsberg, and the angry young John Osborne, his unpunctuated diatribe begins:

Television The daily nausea Nausea
Of prefabricated babble Of decreed cheer
How do you spell GEMÜTLICHKEIT
Give us this day our daily murder
Since thine is nothingness Nausea

Several similar lines later, this cheerfully prefabricated cheerlessness unwittingly echoes the Monty Pythonesque lament "My brain hurts," rather more wittingly quotes Warhol's aspiration to be a machine, and winds down with the complaint:

My brain is a scar. I want to be a machine.
Arms for grabbing legs for walking, no pain, no thought.

Section 4 ends as its stage directions juxtapose images of ruptured technology and bizarre ideological synchronicity:

TV screens go black. Blood oozes from the refrigerator. Three naked women: Marx, Lenin, Mao . . . speak simultaneously, each one in his own language, the text:
THE MAIN POINT IS TO OVERTHROW ALL EXISTING CONDITIONS .
. .

Resuming his costume, the Hamlet-Player predicts that "A BLOATED BLOODHOUND WILL CRAWL INTO THE ARMOUR," then "*Steps into armour*" and "*splits with axe the heads of Marx, Lenin, Mao, Snow, Ice Age.*" Emerging amid "MILLENIUMS" and from within "GRUESOME ARMOUR," the final section of *Hamletmachine* reverts to pastiche Eliot, as Ophelia announces "This is Elektra speaking. In the heart of darkness," and then makes her way to the final Mansonian invocation:

> Long live hate and contempt, rebellion and death. When it walks through your
> bedrooms with butcher knives you'll know the truth.

Heiner Müller's program notes tend to obscure the poetic quality of his play's stage directions and utterances by drawing attention to the text's allegorical and philosophical functions. Quoting, and apparently sharing, Ferdinand Freiligrath's observation that "Germany is Hamlet, never quite knowing how to decide and . . . always making wrong decisions," and conceding that his references to T. S. Eliot, Andy Warhol, and Coca-Cola make *Hamletmachine* his "most American play," Müller invites its interpretation as "a pamphlet against . . . illusion," particularly "the illusion that one can stay innocent in this our world."[21]

Viewed very generally, this statement seems at odds with a number of aspects of Wilson's aesthetic, particularly his work's enthusiasm for—and integration of—the "behaviour patterns of autistic children . . . repetition, echolalia, wordplay, imitation," which Bonnie Marranca associates with Wilson's collaboration with the autistic "natural wonder-child" Christopher Knowles, whom Wilson appears to credit with precisely the kind of "innocence" that Müller deems illusory.[22] Wilson's preface to *A Letter for Queen Victoria* (1977), records his empathy for Knowles's repetitive explorations of both "the sound and . . . the way the words looked on the page"—a technique "similar to the way I had been writing in my notebooks."[23] In his turn, Stefan Brecht, one of this play's cast, gives some idea of the way in which Wilson's deconstruction and reconstruction of declamation drew inspiration from Knowles: "Wilson's idea, when rehearsals (and the gathering of the text) started, seemed to be that we, the performers, were to learn from Chris, by talking to and being with him . . . by attempts at communication with him, and by imitation of him. This would within us hollow out/fill out what was to be the show piece of the piece, the form of rational verbal intercourse, would make it vibrate by and put it in counterpoise to a non-verbal, arational communication taking place (so Wilson seemed to suggest) by harmonious sensed reverberation."[24]

The notion of "harmonious sensed reverberation"—some sort of "good vibes," one might say—may smack a little of hippie mysticism, but it usefully highlights Wilson's apparent interest in "arational communication," and what

Stefan Brecht defines as Wilson's attempt "to relate,—communicate,—vocally without relying on or without concern for the meaning of what we said or of what was said to us."[25] The consequences of this concern to register vibratory communication seem to be at least twofold.

On the one hand, it accounts for Wilson's use of prolonged, repetitive verbal or vocal interaction between his performers; an impulse towards discursive deceleration, as opposed to the accelerated choreography that appears to derive from the example of video-editing. Wilson associates this process with states in which "you're very much tuned in to everything around you"; with a kind of "body energy experience" in which time is "much more drawn out."[26]

On the other hand, Wilson's interest in unexpected, arational modes of awareness seems to precipitate his compulsion to juxtapose a vast array of divergent images and performers, all presumably "tuned in" to one another, one way or another. Discussing his production of *The King of Spain* (1969), Wilson suggests that this early use of "totally different" figures arose in part from his experience as an adventurous host: "I kept thinking too that certain people I knew had never . . . seen a different kind of people (or persons) other than themselves. Then I also kept thinking about what I've done at parties—getting different people together—and it's curious how at parties totally dissimilar persons get together unexpectedly . . . so I guess that's really how I got the idea for my play."[27]

Slow or fast, different or the same, the actions, images, and protagonists in Wilson's theater all seem to contribute to the dramatization of potential modes of communication, be these rational, verbal, or arational, extraverbal and vibrational. Contrasting the superficial meaninglessness of Wilson's choreography with the hypothetical polemical precision of Müller's text, critics have tended to dismiss Wilson's work as "more concerned with form than expressive content,"[28] and more seriously, as inclined to "play up the atmospheric and rhythmic possibilities of lighting, music, mime and murmurs," and to "play down the spoken word to the point of extinction."[29]

By accident or design, Müller encourages this response, when, acknowledging his gratitude to Wilson's idiosyncratic fantasy, he tellingly observes: "I am glad that Robert Wilson does my play, his theater being a world of its own."[30] Perhaps I am mistaken here, but one seems to catch the pot thanking the kettle for being black, as Müller more or less emphasizes the political sobriety and public accessibility of his "pamphlet against . . . illusion," while praising the poetic integrity of Wilson's private vision. My point here is not so much that Wilson's art is not predominantly idiosyncratic and that Müller's concerns are not primarily social. Rather, it is that Müller's *Hamletmachine* is often much more "atmospheric" than his critics suggest, while Wilson's theatre is in turn far more "meaningful" than his critics allow, if one extends meaning to encompass both traditional rational and verbal meaning, and the less traditional arational, extra-verbal, and vibrational modes of meaning explored by Wilson's theatre. In this respect, it could well be argued that it is Müller—not Wilson—who tends to "play down the spoken word to the point of extinction" by insisting that "drama doesn't happen any more."

The immediate difficulty for the critic is that Wilson's experiments resist easy definition, save in terms of such clichés as the well-meaning allusion to his "weird but sometimes wonderful attempts to turn the theatre on its head."[31] Once again, the formulae of Wilson's critics seem more successful when applied to Müller's rather tired, rather European, anti-narrative. In many respects, Müller stands theatrical conventions on their head without really extending them or adding to their compass.[32] To commence a variation of *Hamlet* with the avowal "I was Hamlet" or to have one's Hamlet figure announce "I want to be a woman," and then to transmute into a "Hamlet Player" declaring "I am not Hamlet" is merely to reverse the "ping-pong" structure that Wilson associates with traditional theatre into simple "pong-ping" provocation. Likewise, the presentation of Marx, Lenin, and Mao as three naked female figures seems a rather predictable neo-Dadist or neo-Surrealist jape in the tradition of Duchamp's Rrose Sélavy.[33]

Wilson's evaluation of Müller's theatre is more generous, indeed, Wilson credits Müller with transcending traditional modes of dramatic structure, remarking: "Most plays are like ping-pong. . . . You know, it's all 'How are you today?' 'Oh, I'm all right.' . . . In Heiner's play you don't have that structure, you have a lot more freedom."[34] When asked to offer an image characterising Müller's alternative to the "pik, pok, pik, pok" dialectic of conventional drama, Wilson compared Müller's *Hamletmachine* to a "labyrinth," and to "pinball"[35]— an image more suited, perhaps, to his own work's tendency to fragment character into the individual or concurrent live and/or technologically modified utterances and gestures of his performers.

Containing no such characters as Hamlet or Ophelia, nor any specific anti-characters, such as Müller's Hamlet-Player, Wilson's production depicts a brigade of all-purpose "Players" identified by pose or position as "woman in swivel chair," "woman leaning into tree," "man peering over wall," and so on. Like Müller's atmospheric images of "woman dangling from the rope" and "woman with her arteries cut open," these figures owe much to the Surrealist cookbook; "man peering over wall," for example, seeming a twin brother to "figure peering out of window" in Luis Buñuel's *Un Chien andalou.*

But whereas Müller's text does little more than subvert traditional dramatic rhetoric by converting its well-jointed realist linearity into disjointed surrealist linearity, Wilson projects postmodern performance into the far more revolutionary realm of multilinear, multimedia narrative, or what he characterizes as "multi-dimensional realities."[36] Put more figuratively still, Wilson creates a partially coherent, partially incoherent, theatrical pinball machine, wherein utterance and identity spin to and fro, from individual or collective "man" and "woman," to the varied accompaniment of different combinations of amplification, live and recorded sound, filmic and video image, and a virtually inexhaustible range of ever-fluctuating accent, intonation, illumination, and gesticulation.

As accounts of his work suggest, Wilson's muse is often surprisingly traditional. His interest in verbal repetition and variation seems to be inspired by the speech patterns of autistic children, while his enthusiasm for notionally discordant materials may reflect his bemusement before the bonhomie between notionally incompatible guests attending his parties. At the same time, however, Wilson's work seems the quintessential child of an age of remotely controlled, multi-channel cable television, broadcasting ever-changing images tailored with digital precision. Just as the viewer may reorchestrate and repermutate such images with the flick of a switch, Wilson's productions punctuate long stretches of "autistic" repetition or inaction with vertiginous "videoesque" rapidity.

In other words, whereas Müller appears to damn television for its triviality, appears to deplore the exhaustion of his own drama in particular and of language in general, and only cites Warhol as an archetype of the decadence and despair of his Hamlet-Player, Wilson, like other more adventurous postmoderns, appears admirably sensitive to the positive potential of contemporary media. Müller's dismissal of television, language, and upmarket gurus like Warhol is seductive, but simplistic. For all its studied cynicism, Warhol's work typifies both the dead end and the live end of postmodern creativity. For example, as Cynthia Goodman points out in her study of *Digital Visions: Computers and Art,* "Warhol was intrigued by colorizing video-digitized images," and seems happily to have employed the computer to modify both the technological and the conceptual basis of his art.[37]

Advocating the same kind of change, and acknowledging that the eighties offer quite different technological and conceptual possibilities from those of the sixties or the thirties, the New York graffiti artist Keith Haring equally illuminatingly observed: "Living in 1984, the role of the artist has to be different from what it was fifty or even twenty years ago. I am continually amazed at the number of artists who continue to work as if the camera was never invented, as if Andy Warhol never existed, as if airplanes, and computers, and videotape were never heard of."[38]

It is precisely this quality of popular, mass-mediated change that Wilson's theater reflects, and which, to some considerable extent, Müller's theater suspects. What one witnesses, then, in the transition between Müller's text and Wilson's production of *Hamletmachine,* is the gulf between dead-end and live-end postmodernism, or put another way, the advance from morose literary intertextuality to ebullient multimedia intertextuality.

One's admiration for the live-end of postmodernism's multimedia creativity is modified by one's apprehension before its "loose-ended" quality. Like Laurie Anderson, perhaps the only other post-Cage multimedia artist to receive substantial commercial and critical acclaim, Wilson might well be criticized in terms of his work's apparent subservience to a certain "magpie" instinct characterized by the accumulation of innovative effects for accumulation's sake.

This is not the place for comprehensive analysis of either Anderson's or Wilson's research. Suffice it to remark, perhaps, that Anderson's most recent large scale project, her live and cinematic versions of the performance piece *Home of the Brave,* struck one primarily as a rapid succession of virtuoso samplers of new, multimedia discursive possibilities, rather than as a more deeply motivated narrative selecting these possibilities in order to evoke a specific existential vision. Wilson's production of *Hamletmachine* seemed to beg the same criticism. The very momentum of Wilson's dazzling display of ever-varied permutations of word, sound, image, gesture, and lighting made one wonder if this production obeyed any principle of selection save that of avoiding repetition.

It is obviously unfair to equate Wilson's work as a whole with such initial, and perhaps inaccurate, first impressions of his adaptation of Müller's *Hamletmachine.* More significantly, as Wilson's own interviews and past productions suggest, his multimedia explorations seem motivated by far more complex ambition than the attempt to juxtapose as many media as possible. As Stefan Brecht intimates, Wilson's work also seems informed by the aspiration to identify and employ arational, vibrational modes of meaning and communication. Nevertheless, it seems legitimate to ask *how* and *why* these unfamiliar modes of meaning are employed in Wilson's multimedia theater.

Other, less celebrated postmoderns, such as the Parisian sound poets Henri Chopin and Bernard Heidsieck, have already used more modest selections of these materials to considerable effect, evincing traces of personal vision, rather than appearing to present primers exemplifying a whole range of multimedia discourse.[39] The virtuoso overkill of Wilson and Anderson begs comparison— and evaluation—with regard to more single-minded contemporaries exploring similarly technological terrain.

At the same time, Wilson's experiments, like those of Cage, deserve recognition in their own right, as the polemical—rather than explicitly functional— innovations of the "wilful visionary."[40] To the extent that such innovations sometimes pander to commercial factors and generate—or degenerate into— modes of "mass" avant-gardism, they tend to lose one's respect. Such, perhaps, is the fate of some of Laurie Anderson's work. But as the Australian sound poet Allan Vizents suggests, there is no reason to expect avant-garde experiments to share the neatly conclusive quality of more conventional creativity. Artists are "avant-garde" precisely because their work has exploratory loose ends. Vizents puts it this way: "What they're all on about . . . is the notion of finding problems. An artist is a problem finder, not a problem solver . . . they're creating, creating and finding problems, not solutions. And it's that dead, linear approach to solutions that they tend to side-step and question. . . . That's what keeps that critical edge to their work. It doesn't settle into obvious answers."[41]

It is this provocative "critical edge" that gives the "hybrid" theatrical experiments of Robert Wilson their compelling relevance. One may well deplore their limitations as balanced, substantial, individual works, and one may well suspect that their seductive orchestration of *son et lumière* sedates rather than stimulates sensitivity to the political and ideological problems of the here and now. Nevertheless, viewed from an aesthetic point of view, it is precisely their exasperating but exhilarating identification and exemplification of new theatrical problems and new theatrical possibilities—particularly international collaborative possibilities, such as his work with Müller's firey texts—that makes Wilson's works of value to anyone interested in the positive, innovative potential of postmodern creativity.

Perhaps Wilson's mature works will realize this potential comprehensively, both in terms of existential vision and aesthetic exploration. If not, other writers will certainly follow in his wake. What is most significant for present times is that Wilson's experiments and collaborations leave considerable inspiration and provocation in their wake, and demonstrate—despite all alarmist arguments to the contrary—that innovative drama still "happens" once one looks beyond the tried and trusted (or tired and untrusted) modes of linear narrative and antinarrative, and considers the multilinear narratives peculiar to postmodern culture's multimedia sensibility.

baudrillard, modernism, and postmodernism 7

JEAN BAUDRILLARD'S DISCLAIMER "I HAVE nothing to do with postmodernism" is rich with irony.[1] Considered in terms of his general arguments and assertions, Baudrillard has *everything* to do with postmodernism. For Arthur Kroker, for example, Baudrillard is "the very first of the *postmodern primitives*."[2] For Steven Best and Douglas Kellner, "He has achieved guru status throughout the English-speaking world ... as the *superthe-* orist of a new postmodernity."[3] For Marshall Berman, he is "the most recent postmodern pretender and object of cultic adoration in art scenes and universities all over America today," and the very Anti-Christ of those who consider that "modernism still matters."[4]

At the same time though, Baudrillard's concurrent appeal to "art scenes and universities" hints perhaps at the way in which his impact is both aesthetic and academic, rhetorical and theoretical. In Baudrillard's own terms, his kind of theory is "in many respects indefinable. ... It's not really an aesthetic, it's not a philosophy, it's not a sociology, it's a little volatile. Perhaps this corresponds to a certain kind of floating instability with more in common with the contemporary imagination than with any real philosophy. Possibly that explains why it is not someone like Derrida—who has had great academic success throughout American universities—why it is not so much his references to deconstruction and so forth that have been taken up by artists, as notions of simulation."[5]

What is it that makes Baudrillard's ideas so appealing? Conversely, why do so many of Baudrillard's opponents find his popularity so disturbing? As these pages will suggest, most favorable and unfavorable responses to his work focus predominantly upon its rhetorical play rather than upon its specific accuracy and applicability. While Baudrillard's writing obviously displays a curious mixture of analytical acuity and fictional fantasy, and invites investigation in terms of its slippage from sociological to symbolist rhetoric, it is perhaps most compelling in terms of its visionary—if frequently flawed—sensitivity to many of those mutant values now most at stake within the late postmodern condition.

Like Lenny Bruce, Baudrillard commands attention in terms of his rhetorical excess—in terms of the register, rather than the substance, of his patter. Indeed, Baudrillard happily asserts that "The form of my language is almost more important than what I have to say within it. . . . It's not a question of ideas—there are already too many ideas!"[6] On the contrary, it seems extremely important to consider the substance of Baudrillard's ideas. To the rather general question "What analytical and fictional strategies does Baudrillard deploy in his accounts of the postmodern condition?" one must surely add the far more demanding question "*With what accuracy does Baudrillard write about the postmodern condition?*"

More often than not, Baudrillard's critics seem happy to trounce him for philosophical or theoretical misdemeanors, while holding fire regarding the factual accuracy of his observations. In consequence, Baudrillard is more or less granted poetic license to fictionize to his heart's content regarding the present and the future, so long as he makes no serious philosophical or theoretical claims. While this response effectively lets Baudrillard off the hook by declining to evaluate the specificity of his claims, it concurrently releases his critics from any obligation to suggest just what an accurate assessment of postmodern existence might address. Having established the madness of Baudrillard's methods, his contemporaries frequently seem quite happy to add that, all things considered, Baudrillard is still an okay kind of guy, generally or fictionally speaking.

Christopher Norris, for example, stipulates that Baudrillard is "thoroughly inconsequent and muddled when it comes to philosophising on the basis of his

own observations," but also freely concedes that "Baudrillard is a first-rate diagnostician of the postmodern scene."[7] Writing with almost unbridled enthusiasm
for Baudrillard's evocations of the rhetorical and the conceptual muddle "between
delerium and anxiety, between the triumph of cyberpunk and the political reality of cultural exhaustion," the Kroker-Kroker-Cook *Panic Encyclopedia* concludes
that "*Jean Baudrillard . . . is* the postmodern commotion."

Fredric Jameson similarly locates the postmodern sensibility somewhere
between the poles of cultural exhaustion and the energy of cyberpunk fiction,
"henceforth, for many of us, the supreme *literary* expression . . . of postmodernism."[9] Placing Baudrillard's relevance within a similar cosmos, Best and
Kellner deplore the ways in which Baudrillard's theory "tends to degenerate into
sloganeering and rhetoric without any systematic or comprehensive theoretical
position," but suggest nevertheless that "Baudrillard's best work can . . . be read
along with the novels of . . . cyberpunk fiction as projecting visions of futuristic
worlds which illuminate the present high tech society."[10]

At its best, in works such as David Blair's remarkable film *WAX or the discovery of television among the bees* (1991),[11] cyberpunk culture evokes many of
the most challenging issues raised by postmodern technology. In this respect, the
cyberpunk movement is but the most recent manifestation of the frequently
neglected lineage of postmodern high tech creativity, and, as such, a further
reminder that the alleged "reality" of *cultural exhaustion* is perhaps more symptomatic of academic myopia than of the high tech cultural climate as a whole.

In other words, if Baudrillard's writings may well reflect the "commotion"
within academia—or within those sections of academia preoccupied with
symptoms of cultural exhaustion, such commotion may itself be merely a footnote to the more understated but more substantial positive cultural energies of
the postmodern condition. Put another way, much of the postmodern cultural
theory detecting cultural exhaustion seems likely to prove to be a kind of *flat-
culture mythology* with as much conviction as earlier flat-earth theories.

As I have argued elsewhere,[12] postmodern culture is repeatedly misrepre-
sented as an era of cultural and theoretical confusion neutralizing the more positive energies of cultural modernism and accelerating the supposed "death" of
aura, authoriality, avant-garde integrity, and referential reality. Predicated upon
the more extreme assertions of Walter Benjamin, Roland Barthes, Peter Bürger,
and Baudrillard, this misreading of the potential of postmodern culture culminates in the mythology that I would term the "B-effect." While this emphasis

upon cultural exhaustion and entropy obviously constitutes *one* impulse within mass culture and within what one might think of as "B-grade" mass misreadings of the postmodern condition, other more rewarding forms of postmodern creativity—particularly postmodern multimedia creativity—are frequently exemplary of the positive energy that I would associate with the "C-effect," or the technological confidence and flair of pioneer American postmoderns such as John Cage, and of younger contemporaries such as Laurie Anderson, Robert Ashley, David Blair, Philip Glass, Meredith Monk, Yvonne Rainer, Bill Viola, and Robert Wilson.

In this respect, the postmodern condition, viewed as an increasingly distinct cultural era emerging from the mid-1930s and becoming most evident across the arts from the mid-1950s, might best be conceived of as a plurality of successive cultural impulses. At times these impulses negate those of modernism; at times these impulses extend and mutate modernist aspirations across the new media. At worst, such impulses culminate in commercial dross and theoretical cynicism; at best such impulses provoke highly challenging conceptual and creative initiatives.

As the twentieth century draws to an end, it seems increasingly urgent that the cultural practices of the postmodern era be evaluated both in terms of their mediocrities and in terms of their more mature and masterly precipitates. While there is obviously every reason to reconsider potentially repressive concepts of mature and masterly creativity, it seems equally evident that repressive politically correct resistance toward the qualitative analysis of our culture, and repressive theoretically correct subscription to accounts of the "deaths" of assorted modernist and premodernist values, compound the counterproductive intellectual indifference that the late Félix Guattari denounced as "the virtual ethical and aesthetic abdication of postmodern thought."[13]

The American multimedia artist Dick Higgins diagnoses much the same malaise when he detects "a sort of failure of nerve" among artists and academics over the last two or three decades, although, as Higgins also points out, "there are some individuals who have kept the nerve, kept the vision and kept the energy together."[14] The history of the postmodern mentality is in many respects the chronology of variously maintained, variously lost, and variously regained kinds of "nerve" during five or more decades of increasingly complex social, political, cultural, and theoretical transition. Within the rather restrained parameters of the cultural and theoretical contexts addressed by these pages, the most significant "commotion" within the postmodern cosmos appears to have been generated by those who have kept or recovered their ethical and aesthetic nerve, and who have nurtured and negotiated the potential of old and new kinds of creative and conceptual energy.

Baudrillard's writings fit very uneasily within this spectrum, in the sense that his emphasis upon "delusional" reality and upon mass culture leads at best to what one might think of as a first-rate analysis of second-rate "extreme phenomena." More specifically, Baudrillard proposes that "the world is on a delusional course" and that it therefore makes best sense to "adopt a delusional standpoint towards the world."[15] Taken literally, such studiedly apocalyptic assertions rapidly lead to what Gene Youngblood defines as the "numbing powerlessness" resulting from overexposure to Baudrillard's hypotheses."[16] Yet, as Youngblood remarks, while it may at first sight appear that Baudrillard "laments the loss of the original, the authentic, and with them the possibility of Reality and Truth," it also frequently seems to be the case that "Although he doesn't actually say so, it is clear that Baudrillard longs for the recovery of Walter Benjamin's 'aura.'"[17]

To carp about the underly philosophical, underly theoretical, and overly fictional registers of Baudrillard's rhetoric is to miss the still more significant tension between his writing's explicit denial of reality and truth and its almost unerring emphasis upon what one might think of as prime sites of new—or mutant—cultural realities and truths. More often than not, Baudrillard is not entirely a first-rate diagnostician of the postmodern scene, because he consistently—and perhaps self-consciously—gets things wrong by converting evidence of illumination into confirmation of delusion. Likewise, his theoretical fictions command partial rather than total respect, insofar as they seem programmed to project "panic" paradigms upon high tech society, deflecting critical attention from the subtleties of emergent practices. Yet, on occasion, when Baudrillard preaches from practice (as in his recent comments upon photography) rather than from prose, his insights offer unambiguously required reading.

Commenting upon the curious way in which "the best Dadas . . . seem least Dada," the veteran Dadaist Marcel Janco discussed the way in which the Dada movement is usually caricatured in terms of its initial "negative speed," rather than viewed more panoramically in terms both of this initial momentum and its subsequent impulse "beyond negation."[18] Like Dada, Baudrillard's work seems characterized by two speeds, the one self-evidently and seductively destructive, the other unexpectedly perceptive and affirmative and, as such, a sporadic source of marvelous exceptions to his more mundane general rules. In turn, postmodern culture and the postmodern condition as a whole require consideration not simply in terms of mass culture's negative speed, but also in terms of those less obvious practices reaching at once both beyond modernist conventions and "beyond negation."

Considered very generally, Baudrillard appears to be an exemplary post-modern, or antimodern—or *past-modern*—thinker in terms of his avowed opposition to the Enlightenment-inspired "communicative rationality" that Jürgen Habermas associates with the modernist project.[19] Yet, as Baudrillard himself remarks, the act of opposition is a relatively indolent gesture, and offers no particular guarantee of any more pragmatic alternative. If most intellectuals "feel very, very comfortable when they are in opposition," they usually "do not know how to define themselves when they are no longer in opposition and have to participate."[20] At his most pessimistic, Baudrillard tends to remark that the 1980s and 1990s leave him in precisely this kind of dilemma, insofar as he cannot identify "a new position, one that is original and credible."[21]

Discussing his work in a more confident register, Baudrillard repeatedly emphasizes, firstly, that his writings are not modernist, and secondly, that they aspire toward some kind of catalytic initiative reaching beyond the "total eclecticism" of a postmodern culture "acquainted with neither hard ideologies nor radical philosophies."[22] Baudrillard's apparent indifference to postmodern culture seems surprising, to say the least, when one considers that his own writings have obviously made major contributions to the analysis of the chronologically postmodern condition. What seems most revealing here is Baudrillard's impatience toward the dead ends of postmodern mass culture: in this instance, what he convincingly identifies as the gravitation of its "banal energies" toward "total eclecticism." Put another way, Baudrillard's most valid writings point away from indiscriminate eclecticism toward those more substantial problems and practices that one might think of as the *live ends* of postmodern culture; the exceptions, as it were, to the "critical vices" underlying Baudrillard's seductively apocalyptic general rules.

Considered in terms of his most substantial insights, and in terms of his sensitivity toward the most challenging developments of the 1980s and the 1990s, Baudrillard is without doubt a major cultural cartographer of the post-modern cosmos. Thematically, Baudrillard's subject matter is frequently thrilling. Rhetorically and conceptually, however, Baudrillard's accounts of this subject matter frequently appear slightly antiquated. Paradoxically, Baudrillard's rhetorical and conceptual tropes seem predicated upon a curiously *modernist* cultural logic (or poetics). To read Baudrillard's writings on contemporary culture is to confront the new and the *déjà vu*, as one is both guided toward emergent problems and yet, at the same time, distracted from the specificity of their implications by curiously anachronistic commentary.

More specifically, Baudrillard's arguments successively repudiate the logic of Enlightenment modernism, consciously or unconsciously invoke the poetic logic of cultural modernism, direct attention to key developments in the chronological postmodern social and cultural condition, and then—like other theorists such as Jameson and Andreas Huyssen—misguidedly overemphasize the negative impact of mass culture, and misguidingly underestimate the positive potential of the postmodern era's new mainstream and avant-garde practices.[23] Significantly, Baudrillard himself now acknowledges such shortcomings in his writings and suggests that he is increasingly concerned to identify alternatives to the predictable apocalyptic register of most accounts of postmodern technoculture: "Up to now I think that technology has been analysed in too realistic a way ... it has been typecast as a medium of alienation and depersonalisation ... it's possible to continue forever in this sort of direction. But I sense now that a sort of reversal of focus is taking place.... I'll always continue to offer a radically critical analysis of media and technology.... But it's also necessary to identify another form of analysis—a more subtle form of analysis than that one."[24]

Ironically, the terms of Baudrillard's emergent positive focus frequently seem as nostalgic as his initial negative focus. Just as Baudrillard's preceding analyses of mass culture—like those of Jameson and Huyssen, moreover—frequently remind one of the rhetoric of Max Nordau's "panic" reading of late-nineteenth-century cultural transitions in *Degeneration*,[25] Baudrillard's recent positive appraisals of technology seem similarly *fin-de-siècle* in register. In much the same way as Stéphane Mallarmé's notes on "Music and Literature," for example, associate the creative process with the transition from states in which artists "elicit emptiness," to "celebrations" in which "sublime" forces "lovingly ... shed glittering lights ... through empty space,"[26] Baudrillard describes his practice as a photographer as one in which "I isolate something in an empty space and then it irradiates this emptiness—there's the irradiation of the object within this emptiness." Qualifying his seemingly symbolist process in self-consciously surrealist terms, Baudrillard adds that it is a kind of "automatic writing." "I enter into this second state—this kind of rapid ecstasy—much more often in my photography than in my writing. The ecstasy of photography . . . is much stronger, much more spontaneous and automatic. For me photography is a kind of automatic writing. . . . I've experienced what I'd have to call my greatest sense of pleasure—indeed, my strongest sense of passion—in the realm of images, rather than in the realm of texts."[27]

Perhaps, after all, modernist cultural rhetoric *is* the most effective discourse for describing the kind of "ecstatic" technological creativity that Baudrillard has in mind. My point here is that Baudrillard often appears at a loss to describe postmodern culture in anything other than the prior discourse of the modernist arts: a paradox which perhaps points to two dilemmas which still await adequate resolution. On the one hand, it may well be the case that the notorious ruptures widely perceived between modern and postmodern mentalities are neither as terminal nor as topical as many have imagined. Perhaps the 1980s and the 1990s signal not so much the supposed *disappearance* or *termination* of modernist values, as their *reappearance* or *transmutation* through new eyes and new technologies. Theories of the great "divide" between modernism and postmodernism require more careful delineation.

On the other hand, definitions of the postmodern theoretical temper also now require reconsideration. Too often, the postmodern is equated with the early, somewhat impatient and intemperate avowals of Parisian theoreticians. Significantly, both Barthes and Baudrillard have gradually acknowledged that postmodern technological practices may well be surprisingly compatible with the very notions of singularity, originality, subjectivity, and creativity which their earlier writings—like those of their followers—dismissed, displaced or deconstructed beyond recognition. In this respect, Baudrillard's recent emphasis upon what he terms the "ecstasy" and the "singularity" of photography offers a welcome alternative to his earlier rather tiresome insistence upon the notionally neutralizing effect of the media. Like Barthes, Baudrillard now comments: "I'm considerably in favour of *punctum* in the sense of the singularity of the object at a given moment."[28]

Were this the whole story, Baudrillard's present writings might well appear to adumbrate an unexpected happy ending to his earlier accounts of the postmodern misadventure. Ironically, and somewhat perversely, Baudrillard not only invariably qualifies his own most affirmative ideas, but also almost always

compulsively *disqualifies* such insights, indulging in a kind of conceptual infan-
ticide, for fear, perhaps, of manifesting explicit commitment to aesthetic, poetic, or ethical ideals. Whereas Marcel Proust, for example, elegiacally invoked
John Ruskin's genius in terms of "one of those extinguished stars whose light still
reaches us,"[29] Baudrillard insists that his seemingly romantic allusion to "the
scintillation of being" in *The Transparency of Evil* has no such transcendental
overtones. Rather, it seems to denote detached uncertainty, not unlike the whimsical reference to "the star whose ray/ announces the disappearance/ of its master by the presence of itself," in the American poet Ed Dorn's magic realist epic
Gunslinger.[30] Like Dorn, Baudrillard seems to have an eye for the cool, slightly
surreal paradox.[32] "I use the term 'scintillation' in terms of the way that it's used
with reference to stars—for very distant stars which perhaps have died, but which
still seem to shine . . . there are two alternatives here, there seems to be light, but
perhaps there isn't any light, and perhaps it's just an apparition."[31]

At his most positive, Baudrillard suggests that his most credible position is
that of the conceptual *agent provocateur*—the master of "this art of appearance,
this art of making things appear."[32] Acknowledging that this "art" has something
in common with science fiction, but little in common with either postmodernist
or modernist mentalities, Baudrillard typically explains: "It's not postmodern. I
don't know what one means by that. But I'm no longer part of modernity, not in
the sense where modernity implies a kind of critical distance of judgement and
argumentation. There is a sense of positive and negative, a kind of dialectic in
modernity. My way of reflecting on things is not dialectic. Rather it's provocative,
reversible, it's a way of raising things to their 'N'th power, rather than a way of
dialectizing them. It's a way of following through the extremes to see what happens. It's a bit like a theory-fiction. There's a little theoretical science fiction in it."[33]

Considered in terms of a modernity based upon critical distance, judgment
and argumentation, nothing could be less modern than Baudrillard's commitment to "following through the extremes to see what happens." If the
Baudrillardian project pivots upon the fatal strategy of "raising things to their
Nth power," the Habermasian project of modernity emphasizes instead the
Enlightenment ideal of furthering "rationalized everyday life" by cultivating
"objective science, universal morality and law, and autonomous art according to
their inner logic."[34]

As Stjepan G. Mestrovic suggests, debates regarding the respective absolute
merits of rationalized inner logic and accelerated Nth-power hyperlogic seem

surprisingly dated if one considers the way in which the majority of contemporaries cheerfully accommodate and reconcile both forces. Arguing that "the Enlightenment 'project' is an illusion" that "died long ago," and which was fully "discredited ... during the previous turn of the century," Mestrovic concludes: "All the concern expressed by postmodern theorists with this 'project' constitutes an anomic aberration, a long-standing collective neurosis that stems from repression of the irrational. The proof is that while intellectuals write about completing the Enlightenment project, the rest of humanity turns to irrationalities of every sort to satisfy its collectively hungry heart—religion, nationalism, cults ... and all kinds of sentiment thrive in postmodern culture."[35]

Whether one likes it or not, it seems evident that a major—and doubtless enduring—dimension of postmodern culture consists of *irrationalized* or *extrarationalized* everyday life: the consoling fictions that Don DeLillo's novel *White Noise* associates with "The tales of the supernatural and the extraterrestrial. The miracle vitamins, the cures for cancer, the remedies for obesity. The cults of the famous and the dead."[36] Mestrovic's central argument is that the rational cult of the Enlightenment project is more likely to do harm than good in present circumstances, in which "the West needs a new faith," rather than "the collective repression of the heart in favour of excessive intellectualism, the mind."[37] Accordingly, it appears redundant to engage in obsolete debates regarding the merits of the Enlightenment project, irrelevant to waste time pondering the ambiguities of the term postmodernity, but essential "to confront and tame the irrational, and reach the goal of a cosmopolitan society of humankind."[38]

To be fair to Baudrillard, his own arguments frequently express contempt for the "self-verification," "tautology," and "permanent recurrence" that he associates with irrelevant debates in which "nothing will ever put itself into question."[39] Nevertheless, his enthusiasm for projecting his attention "somewhere else, to see what is going on elsewhere,"[40] by peering "through the extremes,"[41] beyond "the end of linearity, the end of finality, of the final perspective,"[42] is itself something of a conceptual trap.

Despite his distaste for fixed rhetoric and for inflexible references, and despite his reluctance to promote "complacent catastrophism,"[43] Baudrillard's fundamental conviction that he inhabits "a world that has lost all sense of perspective, where sight, distance and judgement have been lost,"[44] repeatedly culminates in complacent indifference toward notions of theoretical, social, or cultural progress. While he often refers to his "serious" concern for various issues "at stake," his aversion to referential and judgmental categories usually leaves him more or less literally at a loss for any words save those of disbelief and dissociation.

What is at issue here, then, is the question of whether the so-called post-modern critique of modernist formulations of particular values and categories necessarily negates them. Baudrillard consistently takes this to be the case. But as others such as Mestrovic, Jean-François Lyotard, Berman, and Linda Nicholson all suggest, it has become increasingly evident that the postmodern condition does not so much negate the legitimacy of modernist values as *reinstate* these values by offering them more flexibility with regard to contemporary "differences."[45] This conciliatory impulse is frequently anticipated by the more progressive forces of cultural modernism. In this respect, the priorities of mainstream postmodern theory often appear to offer belated confirmation to the ideals of the modernist cultural avant-garde.

Consider, for example, the following extracts from the Dadaist poet Tristan Tzara's "Lecture on Dada." Initially questioning the legitimacy of those "intelligent movements that have stretched beyond measure our credulity in the benefits of science," Tzara commends "the point where the yes and the no and all the opposites meet, not solemnly in the castles of human philosophies, but very simply at street corners, like dogs and grasshoppers."[46] Subsequently claiming that "Only the elasticity of our conventions creates a bond between disparate acts," Tzara concludes: "The Beautiful and the True in art do not exist; what interests me is the work; the man and his vitality; the angle from which he regards the elements and in what manner he knows how to gather sensation, emotion, into a lacework of words and sentiment."[47]

Significantly, Tzara not only rejects monolithic categories such as "The Beautiful" and "The True." At the same time he calls for the coexistence of "all the opposites" and proposes alternative, more elastic "conventions," placing considerable value upon concepts of creative "intensity" and "vitality."

At his most positive extreme—or, one might say, at his most *Dadaist* extreme—Baudrillard similarly expresses commitment to "singularities, exceptional events."[48] While many of Baudrillard's writings mechanically reiterate that "it is impossible to distinguish between good and bad excess,"[49] it seems significant that he frequently acknowledges the aesthetic value of contemporaries such as the filmmaker Jean-Luc Godard: "You can *live* in a Godard film. It is at the same time a different dimension and a way of handling images, which is the only one worth calling modern to my mind."[50]

Baudrillard's nihilism, like Tzara's nihilism, is clearly tempered by aesthetic insights; by his unexpected discovery that in a world which should logically lack value, new—or unfamiliar—modes of handling images, words, and sentiment suggest that certain kinds of aesthetic value still survive as they transmute and multiply against all odds. Discussing the novelist Elias Canetti, Baudrillard, again rather hesitantly, acknowledges that all is not quite so grim as he usually intimates. Cautiously prefacing his comments with the stipulation that "it is not the ensemble of his work but fragments of it that have excited me," Baudrillard continues: "The fragment is like a nucleus of an ephemeral destiny of language, a fatal particle that shines an instant and then disappears. At the same time, it allows an instantaneous conversion of points of view, of humours and passions."[51]

Parisian postmodern theory would doubtless relate this kind of emphasis upon the ways in which language's "fatal particles" afford an "instantaneous conversion" of points of view to Barthes's notion of the text as "the *stereographic plurality* of its weave of signifiers;" to Derrida's focus upon "the traces of differences . . . the *spacing* by means of which elements are related to each other;" to Michel Foucault's attention to the ways in which texts generate "discontinuity . . . rupture, break, mutation, transformation"; or to Gilles Deleuze and Félix Guattari's ideal of "a book made of plateaus, each communicating with the others through tiny fissures, as in the brain."[52] Considered in such contexts, Baudrillard's admiration for Canetti's fragments seems both predictable and respectable, and altogether typical of the Parisian postmodern intellectual temper.

Yet, at the same time, this sensibility is itself still more typical of the modernist poetic sensibility, which is perhaps simply another way of suggesting that far from representing the cutting edge of the postmodern mind, the Parisian postmodern intellectual temper is best understood as a manifestation of academia's embarrassingly belated assimilation of the dominant insights of modernist poetics. Writing a whole century before the rhizomic rhetoric of May 1968, the aesthetician Walter Pater contrasted the multiplicity of "impressions, unstable, flickering, inconsistent" with the apparent "solidity with which language invests them" concluding that "our one chance lies in expanding" the "interval" of existence, and "in getting as many pulsations as possible into the given time."[53]

Stéphane Mallarmé's writings in "Crisis in Poetry" similarly adumbrate an aesthetics of "hesitation, disposition of parts, their alternations and relationships—

all this contributing to . . . rhythmic totality."[54] In turn, Virginia Wolfe's essay "Modern Fiction" concludes that the modernist novelist's task is to "trace the pattern, however disconnected and incoherent in appearance, which each sight or incident scores upon the consciousness," irrespective of "whatever aberration or complexity it may display."[55]

Not surprisingly, perhaps, both modernist novelists such as Joris-Karl Huysmans, and postmodern Parisian theorists, such as Baudrillard, share particular enthusiasm for the traces of intertextual plurality, difference, discontinuity, and interconnected fissure within the prose poem and the condensed literary fragment. Recounting the poetic aspirations of Des Esseintes, the hero of *Against Nature,* Huysmans relates: "Of all forms of literature, the prose poem was Des Esseintes' favourite. Handled by an alchemist of genius it should, he maintained, contain within its small compass and in concentrated form the substance of a novel, while dispensing with the latter's long-winded analyses and superfluous descriptions . . . every adjective . . . would open up such wide vistas that the reader could muse on its meaning, at once precise and multiple, for weeks on end."[56]

For his part, Baudrillard has almost exactly the same to say regarding his exploration of partially precise, partially multiple, discourse in *Fatal Strategies.*[57] Discussing this volume in the year of its publication, almost exactly a century after the publication of Huysmans's *Against Nature,* Baudrillard comments: "You could almost make each paragraph into a book . . . I want to slim things down . . . to get rid of things . . . to create voids between spaces so that there can be collisions and short circuits. For the traditional imagination that is not acceptable. It's a sacrilege."[58]

Both the traditional realist imagination and the "purposive" mindset of the Habermasian modernist project would undoubtedly judge such discourse "sacrilege." Dismissively alluding to what he terms the "nonsense experiments" of the "hopeless surrealist revolts," Habermas, for example, insists that "destructured form" is "altogether incompatible with the moral basis of a purposive, rational conduct of life."[59] Yet, as Mestrovic remarks, such "repression of the irrational" appears puzzlingly anachronistic.[60] To all intents and purposes, irrational or destructured forms of thought became assimilated into the twentieth-century mentality decades ago. As the novelist William S. Burroughs puts it, "It must be remembered that the unconscious was much more unconscious in Freud's day than in ours."[61]

Baudrillard makes much the same point in *America,* where he emphasizes that everyday aspects of American culture "simply are extraordinary." "They have that extravagance which makes up odd, everyday America. This oddness is not surreal-istic (surrealism is an extravagance that is still aesthetic in nature and as such very European in inspiration): here, the extravagance has passed into things."[62]

In much of his writings there is something seductively contemporary in Baudrillard's conscious attention to the semiotics and semantics of everyday life in the 1980s and 1990s.[63] Yet, at the same time, Baudrillard's arguments fre-quently appear limited in terms of the ways in which their subversive project pivots upon such substantially passé, cultural modernist categories as the Surreal, or upon such latter day Dadaistic or semi-Situationist antiaesthetic ges-tures as his avowal "I don't want culture; I spit on it."[64]

As the veteran Dadaist pioneer Raoul Hausmann remarked with regard to the various "neo-Dada" movements of the 1960s, "Renaissances are, for the most part, sad and without issue."[65] Viewed with hindsight, much of the momentum of Parisian postmodern theory seems informed by this kind of oddly nostalgic, and ultimately unproductive register, characterized as it is— as Foucault observed—by the afterglow of the surrealist dream, "the dream that cast its spell, between the First World War and fascism."[66] What one sens-es here is the retrospective illumination of the cultural *archeologist,* as opposed, say, to any special sensitivity to the cultural potential of the present work-in-progress that writers such as Burroughs have associated with "*astro-nauts* of inner space."[67]

To be sure, the surrealist dream may well have appeared a very revolution-ary vista to the mandarins of the French academy when compared with the aca-demic "ethics" that Foucault associates with the three decades preceding May 1968.[68] But to those already versed in the poetics and politics of cultural mod-ernism, and to those alert to the positive potential of early postmodern techno-logical culture, a revival of the surrealist temper, with its cult of destructured textuality, appeared something of a mixed blessing.

On the one hand, the poetics of surrealism already seem a little dated, when compared with subsequent poetics born of the electronic media: the domain of technopoetics. On the other hand, as the multimedia sound poet Henri Chopin points out, the cultural politics of surrealism were still more restrictive than the parameters of surrealist poetics, in the sense that surrealism monopolized the attention of Parisian intellectuals and decelerated recognition of concurrent developments in modernist culture, such as the Dadaist and Futurist artists' exploration of emergent modes of mechanical *production* which only became readily available with the advent of new recording and printing technologies in the late 1950s and early 1960s.

Reflecting upon the "ethics" of the Parisian avant-garde in the 1950s, Chopin revealingly emphasizes the extent to which the creative community ignored the technological modernist experiments and aspirations of Surrealism's "other"—the Futurist and Dadaist movements of Italy, Russia, Switzerland, and Germany: "In 1949, Dada was completely unknown and completely eclipsed by Surrealism . . . It was all very vague—nobody knew what Dada was, and nobody much about Italian Futurism or Russian Futurism. . . . When Surrealism appeared, artists like . . . Raoul Hausmann were completely forgotten and neglected. . . . I had to visit the artists themselves before I finally learned that their world was much more creative than Surrealism, and discovered the true art of the twentieth century."[69] Chopin's fellow sound poet, Bernard Heidsieck, hints at the same kind of general problem, when remarking that the recent Musées de Marseilles exhibition, *Poésure et Peintrie*—the first ever major French survey of modernist and postmodernist developments in visual poetry, may finally "clarify the situation" and "present forty years of a different history" by examining the present in terms of "the vanguards of the early twentieth century, Futurism and Dada."[70] The prevalence of surrealist references and rhetoric within poststructuralist theory, and the failure of this theory to offer any informed analysis of multimedia elaborations of the Dadaist and Futurist vanguards, tell their own story.

Like many French intellectuals of his generation, Baudrillard frequently appears trapped behind conceptual and rhetorical blinkers. Refreshingly, though, he cheerfully claims to be "a very bad analyst" of art's "foreign domain,"[71] while writing many of the most provocative general accounts of this domain, and indeed, while attaining increasing recognition as a photographic artist in his own right.[72] Clearly, Baudrillard's relationship with his subject matter is far more complex than one might initially suppose.

On the one hand, Baudrillard seems neither willing nor able to address the positive potential of the innovative postmodern technological practices that Chopin emphatically identifies as the "true art" of the last four decades. But, on the other hand, Baudrillard appears compelled to confront the present as best he may. As the lines below from his essay "Xerox and Infinity" indicate,

Baudrillard's "best" culminates in marvelous discursive bravado—not unlike that of the gentle giants of the World Wrestling Foundation. Both defusing and diffusing defiance within deftly formulaic generalization, Baudrillard seems to steer his way to the heart of the problem—in this instance, the exact quality of electronic communication—by a process of energetic exaggeration and elimination. Catching his argument in mid-stride, one reads: " . . . just as the sudden and fabulous expansion of communication and information techniques is connected to the undecidability which circulates in them—the undecidability of knowing whether there is knowledge in there—so the undecidability in communication is of knowing whether or not it is a genuine form of exchange . . . I defy anyone to decide this—rather, to go on to believe that all these finally lead to real use of the world, to real encounters, etc."[73]

At this point, Baudrillard's argument dramatically changes gear from what one might think of as Nth-power analytical exaggeration and defiance, to registers of Nth-power fabulation and affirmation. Having asserted the implausibility of yet another aspect of contemporary culture (a hypothesis, moreover, quite at odds with the confidence with which artists, such as Diamanda Galas claim that they "dominate" their technology),[74] Baudrillard's pessimistic description transmutes into optimistic emphasis upon the "crucial" dilemma that he now perceives in terms of the spectacular "race-chase" between "man and his virtual clones on the reversible track of the Moebius Strip."[75]

Against all odds, perhaps, the paradoxical impact of Baudrillard's fusion of calculated incredulity and enthusiastic theoretical fantasy appears strikingly relevant. Even if Baudrillard's accelerating antitheses seem both to misunderstand and misrepresent their subject, they compel the reader to reconsider some of the most "fascinating" facets of contemporary culture. Claiming that "No one understands the stake of these techniques any longer," Baudrillard challengingly concludes: "No, the crucial stake, and the actual one, is the game of uncertainty. Nowhere can we escape it. But we are not ready to accept it, and worse still, we expect some sort of homeopathic flight of fancy by reducing this uncertainty with yet more information and yet more communication, thereby aggravating the relationship with uncertainty. Again, this is fascinating: the race-chase of techniques and their perverted effects, has started, the race-chase of man and his virtual clones on the reversible track of the Moebius Strip."[76]

The disadvantages and the advantages of such Nth-power speculation and fabulation become still clearer in the context of another of Baudrillard's contemporaries, the late multimedia composer, John Cage. Resisting Baudrillard's assumption that postmodern technology axiomatically generates uncertainty, Cage posits that "our souls are conveniently electronic,"[77] and are well able to work with contemporary media. If Cage's balanced optimism points to the perils of Baudrillardian oversimplification, Cage's defense elsewhere of forms of "purposeful purposelessness,"[78] as opposed, for example, to Habermas's commitment to "purposive, rational conduct,"[79] highlights the heuristic value of Baudrillard's ludic provocations, as texts initiating further debate and disrupting rationalist discursive stagnation.

As Baudrillard observes, his Nth-power rhetoric tends to prompt both celebration and denegration. "Everything I write is deemed brilliant, intelligent, but not serious."[80] As becomes increasingly apparent, Baudrillard's calculated defiance toward available concepts of the serious coexists with his frequent claim that his work is "serious just the same."[81] In Linda Nicholson's terms, Baudrillard appears overly dependent upon the elements of "human ingenuity or luck" which seem to prevail when all conventional models of communication break down.[82] Bypassing referential analysis, Baudrillard gambles with "little stories . . . little things which start and which have often been the sites of emergence: situations, wit, dreams."[83]

While Baudrillard prefers to present his writings as intimations of extinction charting "the curvature of things, the mode in which things try to disappear,"[84] his work seems most interesting as what he would term a "wager,"[85] one intent upon identifying—and in a sense predicting—significant "sites of emergence." Pondering upon the quality of that which has not yet been referenced, and resisting the rhetoric of present references, Baudrillard's writings offer a series of theory-fictions calculated to evince their subject matter's most compelling contradictions and challenges.

With luck or with ingenuity, Baudrillard seems to imply, a certain kind of consciously nonreferential theory-fiction, rigorously at odds with conventional truth claims, and inclined to examine the evidence of "things" as opposed to subjectivities, may possibly hit the mark in terms of its contemporaneity. Such, at least, is Baudrillard's avowed strategy for attaining—and perhaps communicating—some sense of "the scale" of contemporary reality: "In reality, things happen in such a way that they are always absolutely ahead of us, as Rilke said . . . things are always much further along than theory simply by virtue of the fact that the use of discourse is in the domain of metaphor. We can't escape it. In language we are condemned to using ambiguous extrapolations. If we claim a truth, we push effects of meaning to the extreme within a model. All that theory can do is be rigorous enough to cut itself off from any system of reference, so that it will at least be current, on the scale of what it wishes to describe."[86]

As Baudrillard remarks, his attempt to work to one side of referential analysis, "on the scale" of his subject matter, places him "on the margin" of mainstream intellectual writing; a position that he feels he shares with "the artists of the nineteenth century."[87] Like the American novelist Kathy Acker, Baudrillard seems to locate himself within something very close to the "*poète maudite* lineage" of those who "posit themselves as being *against* the ongoing society and culture."[88]

If it is the case, as Linda Nicholson argues, that many of the transitions between mainstream modernist and postmodernist thought involve "only . . . a shift in how we understand and use categories,"[89] Baudrillard can best be understood as an impatient thinker unwilling merely "to watch the extension, the adaption, generalized reconversion of all these things."[90] Dismissing the banality of "people in the sociological sense;"[91] dissociating himself from academia—"as soon as I see three intellectuals together I run away;"[92] deploring notions of social progress—"I detest buoyant activism in fellow citizens, initiatives, social responsibility;"[93] and at the same time declaring himself a voluntary exile on the main street of art—"I want to remain a foreigner there;"[94] Baudrillard appears to oscillate between the aristocratic and plebian poses that Renato Poggioli associates with the antagonistic impulse in the modernist *fin-de-siècle* mentality.

In other words, somewhat as Nicholson defines the transition between modernism and postmodernism in terms of shifts between different deployments of "common values" and "big categories,"[95] Baudrillard's subversive tactics ultimately appear little more than updated and slightly modified variants of the two heroic attitudes that Baudelaire associated with modern life—what Poggioli calls "the dandy and the criminal . . . aristocratic secession and plebian transgression."[96] Neither of these attitudes really places Baudrillard's work among the great discursive innovators of cultural postmodernism. Rather, his writings rank among the most brilliant conceptual catalysts of postmodernism, as opposed to those whose work progresses beyond the negativity that Poggioli associates with "*anti-*" discourse, via the radical experiments of "*ante-*" discourse, to "the moment of creation" when substantially new practices come into being.[97]

Discussing the more or less plebian sense of transgression in his "brutal reaction" toward the contemporary arts, Baudrillard characteristically defends his position as a theoretical terrorist on the grounds that he "can't envisage any other," adding: "It's something of an inheritance from the Situationists, from Bataille, and so on. Even though things have changed and the problems are no longer exactly the same, I feel I've inherited something from that position—the savage tone and the subversive mentality. I'm too old to change, so I continue!"[98]

Baudrillard's sense that he is "too old to change" and his reliance upon past cultural models accrue still more poignancy in the context of his suggestion that he would have preferred to live in the era "between Neitzsche and the 1920s–1930s," when "people like . . . Benjamin lived through the high point of a culture and the high point of its decline." Persuaded that "Postmodernism registers the loss of meaning" in a world in which "all that remains is a state of melancholia," or post-1930s sadness, Baudrillard concludes: "Today, we see the result of this process of decline and everyone is wondering how to remake a drama out of that. Personally, the only rebound that I found is America."[99]

As I have argued elsewhere,[100] Baudrillard's account of America drifts between symbolist and surrealist frames of reference, rather than ever coming to terms with the specific contemporaneity of American postmodern culture. The first three pages of *America,* for example, ponder upon such aspects of *Amérique sidérale*—"sidereal" or "astral" America—as: "the magic of the freeways;" "the fascination of senseless repetition;" "the timelessness of film;" "the transparency and supernatural otherworldly cleanness of a thing from outer space;" "magic, equal and opposite to that of Las Vegas;" "magical presence, which has nothing to do with nature;" and "the surrealistic qualities of an ocean bed in the open air."[101]

At best, *America* offers a sparkling account of American mass culture as seen by a postmodern descendant of the surrealist poet Louis Aragon's *Paris Peasant.*[102] At worst, as Kathy Acker observes, "It becomes a celebration of consumerism and of the culture we've got," and "a celebration of . . . the disappearance of value."[103] Considering the impact of video in terms of the ways in which discos like Roxy emulate "the effects you find on screens," Baudrillard reduces the entire potential of video to this kind of neutralizing illusion, insisting: "Video, everywhere, serves only this end: it is a screen of ecstatic refraction."[104]

While *America* initially charms the reader as a witty travelog, written with imaginative flair by an "Aeronautic missionary" leaping "with cat-like tread from one airport to another,"[105] it finally seems flawed for precisely the same reasons that Baudrillard judges Pierre Bourdieu's sociology to be inadequate—as an exercise in "self-verification" with every potential for becoming a sort of stereotype, an analysis which is going to produce the obvious for us."[106] As Baudrillard observes: "All of the themes that I first examined in my previous books suddenly appeared . . . stretching before me in concrete form . . . all the questions and the enigmas that had first posited conceptually. Everything there seemed significant to me, but at the same time everything also testified to the disappearance of all meaning."[107]

Not surprisingly, Baudrillard's infatuation with America—or with America's exemplification of his own worst suspicions—was short-lived. Baudrillard now admits: "I have lost my exaltation over America. It's become trivial."[108] Reciprocally, whereas Baudrillard's *America* testified to the pleasures of discovering and effortlessly decoding foreign vistas—"I know the deserts, their deserts, better than they do"[109]—Baudrillard now seems to prefer the kind of armchair travel advocated by Huysmans's Des Esseintes. Somewhat as Huysmans's hero reasons, "After all, what was the good of moving, when a fellow could travel so magnificently sitting in a chair?",[110] Baudrillard defends the fictional register of his book *La guerre du golfe n'a pas eu lieu* (1991), on the grounds that all of the "sentimental ideological pathos"[111] of debates about the Gulf War were themselves little more than a fiction which actual travel would appear unlikely to ameliorate: "*Les Presses de la Cité* invited me to go to the Gulf and cover the war. They were going to give me everything: money, documents, flights, etc. I live in the virtual. Send me into the real, and I don't know what to do. And, anyway, what more would I have seen? Those who went there saw nothing, only odds and ends."[112]

The strengths and weaknesses of such "virtual" hypotheses are, of course, that they accelerate more plodding cultural analysis into both illuminating and deceptive excess. Working rather more cautiously, Marshall Berman, for example, has modified Habermasian notions of modernity into a more flexible concept of "modernism today" that comfortably encapsulates every "attempt to arrive at some sort of universal values" by "struggling to break through to visions of truth and freedom that all men and women can embrace."[112] With this conveniently open-ended definition in mind, Berman pronounces that "1989 was not only a great year, but a great *modernist* year."[113] Considered in terms of the lyrics to the song "Imagine," 1989 might-equally well be said to be a great "John Lennon year." Alternatively, considered in terms of Lyotard's definition of postmodern thought as the process of struggling "without rules in order to formulate the rules of what *will have been done*,"[114] 1989 might just as well be defined as a great "postmodernist year."

All that now separates Berman's and Lyotard's utopianism is the shift of emphasis between the former's approval of universal values and the latter's antipathy to "the nostalgia of the whole and the one."[115] Confronted by such pedestrian distinctions, one might well turn with more sympathy to Baudrillard's attempt to look beyond mandarin quibbling over the merits and compatibilities of modernist and postmodernist great years, toward theory "on the scale"[116] of the next millenium. "My wager has been one of anticipation even if it meant making a leap, going forward beyond the year 2000; what I proposed was erasing the 1990s and going straight to the year 2000 to play the game on the other side through excess rather than lack."[117]

Somewhat as William S. Burroughs defines and defends the postmodern avant-garde as "*not setting out to explore static pre-existing data*," but rather, as "setting out to *create* new worlds, new modes of consciousness,"[118] the most utopian of Baudrillard's statements similarly contend: "Everything is involved here: to recreate another space which would be without limit (contrary to the former one) with a rule of play, a caprice . . . And what is being lost at the moment is this possibility of inventing an enchanted space, but a space at a distance also, and the possibility of playing on that distance."[119]

As both Burroughs and Baudrillard appear to discover, rhetorical "play" and "caprice" may well disrupt restricting intellectual ethics or conventions, but seldom suffice to inaugerate radically new alternatives to dominant practices; that is, alternatives which are not simply "shifts" to and from available discourse, but points of entry or "sites of emergence" into new discursive possibilities."[120] In Barthes's terms, such possibilities may well be "born technically, occasionally even aesthetically," long before they are "born theoretically."[121] To cite but one example, one might refer to Henri Chopin's discussion of "sound poetry, made for and by the tape-recorder," and as such, a practice "more easily codified by machines and electricity . . . than any means proper to writing."[122]

Chopin seems to have no doubt that his research identifies what Burroughs and Baudrillard would term new worlds, new spaces, and new modes of consciousness. While he acknowledges that cultural modernism disrupted nineteenth-century realist conventions "by offering poetic language a certain dynamism (Futurism) . . . by resituating discursive thought in more subtle forms

(Surrealism)," Chopin defines the specific innovative quality of postmodern sound poetry in terms of its unprecedented exploration of "electronic (recording) technology, which reveals the multiplicity of the voice, of utterances, of semantic values, etc."[123]

Neither Burroughs nor Baudrillard—or indeed the majority of cultural theoreticians and historians presently attempting to define the quality of postmodern culture—seem to share the confident insights common to the pioneers and practitioners of postmodern technoculture. Nevertheless, as writers who are also involved with other arts (Burroughs as a painter, Baudrillard as a photographer), and who were both represented in the "*Trans-Actions*" section of the 1993 Venice Biennale, among other artists "whose work is based on the merging of different disciplines,"[124] Burroughs and Baudrillard frequently evince considerable sensitivity to the multidisciplinary cultural temper of the 1990s.

Burroughs, for his part, evokes his position as that of someone who has metaphorically "blown a hole in time with a firecracker," but who feels "bound to the past," and who finally resigns himself to "Let others step through."[125] Baudrillard seems to experience a similar dilemma. His most optimistic polemic asserts that one way or another "we must try to jump over the wall"[126] of psychology and sociology, to go "through the wall of glass of the aesthetic,"[127] and to "pass through all disciplines."[128] But having proposed such initiatives, Baudrillard often appears unwilling or unable to follow them through. Speculating that "Perhaps the only thing one can do is to destabilize and provoke the world around us," Baudrillard concludes: "We shouldn't presume to *produce* positive solutions. In my opinion this isn't the intellectual's or the thinker's task. It's not our responsibility. It might occur, but it will only come about by reaction. . . . It needs to be provoked into action."[129]

What seems most significant about Baudrillard's ambiguous writings is the fact that even when compulsively asserting "the disappearance of all meaning,"[130] they continue to assert the "crucial," "actual," and "fascinating" nature of the search for meaning."[131] Despite all protests to the contrary, he repeatedly posits that intellectual inquiry should be serious and should have something at stake. For example, when Baudrillard rejects "ill-digested rationalities, radicalities," it is because they have "no support, no enemies and . . . nothing at stake."[132] Elaborating this discrimination in the following unusually assertive avowal, he specifies: "I need a challenge myself, there's got to be something at stake. If that is taken away, then I will stop writing. I'm not mad. At a given moment, however, you cause things to exist, not producing them in the material sense of the term, but by defying them, by confronting them. Then at that moment it's magic."[133]

Here, I think, we see Baudrillard in his true colors, seeking challenges in a world that he contends to be bereft of challenges, asserting that values can be at stake in a world that he associates with the disappearance of values, and aspiring to create magic in a world in which, apparently, "The maximum in intensity lies behind, us; the minimum in passion and intellectual inspiration lies before us."[134] Like Des Esseintes, the hero—or antihero—of Huysmans's *Against Nature*, Baudrillard offers the spectacle of the hesitant utopian, "the unbeliever who would fain believe . . . the galley-slave of life who puts out to sea alone, in the night, beneath a firmament no longer lit by the consoling beacon-fires of the ancient hope!"[135] In Baudrillard's terms, even if utopia "does not exist," and "may even be impossible," it is the intellectual's fate and privilege to continue "raving a little . . . going beyond their objective situation and creating utopia." For, in his rather chilling judgment, "This is the only positivity they can have."[136] Like that of any other significant theorist or artist, Baudrillard's position in the postmodern cosmos is far from simple. Considered in the relatively banal context of what Foucault called "the transformations that have actually been produced" and the systems "according to which certain variables have remained constant while others have been modified,"[137] Baudrillard offers the spectacle of a predominantly *modernist* postmodern; a theoretical revolutionary whose rhetorical variables have not really modified to any great extent.

At first glance, the titles of Baudrillard's essays and books may well seem highly topical and contemporary in their focus and theme. But, as I have suggested, Baudrillard's voluntary stance as a marginal oppositional figure, and his emphases upon the paradoxical, the magical, the surreal, and the hyperreal, are all continuous both with the early postmodern subversive tactics of the Situationists,[138] and with the still earlier strategies of a succession of modernist generations ranging from such *fin-de-siècle* writers as Pater, Mallarmé, and Huysmans, to the subsequent prewar mainstream modernism of Woolf, and the postwar avant-gardism of the Dadaists and the Surrealists.

While Baudrillard's recent photographic work appears to have modified many of his early hypotheses, Baudrillard's overall vision seems to lack the radical audacity of such modernist *"Primitives of a completely renovated sensitiveness"* as the Italian Futurist Umberto Boccioni and the Berlin Dadaist Raoul Hausmann;[139] those whom Benjamin associates with the prophetic aspiration toward new practices requiring a "changed technological standard,"[140] and whom Chopin regards as "a beginning" as distant from present postmodern multimedia practices as "the plane piloted by Blériot" is distinct from "supersonic planes like the Concorde."[141]

It is precisely this kind of discursive *beginning*, aspiring toward, arising from—and then once again demanding—*changed technological standards,* that reflects postmodern culture's most vital technical and conceptual energies. As Howard Rheingold suggests, such discursive innovation is significant both as an initial avant-garde exception to the general rules of the postmodern condition, and as a subsequent conceptual and technical catalyst serving "to enhance the most creative aspects of human intelligence, for everybody, not just the technocognoscenti."[142] If the work of those whom Burroughs term the "astronauts of inner space"—and those whom Rheingold terms the "*infonauts*"—is of crucial relevance to an understanding of our time, then as Rheingold concludes, it is because "some of them may provide clues to what (and how) everybody will be thinking in the near future."[143]

Not merely pointers to new ways of *thinking,* new communications technologies also obviously adumbrate new forms of practical *activity* and *interactivity.* In this respect, neither Baudrillard's accounts of vertiginous cycles of technological simulation devoid of "real use," "real encounters," and any "genuine form of exchange,"[144] nor Gene Youngblood's diagnoses of more positive systems of technological simulation that incarnate "freedom in the digital age," but which apparently "refer to nothing outside themselves except the pure, 'ideal' laws of . . . the dematerialised territory of virtual space," seem commensurate with the "*real situations*" which Morris Berman distinguishes from the cybernetic fantasy-world of self-contained "circuits" and "feedback loops."[145]

What postmodern cultural theory needs, in other words—over and beyond the *analytical* rigor demanded by those who see Baudrillard's work as "grossly undertheorized,"[146] and the *speculative* spontaneity that Baudrillard opposes to the grossly overtheorized caution of those incapable of looking toward—and beyond—the year 2000, is *empirical* sensitivity to the specific liberating potential of emergent practices enriching postmodern *real time* in the here and now of the late 1990s. Put another way, both the analytical and the speculative impulses in postmodern cultural theory and postmodern cultural fiction run the risk of neglecting those positively innovative discourses-in-progress that exceed their respective categories, and which, in Barthes's terms, exist technically and aesthetically long before obtaining adequate theoretical—or fictional—formulation.[147]

Arguably, the cartography-in-progress of innovative discourses-in-progress—as opposed, say, to the more mundane cataloging of "transformations that have actually been produced"—constitutes one of the most challenging tasks for those confronted by what Foucault terms the "abundance of things to know: essential or terrible, marvelous or droll." As Foucault concludes, there are still "too few means to think about all that is happening."[149]

Whatever other reactions his writings and utterances may provoke, Baudrillard continually commands respect in terms of the unusual tenacity and vivacity of his attempts to identify "means to think about all that is happening." Once one acknowledges that cultural and theoretical variants of modernism and postmodernism extend across several generations and advance at differing speeds across several contradictory fronts, it becomes evident that Baudrillard is no more typical of the postmodern mentality as a whole than Habermas is typical of its modernist equivalents. Rather, Baudrillard, like Habermas, has moments of partial lucidity, "on the scale"[149] of what he wishes to describe.

At times, Baudrillard seems altogether reluctant to describe the present in anything other than rather restrictive apocalyptic rhetoric. Nevertheless, even though Baudrillard's discursive and conceptual prejudices frequently deflect his vision away from their unerringly topical targets, toward the nostalgic never never land of modernist poetics and nineteenth-century agonistic posture, there is frequently something profoundly engaging and inspiring in Baudrillard's idiosyncratic attempts to grapple with those issues he finds most challenging and most at stake. Compared with the unadventurous ways in which other cartographers of postmodern culture carefully sift elementary shifts within the familiar shallows of twentieth-century discourse, Baudrillard's finest "virtual" descents into uncharted contemporary depths offer models of passionate engagement with the most crucial developments within the postmodern condition.

"apocalyptic"? 8
"negative"?
"pessimistic"?
baudrillard, virilio,
and technoculture

A creator who creates, who
is not an academician, who
is not someone who studies
in a school where the rules
are already known . . . is
necessarily of his generation. His generation lives
in its contemporary way
but they only live in it. In
art, in literature, in the theatre, in short in everything
that does not contribute to
their immediate comfort
they live in the preceding
generation

—Gertude Stein
Picasso

As Gertrude Stein's *Picasso* (1938, 30–31) observes, one of the greatest problems for the cultural cartographer is the task of identifying appropriate conceptual, theoretical, and aesthetic points of reference in order to chart ongoing

technological work-in-progress. Confronted by contemporary mutations in and across mass-market publicity, photography, film, television, video, and computer art—not to mention hybrid forms of multimedia installation and performance—it is difficult to discern good from bad, substantial from superficial, innovation from entropy, originality from banality.

Indeed, as French theorist Paul Virilio remarked in an interview of January 1995, "The problem is that so far as technological art is concerned, there is virtually no critical theory." (Virilio, 1996, 117) As becomes obvious, theorists such as Virilio and Baudrillard frequently focus upon the negative implications of mass-technoculture, although both authors also insist that their analyses of the postmodern condition are not necessarily negative in spirit. Baudrillard has observed: "I'm far from being a pessimist," (1993a, 133) and Virilio now rather similarly specifies, "People say 'You're opposed to technological creativity!' But it's not the case at all. On the contrary, its quite evident that my writings on art are all clearly in favour of technology! It's absurd to separate art from technology! I realise that many people claim that I am apocalyptic, negative, pessimistic. But all of that is out of date—it doesn't rise to the heights of the situation!" (1996, 117).

Reading the most accessible, the most seductive and the most influential writings of Baudrillard and Virilio, one might be forgiven for typecasting their responses to technoculture as "apocalyptic, negative, pessimistic." It's all too easy to misread postmodern culture as a whole in terms of highly polemical, highly partial accounts of mass culture's bewildering superficialities. Or, if one's optimistically inclined, perhaps it's all too easy to overemphasize the positive potential of other—equally partial—exceptions to mass-cultural mediocrity.

Nevertheless, as these paragraphs will suggest, Baudrillard, Virilio, Roland Barthes and William S. Burroughs all seem to make best sense when they consider technoculture and techno-imaging in terms of those emerging positive practices that offer crucial exceptions to the kind of hyperaccelerated confusion that journalistic polemic all too readily attributes to every facet of contemporary experience.

For example, according to some of the more hallucinatory pages of Baudrillard's *The Transparency of Evil* (1993), we have now reached a cultural condition in which it is impossible to make value judgements; a situation in which "there is no point of reference at all, and value radiates in all directions, occupying all interstices, without reference to anything whatsoever, by virtue of pure contiguity ... there is no longer any equivalence, whether natural or general ... no law of value, merely a sort of *epidemic of value* ... a haphazard proliferation and dispersal of value ... (a) chain reaction (which) makes all valuation impossible." (Baudrillard 1993b, 5)

Why should the possibility of valuation disintegrate into this sort of epidemic of haphazard proliferation and dispersal? According to Baudrillard, points of reference and concepts of cultural value proliferate and disperse because of their unprecedentedly accelerated speed: a speed which—like that of microphysical particles—resists calculation, comparison and evaluation: "It is as impossible to make estimations between beautiful and ugly, true and false, or good and evil, as it is simultaneously to calculate a particle's speed and position. Good is no longer the opposite of evil, nothing can now be plotted on a graph or analysed.... Just as each particle follows its own trajectory, each value or fragment of value shines for a moment in the heavens of simulation, then disappears into the void along a crooked path that only rarely happens to intersect with other such paths. This is the pattern of the fractal and hence the current pattern of our culture." (1993b, 5–6).

Why, we should surely ask, is the "current pattern of our culture" necessarily either "crooked" or "fractal"? *Why,* in other words, should we accept Baudrillard's hypothesis that microphysics offers the most appropriate conceptual model for our experience of multimedia culture? This question is a crucial one, for obvious reasons, insofar as one's cultural *model* more or less pre-cooks one's books, and a "fractal" reading of media culture necessarily *fractures* all hope of locating permanent signs of cultural coherence and value.

Reiterating this rather mechanical diagnosis of contemporary culture at the end of *The Illusion of the End* (1994), Baudrillard suggests that we now inhabit a curiously neutral timeless zone, without past, without future and in consequence a realm without finite or final possibilities: a de-finitive realm characterized by a sense of melancholia, resentment and disappearance. In Baudrillard's terms, "We are, then, unable to dream of a past or future state of things. Things are in a state which is literally definitive—neither finished, nor infinite, nor definite, but de-finitive that is, deprived of its end. Now, the feeling which goes with a definitive state ... is melancholic. Whereas, with mourning, things come to an end and therefore enjoy a possibility of returning, with melancholia we are not even left with the presentiment of an end or of a return, but only with *ressentiment* at their disappearance" (1994,120).

What we witness here is a kind of *descendental* surrealism: a world not so much heightened by the fusion of the realms of real and surreal, consciousness and dream, as neutralised by its absence of past and future and of any kind of dreaming. Put another way, Baudrillard lyrically invokes a melancholic world without possibility of end and certainly without the kind of miraculous revelation that Paul Eluard's *Lady Love* (1924) attributes to the influence of the shared omnipresent dreams of the "She" who:

> ... will never close her eyes
> And ... does not let me sleep
> And her dreams in the bright day
> Make the sun evaporate
> And me laugh cry and laugh
> Speak when I have nothing to say.

If Eluard's poem addresses the problem of verbalizing the experience of ecstatic, postverbal communion, Baudrillard's poetic writings more often than not insinuate that we inhabit a post-surreal culture. In such a culture the problem of reformulating ecstatic poetic experience appears virtually irrelevant insofar as we now supposedly exist without poetry, without dreams, without values, without the beautiful and without the ugly, within crooked, incalculable, omnipresent "fractal" acceleration and disintegration.

According to the American novelist William S. Burroughs, such a condition seems likely to be both a domain of melancholia and a domain of imminent death, if it is indeed the case, as Burroughs claims in *Painting and Guns* (1992), that "Scientists have found that dreams are a biological necessity. If you deprive someone of the dream state for more than two months they will die, no matter how much dreamless sleep they are allowed. People hunger for dreams, they need them. Dreams are not some kind of elite luxury" (46). For Burroughs, it follows that artists are providers of what one might very generally call "dream-time": "What do artists do? They dream for other people. We dream for those people who have no dreams of their own to keep them alive" (46).

Put another way, the most unhealthy impact of Baudrillard's writings culminates in what Gene Youngblood terms the "numbing" effect of pseudoscientific accounts of "fractal" culture (1989, 14), or what Burroughs associates with scientific dogma insisting that "nothing means anything to anyone" within a "dead thermodynamic universe where there is no meaning at all" (1992, 23), and which may perhaps be considered a kind of descendental black magic. Burroughs, by contrast, defines his art as the more transcendental white magic that he associates with the *un*numbing impact of artists such as Paul Klee: "When I read Klee, fairly recently after I started painting, I said 'Jesus he's saying just what I'm talking about.' He says the artist's call is trying to create something that has a life of its own" (1992, 33–34).

In Burroughs's terms, this implies that art is a kind of "evocative magic" which, far from "trying to make people sick," tries "to make people aware . . . of what they know and don't know that they know" (1992, 37). In Burroughs's view, the most productive model for analysis of both the present and future potential of our culture is the work of those artists, and creative thinkers who— in his terms—are already exploring "space": "What you glimpse in dreams and out of the body trips, what you glimpse in the work of artists and painters, is the promised land of space" (1986, 103). For Burroughs, these artists, creative thinkers, and one might add, creative explorers of filmic media, "are already waiting, painting and filming space," and "providing us with . . . maps for space travel." More specifically, Burroughs explains, "*We are not setting out to explore static pre-existing data.* We are setting out to *create* new worlds, new beings, new modes of consciousness. As Brion Gysin said, when they get there in their million dollar aqualungs they may find that the artists are already there" (1986, 102; emphasis in the original).

My point thus far is that Burroughs's writings helpfully challenge Baudrillard's pseudoscientific accounts of our culture's apparent demise, if only by reminding us that the black magic of Baudrillardian fractal theory may well be countered by the white magic of multimedia *creativity* and by the possibilities of gradually mapping, invoking, revealing, and recording "new modes of consciousness."

To be fair to Baudrillard, *The Illusion of the End* also sketches precisely this kind of seemingly anti-Baudrillardian "magic" when its final pages posit the possibility of escaping the neutrality of fractal culture and of fractal theory—or in Baudrillard's case fractal fiction, perhaps—by undertaking or provoking what Baudrillard unexpectedly terms "a poetic reversibility of events." Acknowledging that more or less confident artistic and literary experimentation still continues in the face of the apparently anaesthetizing omnipresence of fractal, mass-media cultures, Baudrillard's conclusion to *The Illusion of the End* tentatively observes: "Against this general movement, there remains the completely improbable and, no doubt, unverifiable hypothesis of a *poetic reversibility of events*, more or less the only evidence for which is the existence of the same possibility in language" (1994, 120).

What we witness here is a sort of discursive slippage as Baudrillard hesitantly posits that the possibility of "poetic reversibility" within language perhaps implies that similar reversals may well modify the apparent terminal entropy of the electronic media. More generally, then, the possibility of literary "poetic reversibility" suggests that late-twentieth-century media culture as a whole may similarly undergo such liberating mutation, rather than being locked forever within the kind of over-accelerating fractal fragmentation that Baudrillard usually considers to be the "current pattern of our culture." At his most objective, Baudrillard pragmatically acknowledges that generally speaking, "the effect of something written is nil today," but adds, very significantly, that certain exceptions to this rule exist nevertheless, insofar as there can still be "something at stake": "At a given moment . . . you cause things to exist, not by producing them in the material sense of the term, but by defying them, by confronting them. Then at that moment it's magic" (1993a, 44).

Like Burroughs—for whom "what we call art—painting, sculpture, writing, dance, music—is magical in origin" (1992, 32)—Baudrillard eventually returns to the rhetoric of creative magic or alchemy, insisting moreover that such magic or alchemy is not so much a process of rhetorical reversal (or deconstruction), as more substantial constructive invocation: "Writing . . . and theory as well . . . is not just a simple question of producing ideas or differences. It's also a question of knowing how to cast a spell" (1993a, 45).

As Baudrillard indicates in another interview, he seems to have theorized himself into a corner from which there seems no escape save via alternative discourses to those of theory. If the literary model of "poetic reversibility" offers Baudrillard one such escape route, the surprisingly optimistic "will to create" of the most visionary postmodern artists seems to suggest another alternative to hypertheorized melancholia. Comparing his sense of theoretical indifference to that of creative commitment, Baudrillard observes: "Personally, I'm no longer involved in political analysis or philosophy, nor in sociology . . . whereas the artists, as I see them, are still fascinated by art, they're still within a history, a will to create, to communicate" (1993c, 85).

Somewhat as Burroughs's associate, Brion Gysin, observed that "Writing is fifty years behind painting" in his 1958 manifesto *Cut-Up Self-Explained* (1973, 11),

Baudrillard seems to have made much the same discovery some thirty-five fears later. In this respect, one might suggest that Parisian theory is *thirty-five* years behind avant-garde New York writing, and *eighty-five* years behind painting, in the sense that until very recently, it has relentlessly labored under the illusion that the cultural logic of the late twentieth century can be reduced to updated evocations of the same kind of entropic fragmentation or accelerated confusion that late-nineteenth-century pessimists such Max Nordau attributed to early metropolitan cultures.

What seems most interesting at present is the way in which both relatively apocalyptic writers like Burroughs, and highly apocalyptic theorists like Baudrillard now seem to be in the process of elaborating far more positive accounts of the present in terms of ways in which photographic and filmic media may well take highly effective account of updated "poetic" and "magic" effects, and in the process reveal what Burroughs terms "new modes of consciousness" and what Baudrillard terms the magic process of causing new things "to exist."

Still more significantly, perhaps, what we might now call the impulse of "poetic reversal" in Baudrillard's theory coincides with Baudrillard's own entry into the activity of photographic practice: an initiative prompting his sense that contemporary culture cannot be adequately accounted for in terms of familiar practices viewed from "the standpoint of reason" insofar as what one might call "the standpoint of creative surprise" suggests that things are far more complicated than one might initially have assumed. In Baudrillard's terms, "Perhaps the desire to take photographs arises from the observation that on the broadest view, from the standpoint of reason, the world is a great disappointment. In its details, however, and caught by surprise, the world has a stunning clarity" (1993b, 155).

Burroughs tempers his more anarchic tendencies with similarly surprising qualifications. Asked if his work was essentially an exploration of literally postmodern images which—unlike Proustian modernist metaphors—"didn't cohere," Burroughs disarmingly replied, "Well, that's a little vague because images always cohere by nature, there's a sort of magnetism. If you have an image over here it's going to attract—or attach itself to—similar images. That's simply a matter of the way the words work. There seems to be a sort of magnetism" (Burroughs 1983). As Burroughs suggests, by the mid-eighties, postmodern aesthetics had looked beyond the confusion that I associate (in chapter three) with the kind of "métaphore manquée" evoked by early postmodern fiction, exploring new kinds of extra-rational structural and symbolic harmony and coherence.

Burroughs's sense of the essential potential *coherence* or *magnetism* of contemporary creativity is evidenced particularly clearly in his *Aperture* article on the American photographer Robert Walker. Here Burroughs acknowledges the general fractal quality of New York, insofar as "the whole city is a backdrop which could collapse at any moment," but also insists that Walker's photography "catches... the underlying unities of disparate elements," (1985, 86). Discussing an image of "a young man in striped black-and-white T-shirt and blue jeans" whose "blank" expression seems captured by "something . . . we can't see," Burroughs cites it as a catalyst of subsequent dreamworld revelations: "I had a dream about this picture in which I touched his arm and found it cold, dead cold, and started back exclaiming, 'He is an Empty one! A walking corpse, a body without a soul'" (66).

If Burroughs initially acknowledges Walker's ability to evoke the prevalent fragmentation and confusion of everyday New York, he still more interestingly associates Walker's art with evocations of what Baudrillard would term revelations of "stunning clarity." For his part, Burroughs defines this clarity as "the meaning of meaninglessness, the pattern of chaos, the underlying unities of disparate elements" (66).

Looking in turn beyond the definable domain of everyday codes, Barthes similarly identifies this possibility of recording haunting clarity in Robert Mapplethorpe's portrait of Philip Glass and Robert Wilson. Barthes uses this example to define his concept of photographic "*punctum*" or his apprehension of a photographic detail that he cannot reduce to the kind of "structural rule" that he associates with *studium*." For Barthes, *punctum* implies a quality of emphatic detail that "pricks me ... is poignant to me," (1981, 27), which "rises from the scene, shoots out of it like an arrow, and pierces me" (26). "Wilson holds me, though I cannot say why, i.e. say where. . . . The effect is certain but unlocatable, it does not find its sign, its name; it is sharp and yet lands in a vague zone of myself; it is acute and yet muffled, it cries out in silence" (51–53).

For Barthes, as for Burroughs, this impact is extremely personal. It is what he associates with "Absolute subjectivity" (55) while at the same time evincing "intense immobility" (49), and one might add, a sense of *intense inevitability,* insofar as this kind of image seems to be one that the photographer "could not *not* photograph" (47). As such it evokes what Barthes calls the dimension of "photographic ecstasy," transcending the boredom of "universalised" images (119).

Discussing those images that he associates with a more objective, more material form of *punctum,* or "the sense of the singularity of the object at a given moment . . . where things have no meaning—or do not yet have meaning—*but* appear all the same" (Baudrillard, 1997a, 39), Baudrillard in turn suggests that photographs may transcend "universal banality" (1993b, 151) and attain what he too calls "the ecstasy of photography" (1997a, 37), within a state restoring "the immobility and the silence of the image," irrespective of "the violence, the speed or the noise of its surroundings" in "the thunderous context of the real world" (1997b, 31). For Baudrillard, such images are "the purest of images" because they attain "pure objectality," evoking—ideally—"a universe from which the subject has withdrawn" (1993b, 154). Baudrillard's photograph *Paris* (1989) which depicts his indentations upon a sheet of red fabric covering his chair, perhaps approximates this ideal insofar as it is an evocation of "the absence of the subject—absence modelled within a certain form." Put another way, this photograph might be said to register the same kind of evocative absent presence or present absence as sheets upon which "[a] light body leaves no trace" (1990, 210).

What seems most significant here is surely the way in which Baudrillard—like Burroughs and Barthes—suggests the ways in which photography may triumphantly immobilize the particular quality of a particular perception, isolating it from its "thunderous," "banal," "fragmentary," or purely structural context, with a sense of uncanny authority and inevitability. Thus, for Baudrillard, "an object creates a sense of emptiness" and "imposes itself" (1997a, 34).

What Baudrillard, Barthes, and Burroughs describe, in other words, is an *art of appearance,* a photographic art of appearance or of reappearance, working against the confusions of fractal culture, and culminating—objectively or subjectively—in the kind of mysterious and almost mystical apparition that Virilio's *The Art of Disappearance* (1991) associates with perceptions of "infra-ordinary reality," involving the "passage from the familiar" to "unfamiliar" reality, in such seeming miracles as Bernadette Soubirous's sightings of the Virgin Mary at Lourdes. Soubirous recounts: "I heard a noise. Looking up I saw poplars . . . quiver as if the wind was shaking them, but all around nothing moved and suddenly I saw something white . . . and this white was . . . a white girl . . . a white girl no bigger than me. She greeted me, bowing . . ." (Virilio 1991, 38). And Baudrillard in turn describes the equally unexpected way in which "an object imposes itself—suddenly one sees it, because of certain effects of light, of contrasts, and things like that, it isolates itself and creates a sense of emptiness . . . and then it irradiates this emptiness" (1997a, 34).

For Virilio, the potential for such revelations seems eclipsed by what *The Aesthetics of Disappearance* calls "the *fait accompli* of technology" (1991, 42). By this he means the neutralizing "violence" of the speed which—so far as he is concerned—"dominates the technical world" (100), in much the same way as it dominates the war machine's quest for ever more effective modes of "surprise" attack. For Virilio, "war is the best model" in "the technical domain" (94). Taking us all by surprise in ever more baffling ways, it would seem that "high technological speeds . . . result in the disappearance of consciousness," as the "authority of electronic automatism" allegedly reduces our will "to zero" (104).

Considered in the highly disturbing general context of the war machine, cinema for Virilio is not so much a potentially liberating "seventh art," offering visionaries the opportunity to film what Burroughs calls "the promised land of space" (1986, 103), as a hybrid local anaesthetic causing "the dominant philosophies and arts . . . to confuse and lose themselves" in a state of "decomposition" (105). At worst, as Walter Benjamin observed, quoting Georges Duhamel, it may well be the case that cinema culminates in "a spectacle which requires no concentration and presupposes no intelligence . . . which kindles no light in the heart and awakens no hope" (Benjamin 1979, 241). But at best, as Barthes, Burroughs, and Baudrillard all consolingly imply, media culture may also perhaps isolate forms of provocative *punctum* by retrieving and asserting something "at stake" apart from "the violence, the speed or the poise of its surroundings."

For Virilio, by contrast, the "transformation [of reality] into video signals stored on tape, "appears inseparable from the tendency for high-technical speeds to inaugurate "the disappearance of consciousness" (1991, 104). Indeed, according to *The Aesthetics of Disappearance,* the very act of taking photographs seems *depassé,* since "photography, overcome by indifference, seems from now on incapable of finding something new to photograph," in an age in which modes of "collective thought imposed by diverse media" seem well on the way to "annihilating the originality of sensations" (47-48). According to Virilio, we are the predestined victims of "technical fatality" (95) within a computerized culture comparable to "a reactor that's out of control." At this point it seems that technological culture signals the death of poetry, the death of contemplative control, in a world in which "the technician becomes the victim of the movement he's produced" (96), lost as it were "in motion" and "in transit," and forever exiled and alienated from "unique historical time" (110).

Persuasive as Virilio's general argument frequently appears, it seems to pivot upon the distorted and distorting model of the war game, regarding technology as a force almost exclusively definable in terms of its neutralizing *acceleration*. While Burroughs also considers that "This is a war universe," he rather more interestingly considers the war machine at several speeds: "Some weapons may hit you right away, other weapons may take five hundred years to hit" (1992, 64).

As seems so often the case, Burroughs's seemingly casual asides offer timely reminders of the complexity of notionally self-evident assumptions. Technology is a tri-part source of accelerated speed, of real-time speed, and of decelerated speed, and it makes little sense to typecast it simply in terms of "the violence of speed." As Virilio himself specifies, speed can obviously be both "negative and positive" (1996, 117).

If "the violence of speed" seems to dominate technology, then this is doubtless merely because we are more accustomed to being surprised by acceleration than by deceleration. Superman is after all faster—rather than slower—than a speeding bullet, and we perhaps mistakenly assume that acceleration is the only possible kind of innovative momentum. Exemplifying this tendency, the Australian video artist Peter Callas remarks how he initially found it strategically effective to differentiate his work with video and computers from cinematic art's slower registers: "I was interested in the idea of playing up the characteristics of the medium to distinguish it as much as possible from film. One of these aspects was the idea of speed and bombardment—of thinking about the electronic gun, and the compression of images on the glass surface of the monitor. Virilio's metaphor of the gun, and the image of the electrons that stop on this glass screen . . . to me all that fitted together very well" (Callas 1994, 116).

Looking at the work of Callas one can understand his point. As he observes, it attempts to present what he calls "the idea of the tantalizing image, of things you half see, of flashes in your mind or dream images, that you want to bring back but which remain so perfect in the very fact they elude you when you try to recall them or recreate them" (119). Nevertheless, what Callas does is precisely to *re-create* this sense of fleeting, flashing dream imagery in a format which, as he observes, can be both tantalizingly fast and transparently slow.

On the one hand, viewed in real time, these images enter what Callas terms "a zone of speed created by the editing and the rhythm of the images so that the person watching it had to *let go* of symbolic thought—because if you tried to hold onto it in an attempt to piece it together as you're watching the tape you'd be lost. You'd have to watch it in a different way to the way you might look at a painting" (117).

On the other hand, however, Callas also comments that he makes such tapes "to be seen again"—either in rapid real time or decelerated *reel* time: "I don't mind if someone watches a tape through frame by frame, because I have a reason for the placement of each and every image, or at least I've made a decision to place each image and all the layers mean something to me" (117).

In much the same way, listening to a speech in a Shakespeare play we are unlikely to consciously dwell upon every ambiguity of every image and every wordplay, hearing it differently, as it were, to the way in which we hear someone asking for the time or asking for directions. As with Callas's video and computer compositions, we can return to the text of Shakespeare's plays, confident that Shakespeare probably "had a reason for the placement of each and every image," and confident that "all the layers" potentially "mean" something to which we can perhaps gradually gain deeper access if we read individual speeches at our own pace, beneath our lamp, at our desk, without the accelerated distraction of all the other words and actions advancing in performative real time on stage. Callas notes that when his work is on television "the audience has the opportunity to record it, and to watch it back at their own leisure," adding, "And as I said, I'm not adverse [sic] to that" (119).

Indeed, contemplating more recent forms of image retrieval systems, Callas posits that in many respects we may already be successfully engaging in adequate subconscious mediated interaction with *mediated* culture such as video and computer art, insofar as it seems likely that "the subconscious (of the maker) were speaking to the subconscious (of the audience) on the shared domain of media(ted) culture" (118).

What this effectively means is that—in Burroughs's terms—when it comes to watching seemingly impossibly accelerated images, audiences may well know things that they "don't know that they know," and like Molière's *bourgeois gentilhomme,* may well have been reading certain kinds of poetry or prose—in this instance, *mediated poetry and prose*—without ever realizing it.

Reconsidered in the context of Callas's comments, Baudrillard and Virilio's insistence upon the impossibility of reading, interpreting, and evaluating media texts seems doubly suspect. Firstly, as Baudrillard himself now intimates, it seems evident that certain forms of photography may well retrieve and immobilize subjective and objective *punctum* from their "thunderous" surroundings (1997a, 31). Secondly, as Callas suggests, even high-speed media texts seem likely to inaugurate *some* significant subconscious interchange with their audiences, and may subsequently be examined in decelerated time, as slow, frame-by-frame sequences, as many times as it takes the viewer to decode their symbolic and structural logic.

With such possibilities in mind it seems evident that media art need not always be the art of "disappearance" that Virilio supposes it to be, and that media art—like photography—may often be compatible with that whole range of subjective, objective, interpretive and evaluative responses that many of Virilio's writings appear to designate as obsolete. Roughly summarized, these responses may be identified in seven groupings:

• The sense of viewing texts in "one's own unique historical time."

• The sense of responding to cinema and video and other related media practices as a seventh or eighth art not so much precipitating the "decomposition" of past values as their *recomposition*.

• The sense of being able to exert modes of analytical, interpretative and evaluative "will" in the face of "electronic automation."

• The sense that the "violence of speed" does not in fact dominate the "technical world."

• The sense that the technician and the techno-artist are not so much the "victims" of the "movement" they produce, as the potential masters of such movement.

• The sense that war is not the "best model" for technical culture, since far from always "annihilating" either the artist's or the audience's access to "originality of the sensation," the "diverse media" may well *diversify* and *intensify* the subjective impact of subjective creativity.

• The sense that far from being "overcome by indifference" and far from being *"incapable* of finding something new," the media arts might be said to be undergoing a veritable renaissance of *new* possibilities— some of course obviously more interesting than others—both from the perspective of the artist's pluralistic compositional options, and from the perspective of the audience's potentially pluralistic analytical, interpretative, and evaluative options.

Briefly, there seem very few grounds for referring to the apocalyptic *fait accompli* of technology. All available evidence indicates that new technologies are simply in the process of navigating the most elementary moves within an immense array of options ranging from obvious examples of confusing mediatized acceleration, to those more subtle and less self-evident mediatized variants of mystical "infra-ordinary" revelations that Virilio defines in Proustian terms as "the suddenness of . . . entry into another logic which dissolves the concepts of truth and illusion, of reality and appearance . . . that which pertains to a moment that is singular and, by definition, different" (1991, 35).

In Bernadette Soubirous's terms, these are precisely the kind of moments for which "you'd give a whole lifetime" (39).

It is surely this ideal that André Breton had on his mind in his Surrealist Manifesto's annunciation of the eventual—or seemingly impossible—fusion of the real and the superreal, an eventuality he notes, which would make "death . . . matter little to me could I but taste the joy it will yield ultimately" (Breton 1934, 414). Paradoxically perhaps, it is likewise surely this ideal that Robert Wilson realized in his performance *Deafman Glance.* Discussing this work in terms of surrealism's *unrealised* aspirations, the veteran Surrealist Aragon writes:

"The miracle was produced, the one we were waiting for, about which we talked . . . the miracle came about long after I stopped believing in them . . . I never saw anything more beautiful in the world since I was born. Never never has any play come anywhere near this one, because it is at once life awake and the life of closed eyes, the confusion between everyday life and the life for each night, reality mingles with dream. . . . Bob Wilson's piece which comes to us from Iowa is not surrealism at all, however easy it is for people to call it that, but it is what we others, who fathered surrealism, what we dreamed it might become, after us, beyond us. . . . Distinguished professors, it is not surrealism, that is to say, for you something to be classified, a subject for a thesis, for a class at the Sorbonne, no, no, no. But it is the dream of what we were; it is the future we were foretelling. . . . All scientific conquest is human triumph, for man. His freedom is exercised beyond the fields which were once his: as pipes relieve man from going to the well . . . Man starts each day beyond himself, beyond his past, his efforts and his discoveries. I say that for cybernetics, computers and the use of the atom and this still nameless thing of which, with no doubt in my mind, this spectacle I am writing of is the first dawning. A play like *Deafman Glance* is an extraordinary freedom machine. . . . Never as here, from a dark hole in the theatre, have I ever experienced the feeling, in confronting the spectacle of Robert Wilson, that if ever the world changes . . . it's through freedom man will have changed. Freedom, radiant freedom of the soul and the body" (Aragon 1971).

Significantly, Virilio himself acknowledges that early cinema, especially what he calls slightly disparagingly the "special effects" and "trick photography" of Méliès, allowed cinema—as Méliès himself observed—"to make visible the supernatural, the imaginary, even the impossible" (1991, 15).

This is precisely what Wilson's works for stage and screen achieve, and it should not surprise us that Burroughs, perhaps America's other foremost explorer of new ways of interweaving media in order to evoke "the supernatural, the imaginary, even the impossible," unreservedly celebrates Wilson's "visionary grasp of the complex medium of opera," affirming that "The future of drama and opera rides with Robert Wilson" (Burroughs 1991, 17). In Burroughs's terms, Wilson "is presenting beautiful life-saving dream images on stage and canvas," because "(he) sees what he wants, and is able to translate his inner vision into stage terms, and to circumvent the crippling conventions of dramatic presentation: what he calls 'ping pong dialogue' and soap opera plots" (1991, 17).

Burroughs's distinctions are crucial. For as he suggests, the positive potential of what we might call *poetically correct* multimedia creativity both circumvents available conventions for presenting available perceptions (the domain, in other words, of cripplingly familiar *studium*), and invents unfamiliar, emergent conventions for translating "inner vision." Like any other truly inventive artist—premodern, modern, or postmodern—Wilson looks *beyond* and looks *across* the seemingly fixed parameters of available media, and in the process both invokes—and reinvokes—the visionary potential of his "complex medium," rather than reiterating the banalities of soap opera plots and of what one might think of as generic, highly simplistic, "soap opera theory," annunciating the post-auratic quality of technocreativity.

While it is undeniable that many contemporary media artists ape the ad-logic and the ad-frequencies of high-speed, low-IQ telepublicity confirming Virilio's and Baudrillard's wildest fantasies regarding the omnipresent impact of *self-neutralizing* discursive acceleration, it is equally evident that many of the most interesting—and most *visionary*—contemporary media artists are energetically exploring far more significant modes of *self-empowering* discursive deceleration.

Discussing Burroughs's textual experiments, Wilson comments that Burroughs commands respect because "he's not afraid to destroy the codes in order to make a new language," adding "The language becomes more plastic, more three-dimensional, like molecules that can bounce, combine and are reformed. That interests me a lot. Because essentially that's what all artists do. One invents a language and then once this language becomes discernible, we destroy it and start again. I think that's what Mozart did when he was composing—you know—the theme and the variation. I think that's what we do essentially" (Wilson 1991).

For Wilson, there is nothing especially shocking or new about the alleged narrative discontinuities or ambiguities of postmodern composition. Rather, such imprecisions seem inseparable from all great art's *punctum,* be this the work of Mozart and Shakespeare, or of Wilson and Burroughs. Rejecting the commercial media-logic that he associates with television's simplistic "one-liners," Wilson explains:

"I don't want to draw any conclusions, and I'd rather process it in time, as something we think about, that's a continuum. When the curtain goes down, you don't stop thinking about it. You go home and still think about it. It's part of an ongoing thing, it's a continuum, it's something that never, never finishes. It's something that continues to intrigue or fascinate. Why do we go back to *King Lear?* Because we can think about it in multiple ways. It has no one way of thinking about it. It cannot be interpreted. It cannot be fully comprehended. So it's foolish for us to think that we can understand what it is that we're saying or doing. Because it's far too complex. We can reflect on it and think about it, have understandings. But to assume we can understand what it is we're doing is a lie." (1991)

Wilson's enthusiasm for decelerated visions, processed "in time" and existing as intriguing ongoing kinds of iconic continuum, is obviously a consequence of his own theatrical practice. As he observes, "I can have someone cross the stage in an hour and a half and it can hold the audience." Not all media artists necessarily share Wilson's fascination for decelerated poetry-in-motion. But it seems likely that almost all would agree with Wilson that the new postmodern technologies are most valuable insofar as "*they help us to destroy our codes, to find new languages, and to rediscover the classics.*" (1991)

While the high-tech *tedium* of high-tech *studium* undoubtedly neutralizes our sensibilities, it is surely arguable that the kind of multidimensional poetic *continuum* that Wilson associates with the *punctum* of new high-tech languages revitalizes our consciousness in much the same way that great art has always revitalized its audiences, and in this respect allows us to rediscover the register of "the classics," albeit from a distinctively contemporary point of view.

Discussing Bill Viola's video installation *Nantes Triptych*—a work recently purchased by London's Tate Gallery—Richard Dorment suggests that it typifies all the qualities that I have tried to define in the preceding paragraphs in terms of Wilson's lucid comments upon the overlaps between the new and the old media.

Emphasizing the way in which this "modern masterpiece" both invites and sustains "repeated viewing," Dorment's review observes:

"For all its stark simplicity is not the *Nantes Triptych* merely a repackaging of one of the oldest subjects in art, the cycle of life, for the age of film and video? On one level, the answer has to be yes, but it is also much more. The longer one stays in the room, the more the work begins to exert its hypnotic hold. The slow regular rhythm of the action, the enveloping scale, and the monotonous soundtrack all militate against our trying to understand it through reason alone. After a few minutes we allow our senses to take over, letting go of our conscious thought processes. By the end of the video, our ego or identity has been absorbed into something larger than ourselves: the *Nantes Triptych* represents a journey into new realms of consciousness." (Dorment 1994, 16).

Yet as Dorment adds, such "new" realms of consciousness are themselves the self-same concerns of "St John of the Cross and St Teresa of Avila, both of whom used prayer to experience an exalted sense of mystical union with the Creator." For Dorment, then, Viola's work is most distinctive in terms of the ways in which its tri-part subjects—"birth . . . shown in real time," "death in slow motion," and the unsettling image of the artist floating under water—suggest precisely the kind of "infra-ordinary reality" that Virilio associates with mystic revelation and at times seems to consider extinct within an age of "electronic automation reducing our will to zero" and imposing the supposed "disappearance of consciousness" (1991, 104).

It is a somewhat poignant sign of the times that Dorment feels compelled to defend his account of Viola's installation by anticipating the charge that he has perhaps made it sound "like a trip for superannuated hippies." It may be the case that Viola's sensibility emerges from the sixties ("that much maligned and misunderstood decade") and "is continuing to explore religious and philosophical ideas which have long fallen out of fashion" (1994, 16). But one might equally ask *why* we should restrict our expectations of technocreativity to those post-auratic, post-aesthetic, post-religious, and post-philosophical prejudices presently in fashion in the nineties. Indeed, as Félix Guattari suggested, the intellectual fashions of the nineties may well be still more savagely maligned—and still more justifiably maligned—than those of the sixties, when considered in terms of the "black stain" of their facile "ethical and aesthetic abdication" (Guattari 1996, 116). Happily such "abdication" has become increasingly discredited.

Just as Baudrillard's recent comments upon photography's capacity to restore the object to "the immobility and the silence of the image" (1997a, 31) reassuringly challenge his more extreme polemic, and refreshingly reemphasize photography's capacity to evoke unexpectedly incisive realms of *punctum* beyond the decodable dreariness of *studium,* Virilio freely admits that over and above the predictable domain of "the publicity mentality," he is "interested by two kinds of art at present: dance and video-installation." More specifically, Virilio observes, "I'm interested in video-installation—not in video, but in video-installation—because it poses the question of the relationships between images and space. I tell my architectural students that they need to pay attention to developments in installation art, because the problems confronting contemporary architecture are precisely those of video-installation" (1996, 120).

Still more tellingly, perhaps, when asked whether he agreed that certain video-installations now address the same kinds of questions regarding time and space as earlier writers and artists such as Proust and Turner, and whether he agreed that the new media may well be entirely commensurate with such substantial thematics, Virilio replied "Yes, I think so. There's a quality of truth in the work of the best of these artists that clearly corresponds to that of the great writers, the great painters—and the great architects" (120).

Viola's video-art, like Wilson's work for stage, video and multimedia performance, and like Burroughs's work for page, tape, film, and verbal-visual montage, distinctively exemplifies the ways in which exceptions to postmodern "soap" culture identify and intensify different kinds of "infra-ordinary" experience, and testify to the extent to which the work of art in the age of high-tech mechanical production and mechanical reproduction remains as forcefully an *art of appearance* and an *art of truth* as the art of any other previous era.

To attempt to analyze postmodern culture on the basis of the war machine or the soap machine—as Virilio's and Baudrillard's more seductive writings often do—is to overestimate the significance of superficial half-truths, and to underestimate what Virilio terms "the heights" of a "situation" requiring a far more rigorous "*grande curiosité*" (123). As Robert Wilson suggests, "It's the uncovering of the knowledge that is the learning process" (1991). It is surely time that contemporary media theory became more knowledgeable about those frequently marginalized—but absolutely "central"—contemporary artists curiously mapping and mastering the margins of the technocultural future.

baudrillard, giorno, viola and the technologies of radical illusion

9

Media art, in its possession of new technologies of time and image, maintains a special possibility of speaking directly in the language of our time, but in its capacity of art, it has an even greater potential to address the deeper questions and mysteries of the human condition. This is the challenge to the media arts at the turning point of the century and the passage into the millenium that lies just before us.

—Bill Viola
"Between How and Why"

Contesting the optimism of techno-artists such as Bill Viola,[1] Jean Baudrillard's *The Perfect Crime* is essentially a passionate defense of radical thought and, by extension, of the kind of radical writing that effects "the resolution of the infelicity of meaning by the felicity of language."[2]

It is a book written by a performative writer, alarmed, like the American video artist Bill Viola, by the non-poetic register of rational thinking, but also fearful—unlike Viola—of the apparently post-poetic register of those information technologies that seemingly "wipe out all the supernatural reflexes of thought extirpating all the magic from thought" (18). Put another way, *The Perfect Crime* articulates the anxieties of a *verbal magician*, intolerant toward the past and uncertain before the technological future.

In many respects, this book might be thought of as a kind of "Custer's last stand" by one of the most lucid defenders of the magical illogic of the text. A timely celebration of "poetic" analysis, *The Perfect Crime* typifies text-based theory's continued tendency to reject contemporary media culture in terms of the lowest common denominators of its most prosaic depths, and to neglect those emergent poetic heights presently scaled with ever-increasing subtlety by such *multimedia magicians* as Bill Viola.

Convinced that "Analysis is, by definition, unhappy," whereas "language, for its part, is happy, even when referring to a world without illusion and without hope," Baudrillard speculates: "That might even be the definition of a radical thinking: a happy form and an intelligence without hope. . . . What counts is the poetic singularity of the analysis . . . not the wretched critical objectivity of ideas . . . better a despairing analysis in felicitous language than an optimistic analysis in an infelicitous language that is maddeningly tedious and demoralizingly platitudinous, as is most often the case . . . among those who speak only of the transcending and transforming of the world when they are incapable of transfiguring their own language" (103–4). But how does the writer transfigure their own language? And how does Baudrillard's concept of "transfigured" language relate to the practices of the multimedia avant-garde?

As Bill Viola suggests, the most "radical" recent transfigurations of language (and of the image) combine the electroacoustic poetics and performative sensibility of the sixties, seventies, and eighties, with new modes of "micro-acting" peculiar to the imaging technologies of the late nineties;[3] manifesting the Futurist sensibility that Boccioni evokes as the "completely renovated sensitiveness" of the mind "*multiplied by the machine.*"[4]

Like the English Vorticist Wyndham Lewis, Baudrillard might well have informed F. T. Marinetti, "I am not a Futurist."[5] For Baudrillard, language is (and perhaps, can only be) "multiplied" by textual alchemy, as opposed to mechanical energies. "By its very form," transfigured language "appeals to the spiritual and material imagination of sounds and rhythm, to the dispersal of meaning in the event of language," propelled by what he calls a "passion for artifice, for illusion," for "undoing . . . meaning," and for "letting the imposture of the world show through" (104).

Such writing, Baudrillard seems to suggest, transmutes what he takes to be the inadequate illusions of reason into the felicitous illusions of the *supernatural* or the *magic*. But how exactly is this done? Some thirty years ago, William S. Burroughs's *Nova Express* evoked this kind of cabalistic alchemy (necessitating the disruption and word, photo, and "tourists") with the haunting imperative:

> Partisans of all nations, open fire—tilt—blast—pound—stab—strafe—kill. . . .
> This is war to extermination—Shift linguals—Cut word lines—Vibrate
> tourists—Free doorways—Photo falling—Word falling—Break through in
> grey room—Calling Partisans of all nations—Towers, open fire—"[6]

For his part, Baudrillard appeals to his peers with the encouraging words: "Thinkers, one more effort!" (97), recommending the following predominantly *textual* strategies: "Cipher, do not decipher. Work over the illusion. Create illusion to create an event. Make enigmatic what is clear, render unintelligible what is only too intelligible, make the event itself unreadable. Accentuate the false transparency of the world to spread a terroristic confusion about it, or the germs or viruses of a radical illusion—in other words, a radical disillusioning of the real. Viral, pernicious thought, corrosive of meaning, generative of an erotic perception of reality's turmoil" (104).

What exactly does Baudrillard understand by the *event* of language? Perhaps a kind of verbal "magic," or indeed a kind of photographic "magic," but certainly not high-tech experimentation. For Baudrillard, the event is distinguished above all by its "suddenness," and by its "non-anteriority" as an "emergence from the void" (58).

Breaking "with all previous causality," but at the same time remaining within the domain of more or less familiar verbal/visual intertextuality,

"The event of language is what makes it re-emerge miraculously every day, as a finished form, outside of all previous significations. Photography, too, is the art of dissociating the object from any previous existence and capturing its probability of disappearing in the moment that follows. In the end, we prefer the *ab nihilio*, prefer what derives its magic from the arbitrary, from the absence of causes and history. Nothing gives us greater pleasure than what emerges or disappears at a stroke, than emptiness succeeding plenitude. Illusion is made up of this magic portion, this accursed share which creates a kind of absolute surplus-value by subtraction of causes or by dissolution of effects and causes" (58).

As a process born of "the poetic imagination" the *event* of radical thought, radical language or radical photography is distinct, firstly, from "analytic thought"—which for Baudrillard always "has an origin and a history," and secondly, from the "classical and rational" orders of thought that he associates with the Enlightenment's project of modernity, with its hypotheses of "an evolution and a progress of living forms" (57). In this respect, it is "unintelligible" because it is "without historical continuity"; and as such, a source of protection from the tripartite perils of being, of mortality, and of determinacy.

"Born at a stroke," Baudrillard tells us, "it is not susceptible of having an end set to it—we are protected from its end by this non-meaning which takes the force of poetic illusion. Illusion, being pre-eminently the art of appearing, of emerging from nothing, protects us from being. And being also pre-eminently the art of disappearing, it protects us from death. The world is protected from its end by its diabolic indeterminacy. By contrast, all that is determinate is condemned to be exterminated" (57). Ironically, Baudrillard's concept of a poetic event *without origins*, history, determinacy, or mortality reiterates the ideals of innumerable culturally modernist and postmodernist visionaries, to speak only of its most recent precursors.

One thinks for example, of Walter Pater's advocacy of a pre-Baudrillardian "passion for artifice" in *Studies of the Renaissance* (1873). Here Pater insists that the artist and writer should "burn always with this hard gem-like flame" rather than "form habits . . . relative to a stereotyped world." Explaining that only "High passions give one this quickened sense of life, ecstasy," Pater continues: "Only, be sure it is passion, that it does yield you this fruit of a quickened, multiplied consciousness. Of this wisdom, the poetic passion, the desire of beauty, the love of art for art's sake has most; for art comes to you professing frankly to give nothing but the highest quality to your moments as they pass, and simply for those moments' sake."[7]

Alternatively, one thinks of Burroughs's definition of immortality as a condition informed by "increased flexibility, capacity for change," and by the potential mutation that he associates with "training for space conditions" within a domain in which "you must leave the old verbal garbage behind." For

Burroughs, "Artists and creative thinkers ... are providing us with the only maps for space travel. *We are not setting out to explore static pre-existing data.* We are setting out to *create* new worlds, new beings, new modes of consciousness."[8]

If Baudrillard's final comments to the first section of *The Perfect Crime* suggest that he shares Burroughs's commitment to innovative art insofar as he claims that "Thought has to be exceptional, anticipatory and at the margin" (101), Baudrillard's general critique of "static pre-existing data" and the "stereotyped world" culminates in double derision; first, for the "absurdity" of those "progressive ideologies" that deny that "man is an ambiguous, untamable animal" and "attempt to extirpate evil from him in order to turn him into a rational being" (147), and second, for those progressive artists (like Marinetti, perhaps?) who aspired or aspire to create new worlds, beings or modes of consciousness.

Confirming an earlier confession that he's "too old to change,"[9] and contending that artistic progress cannot really occur—since "We cannot project more order or disorder into the world than there is" and that "We cannot transform it more than it transforms itself"—Baudrillard opens fire upon both philosophic and poetic idealism: "All the philosophies of change, the revolutionary, nihilistic, futuristic utopias, all this poetics of subversion and transgression so characteristic of modernity, will appear naive when compared with the instability and natural reversibility of the world. Not only transgression, but even destruction is beyond our reach"(10).

It is perhaps for this reason that Baudrillard celebrates the work of Andy Warhol as an exemplary "challenge to the very notion of art and aesthetics" (79), or as what one might think of as the work of an artist all dressed up to kill every trace of ideological and aesthetic ambition, but with nowhere to go, and apparently evincing "the minimum pretension to being, the minimum strategy of means and ends" (77).

In Baudrillard's judgement, "Warhol starts out from any old image, eliminates its imaginary dimension and makes it a pure visual product ... Warhol's images ... are products of the elevation of the image to pure figuration, without the least transfiguration. Not transcendence any longer, but the ... sign which, losing all natural signification, shines forth in the void with the full gleam of its artificial light" (76). Bearing in mind that Baudrillard celebrates "an irony which plays not on negation but on empty positivity" and reveres "the splendour of the void" (70), arguing that "Irony is the only spiritual form in the modern world" (73), it is not surprising that he defines Warhol"s "ecstatic, insignificant iconry"

(76) in terms of a distinctively non-sacral aura—"that fetishistic aura which attaches to the singularity of the void" (79). For Baudrillard, Warhol's work radiates a peculiarly descendental *anti-mysticism.*

As the lines below indicate, Baudrillard prefaces his sense of the inevitable vacuity of contemporary, technologically mediated revelation with a brief definition of conventional mysticism. In other words, if progressive thinkers "explore the wretchedness of others to prove our existence "a contrario" (137), his argument tends to first outline and then outlaw the values of others, in order to prove our wretchedness "a contrario": "In the mystical vision, the illumination of the slightest detail comes from the divine intuition which lights it, the sense of transcendence which inhabits it. For us, by contrast, the stupefying exactness of the world comes from the sense of an essence fleeing it, a truth which no longer inhabits it. It comes from a minutely detailed perception of the simulacrum and, more precisely, of the media and industrial simulacrum. Such is Warhol . . . at once both our new mystic and the absolute anti-mystic, in the sense that every detail of the world, every image, remains initiatory, but initiatory into nothing at all" (76).

But why should media and industrial culture culminate in "nothing at all"? Why should techno-culture impose a "state of pure operational intelligence"? And why should those who "persuade us that technology will inevitably produce good" champion the "radical disillusioning of thought" (18)?

Remarking that "*the failure of an attempt at annihilation is, necessarily, vital and positive*" (151), Baudrillard predicts the way in which his scathing account of techno-culture—or his attempt, as it were, to "annihilate" the credibility of techno-culture—prompts reconsideration of such exceptions to his rules as the most recent experiments with video-theater and micro-acting by American artists John Giorno and Bill Viola.

Discussing his performance as Joe in the La Mama Experimental Theatre's January 1995 production of Beckett's *Eh Joe* in New York—in which his offstage gestures were projected live by video onto a wall-sized screen in the theatre, before an audience hearing the play's monologue by individual radio-headsets—New York poet John Giorno argues that in this kind of video-theater, as in any other high tech or low tech performance, "The one ingredient that makes a performance successful . . . is the amount of energy that a person gives from their heart to the audience. It can be done any way—Diana Ross does it in her way, or a poet or an actor can do it in their way. When you understand those things, it's understanding a concept experientially in a visceral way."[10]

Asked whether he felt this blown up video-image had more impact than Warhol's monumental portraits, Giorno (who slept in Warhol's film *Sleep*), suggested both were "equally strong." "Apparently they've rediscovered Andy Warhol's screen tests from the early 1950s, including mine, and someone who saw it in a show in San Francisco . . . was saying how powerful it was. Take anybody's head and show it from chin to forehead, and it's probably powerful!" In Giorno's terms, the "visceral" impact of his own technologically mediated "eyes . . . fifty feet apart . . . tears three feet wide, going down the screen!" generated all the intensity that Baudrillard associates with the creative "event," and when shown in Italy—"it's quite a sad play—a tragic play . . . and you know—Italians and tears!"—proved "a huge, huge success in Rome!"

As Giorno observes, the success of this performance was very much a synthesis or reorchestration of his earlier experience as a sound poet, translating or transforming certain aspects of the electroacoustic sensibility into a new dimension of what one might now call video-theater: "They were casting Beckett's *Eh Joe* and they hadn't found anybody they liked for Joe . . . and so they asked me. I was completely shocked, because I've spent twenty-five years performing my own work all the time! I've developed great performing skills, but I only perform my own work, so when somebody asked me to do . . . this Beckett thing I thought, 'What a wierd idea!' and 'What a great idea!' so I said, 'yes!' Looking back on it now, it seems a brilliant idea, because although a lot of poets develop skills in performance . . . people don't really consider poets as performers."

In turn, Los Angeles video artist Bill Viola similarly traces his present work to the electronic revolution brought about by the postmodern avant-garde of the sixties and early seventies: "The avant-garde film movement was at its peak in America . . . and modern art was being pushed to its limits by people like Cage . . . and I felt all of that served to give me a language with which to start writing short stories, you know. They were literally creating new letters, creating a new alphabet, creating new words, new semantics, a new grammar, and I felt my privileged position was to be able to take that grammar and start to talk with it."

For Viola, this new grammar allows the new kind of performance that he associates with the "micro-acting" of his 1995 Venice Biennale installation, *The Greeting*, in which he explores: "the dynamics of what happens when two people who know each other are happily engaged in conversation, and a third arrives, upsetting the intimacy of the first two and causing what I call the 'third woman'—who doesn't know this new person—to become very unsure of her role."

An "almost sculpturally" triangular structure, partially inspired by the configuration of figures in Jacopo da Pontomoro's painting *The Visitation*, and partially inspired by the "silent dialogue" witnessed "from a distance . . . sitting in my car," the ten-minute sequence of *The Greeting*'s decelerated "choreography of gesture and interaction" culminates in what Viola describes as a distinctive new form of micro-acting: "If they paused for longer than a second, that second would have been ten seconds in screen time. If they miscue by two seconds or if they don't do something right, in a very short amount of time it becomes . . . a big, big problem at the end . . . the whole theme unfolded in about forty-five seconds ."

Like Giorno, Viola asserts his "great faith in the inherent power of images," despite "the onslaught of media images that incessantly confront us and skew our perceptions."[11] Also, like Giorno's 1996 interview, Viola's recent comments emphasize the ways in which techno-performance may both incorporate and mutate the languages of preceding art forms, offering painterly, sculptural, choreographic, and dramatic qualities in a process that he likens to "transposing music, changing keys."

As Viola also remarks in his earlier essays, "One of the most interesting aspects of the recording media is how they tell us so much about the way we perceive the world," offering us "surrogate sensory perceptual systems," that reestablish our links with past cultures, past questions, and past insights: "The new technologies of image-making are by necessity bringing us back to fundamental questions, whether we want to face them or not. . . . Spend time with a video camera and you will confront some of the primary issues: What is this fleeting image called life? . . . And why are the essential elements of life change, movement, and transformation, but not stability, immobility, and constancy?"[12]

While Viola and Baudrillard ask near-identical questions, their answers could not be more different. For Baudrillard, the impact of the lowest common denominators of techno-culture demonstrates that "there is no point taking refuge in the defence of values, even critical ones" (65), and confirms that "we no longer know what to do with the real world" because "the real . . . has been 'laid off'" (42), just as "the machinery of thought . . . is laid off" (27) and "every natural movement of desire, is laid off" (126).

For Viola, utilization of techno-culture's "new words, new semantics . . . new grammar" reveals that "questions of form . . . and the how of image-making drop away", as "You realize that the real work for this time is not abstract, theoretical, and speculative—it is urgent, moral, and practical."[13]

On occasion, however, Baudrillard hesitatingly hints that his superficial cynicism conceals more profound afterthoughts. For example, prompted by Martin Heidegger's suggestion that " 'When we look into the ambiguous essence of technology, we behold . . . the stellar course of the mystery' " (73), Baudrillard seems to concede that techno-culture may sometimes evince unexpected spiritual and ironic depths.

Indeed, somewhat as the American artist, composer, and poet Dick Higgins argues that the most accomplished sound poets, such as Henri Chopin, present performances driven by the particular "vitality" that Higgins describes as "this golem—this demon that's generated by the piece,"[14] Baudrillard speculates that certain kinds of media-culture may well reveal what he calls "the evil demon of technology." "The Japanese sense the presence of a divinity in every industrial object. For us, that sacred presence has been reduced to a tiny ironic glimmer, a nuance of play and distantiation. Though this is, none the less, a spiritual form, behind which lurks the evil genius of technology which sees to itself that the mystery of the world is well-guarded. The Evil Spirit keeps watch beneath artefacts and, of all our artificial productions, one might say what Canetti says of animals: that behind each of them there is hidden someone thumbing his nose at us" (73).

One discovers the same general speculation in Baudrillard's concluding meditation upon Jorge Luis Borges's story of the "mirror people," which prompts his suggestion that behind every reflection or representation "a defeated enemy lies concealed"; a defeated "singularity" that "will one day rebel" (149).

But Baudrillard"s writings seem incapable of exemplifying this evil genius more specifically, and at this point his prophecies grind to a halt, as if trapped within a conceptual vice restraining wider vision. "What will come of this victory? No one knows" (149). "As for art. . . . There must surely be some meaning to it . . . but we can't see what it is" (129).

Can't see, or *won't* see? As his sympathetic references to other artists and writers such as Edward Hopper, Warhol, Borges, Brecht, Elias Canetti, Heidegger, Alfred Jarry, Vladimir Nabokov and so on indicate, Baudrillard, like Viola, situates himself among a distinguished lineage of fellow literary and painterly spirits (although he seems to have more difficulty affiliating himself with techno-culture, and unlike Virilio, for example, never explicitly argues that "technology is inseparable from art" [117]). At most, Baudrillard hints that the best of contemporary art, like any *exceptional* art, attains distinctive "poetic singularity" (103).

Working with the new electronic languages of the late postmodern avant-gardes, and recognizing their continuity both with the experiments of the early postmodern avant-gardes of the fifties and sixties, and with the "radical" vision of "almost every artist who has left his or her mark on the earth",[15] Viola offers timely alternatives to Baudrillard's cynical suggestion that "we have nothing to look forward to, save a native wit . . . surplanted by Artificial Intelligence" (44).

Viola persuasively concludes: "after all these years, video is finally getting 'intelligence,' the eye is being reattached to the brain. As with everything else . . . the limitations emerging lie more with the abilities and imaginations of the producers and users, rather than in the tools themselves . . . . As we take the first steps into data space, we discover that there have been many previous occupants. Artists have been there before. . . . Fascinating relationships between ancient and modern technologies become evident".[16]

It is precisely such "fascinating relationships" that critical voices unrestrained by critical vices should endeavor to address.

zurbrugg's complaint, or how an artist came to criticize a critic's criticism of the critics

10

warren burt

"Postmodernism is a punk band from Oklahoma."

—New York City cab driver

I

Let me declare my interests at the start. I am primarily a freelance composer and video/computer graphics artist who also writes criticism. Critical writing for me is a utilitarian activity. I write criticism for three reasons—exposition, propaganda, and because my friends ask me to. I don't have an academic position, and it doesn't help get me gigs. At best, writing helps me make things clear for myself; at worst, it's distraction from my other work. (As in, "I'm not doing this either for my pocketbook or for my health, you unnerstan' . . .") I say this at the start not to be ingenuous (or insulting), but simply to make clear that my writing is primarily from the viewpoint of a practitioner in the arts, but one who is quite aware of trends in current critical theory.

My expository articles come about because there is some aspect of artistic activity that I notice is being consistently misunderstood or ignored by my colleagues, and so I immodestly write to set the record straight. (And I am ego-maniacal enough to think that I can do this and have enough competence to do so.) An example of this was the series of articles on postmodernism I edited for The Australian Music Centre's journal, *Sounds Australian*, to which Nicholas Zurbrugg was one of the contributors.[1] I had noticed in earlier issues of the journal that a number of my colleagues were maintaining that postmodernism in contemporary Australian art music consisted simply of the use of either appropriation or a neoromantic idiom in an effort to either a) "serve the people," or b) get popular enough to make a living from it. While these may both be understandable motives, it was clear to me that this showed a deep misunderstanding of both the history and nature of postmodernism. Therefore, I wrote and edited a series of articles in which practitioners from different disciplines explained the history and uses of postmodernist thinking in their areas. These included articles from choreographer Nannette Hassall, semiotician/composer Benjamin Thorn, poet/composer Chris Mann, and musicologist/cultural theorist Linda Kouvaras.

As to the propagandistic writing, I attempt to share my enthusiasms with like-minded people, making them aware of things I've enjoyed that they might also enjoy. An example of this was my history of Australian experimental music published in the first issue of *Leonardo Music Journal*.[2] Having experienced much of this work first hand, and having noticed an almost complete lack of interest from other Australian music writers on this topic, I wrote the article to show the rich range of music that existed, and what some of its historical precedents were.

Other than that, my interests in critical writing are limited, and I find that although I possess quite catholic tastes in artistic activity, I have quite narrow ones when looking at criticism. The main theme of my critical articles is that our tastes continually need to be broadened, that we should, in the words of composer Kenneth Gaburo, "convert every either-or statement into a both-and statement."[3] Critics that do not advance this view get very short treatment from me. Further, while understanding the value of criticism as a valid form of literary expression, if, from reading a particular critic, I learn more about their tastes, desires, and prejudices than I do about the object of their criticism, I rapidly become disenchanted and uninterested.

In arts training, negative reinforcement used to be a standard procedure. The pupil would show the teacher their current production, and the teacher would criticize it severely, pointing out the student's inadequacies. This kind of "criticism" trained many students to understand very well their teacher's tastes, and, if they admired the teacher, how to imitate them. It seems to me that the majority of criticism I encounter is still written in that negative mode, which for me mainly illustrates the tastes, personality, and desires of the critic. More recently, several teachers have been using other methods, involving both positive feedback and a radical reorientation of the critical process. Two of these are the Melbourne-based improvisation workshops of choreographer Al Wunder, and the composition seminar given from 1981–92 at the University of Iowa by the late Kenneth Gaburo.

In Wunder's case, after a student's presentation, each member of the workshop must make a comment to the student, but the comments can only deal with that aspect of the performance the observer enjoyed. This has a twofold effect. First, the performers are reinforced to do those things that produce positive reactions in their fellow participants, and second, it focuses the attention of the observers: sometimes they have to work really hard to find something they like. The results of these workshops are impressive. Many of the most active and successful of contemporary Australian dance/theatre improvising performers have passed through Wunder's workshops, and they continue to produce interesting and challenging performers.

In Gaburo's case, the restriction on discussion was even more stringent. The two statements not allowed in discussion were "I liked it because . . ." and "I didn't like it because . . ." Getting rid of personal opinions and dealing with the matter at hand was often difficult for students, but once they adjusted to this, they seemed to thrive, and learn quite rapidly. One of the questions Garburo continually asked students in the seminar was, "Are you criticizing the work you heard, or the work you *wanted* to hear?" Again, the results of this reorientation of critical discourse were impressive. Every time I would visit the U.S. and pass through Gaburo's seminar, I heard and saw some extremely interesting and challenging multimedia works.

Now if advanced teachers of creative activity can use these methods—which involve a rethinking of the purpose and methods of criticism—successfully, is it too much to ask of critics that they adopt these methods as well? Or, to state it more personally, having seen these re-evaluative critical methods work so well in arts training, it becomes boring to then have to put up with old style negative feedback, complaining about methods of criticism in the world of print.

In the end, I find that I'm really not all that interested in what someone else likes or dislikes. It's all so bloody *contingent*, anyway. Someone wakes up in the morning, and their coffee tastes bad, and the result is that they write that someone else's work/idea/activity doesn't correspond to their idea of what it should. And though we're all supposed to be nice boys and girls and accept that our critics have the best and most responsible motives at heart, I've been around too many critics for too long to accept them and their works as anything but all too humanly fallible contingent self-expressions. Too often, when I read criticism, I'm simply reading about the critic's worldview, and not the work. Evaluations I can make for myself (and hopefully, in the interests of good taste, keep to myself). What would really interest me is a critic (or a cultural reporter) who told me what I didn't know, and who alerted me to possibilities and cultural resources I could investigate for myself.

I understand that evaluation is an important part of the life cycle of a creative activity/artifact, but the thought keeps occurring, again and again—how dreary must someone be who, on encountering something, first thinks, "How can I evaluate that?" All too often, I see evaluation being used as a substitute for experience, rather than being an adjunct to it. Further, in the face of much contemporary critical writing that seems concerned solely with its own values and issues, I begin to revert to Marxist methodology and ask, quite seriously, "Whose class interests does all this writing serve?" And while not quite willing to accept an anonymous colleague's irreverent answer of "It serves the interests of the academic class in their quest for [ever disappearing] tenure," I do begin to appreciate the cynicism behind such a reply.

Which brings us to the matter at hand, Nicholas Zurbrugg's specific frustration at a number of contemporary critics who consistently seem to "get it wrong," and his more general frustration at a literary critical environment that refuses to recognize even the validity of those multimedial art forms he has the greatest enthusiasm for. During our many collaborative projects, I have listened many times to Zurbrugg complaining about the attitudes of his literary colleagues, some of whom even reject the notion of creativity as a useful thing. His frustration at having to deal with views of this sort, when there was a whole world of exciting and new activity that he wanted to share his enthusiasm about, was palpable. Adding further to his frustration was the fact that those writers that most consistently seemed to "get it wrong," such as Jean Baudrillard, were held in high esteem, and were, in fact, often taken by the creative community as guides. To state it more crudely, Jean Baudrillard (for example) writes in a wrongheaded way about Andy Warhol, and for the next five years we have to put up with art school students making bad Warhol imitations. For those of us trying to show the joy available in new possibilities of art making, this sort of endless boogie of recycling ideas that were weak in the first place has a tendency to get a bit annoying. So if Baudrillard (for example) is going to (probably much against his own will!) have that kind of influence, can we at least get him to write intelligently about things, please? This seems to be the crux of Zurbrugg's argument, and in the essays contained in this volume, he has articulated a number of examples where critics have, for one reason or another, failed to deal intelligently, if at all, with the wide variety of expressions available in both new and old media. This collection, then, is to be applauded. Not only does it document a debate on the nature of criticism that seemed crucial to us in the eighties and nineties—importantly showing how weak and flawed the arguments of postmodern theory were, and often how inapplicable those arguments were to the cultural activities of the time—it also provides a guide to a lot of very exciting work from artists as diverse as Robert Wilson, Heiner Müller, Samuel Beckett, William S. Burroughs, Brion Gysin, Henri Chopin, John Cage, Bill Viola, and John Giorno, to name but a few.

This frustration Zurbrugg and I have shared is not limited to literary critics, for critics in many other media are similarly guilty of having such a limited scope. For example, in "Do We Really Need More Arts Coverage?", written for the Winter 1990 issue of *Sounds Australian*, I asked why Australian classical music critics did not cover experimental music events when those events took place outside the established venue of the concert hall.[4] Given that much of the most interesting contemporary music activity today is taking place in multimedial contexts—such as installations, radio, art galleries, sound-poetry performances, community music events, and the like—I wondered why music critics expended so little effort in seeking these out. One answer that I got informally from one critic/colleague was that my article was highly offensive to him, that his area of expertise was reviewing concert hall music, and that if I wanted to read writing about non-concert hall activities, I could bloody well do it myself.

If I then decide to temporarily agree with this colleague, I begin to wonder why Zurbrugg is complaining so. Rather than dealing with critics who fail to get the point of those things he is enthusiastic about, why doesn't he just tell us about those things he appreciated, or even enjoys? Or if he believes that criticism is important, why doesn't he just (in his academic role) train a new generation of critics? Leaving the old fogies to their world, why doesn't he just get along with his? For example, he convincingly shows how Fredric Jameson (by his own admission) uses a critical language that is unable to deal with contemporary video art. However, unless Fredric Jameson's approval is important for video art's survival and reception (and I, for one, can't see how it is), why even deal with Jameson's impotent and ignorant responses? Why not just tell us about some video art we might appreciate?

The issues of approval and acceptance, however, seem very important to Zurbrugg. For him, it seems that it's not enough that good work exists and is made available—it's also important that that work be accepted by his colleagues in the academic and critical communities, for it is these writers who often spread information about new works, and provide frameworks of introduction to, and understanding of, those works. This informational role is one that I agree is very important, and it is therefore important that critics do indeed "get it right." This is a matter of prime concern for Zurbrugg, who is concerned that the artistic history of the century be accurately documented, with proper attention being paid to those who originated ideas, or at least combined older ideas in striking and unexpected ways. Therefore, his concerns about the shortsightedness of editors such as D. J. Enright in his first essay, while they may distract us from his main subject matter, the rich and wonderful heritage of experimental and technologically informed twentieth-century poetics, are indeed warranted. (I just wish, at times, that the complaints about Enright didn't have to form the "frame" around the valuable historical material in this essay.)

But there is another, more generalized frustration being manifested in these essays. As a child of the radical artistic thinking of the sixties, it must be very depressing for Zurbrugg to be faced with the unadventurous and conservative criticism of the seventies through the nineties. It is a depression I share with him. As one who was raised on the optimistic and visionary writings of John Cage, R. Buckminster Fuller, Marshall McLuhan, and Edmund Carpenter, to name but a few, the rise of pessimistic and limited thinkers like Jean Baudrillard and Fredric Jameson is indeed cause for a regretful sigh or two. Fortunately, there are other streams of critical writing. For example, any of Guy Davenport's critical anthologies, or Suzi Gablik's *The Re-Enchantment of Art*, which was for me a fine antidote to Fredric Jameson's *Postmodernism, or the Cultural Logic of Late Capitalism*.[5] And the ecological, mystical and even

psychic concerns expressed by much of the art in Gablik's book forms a positive alternative to literary-based theories of culture. Among artists working in
this way might be mentioned the work of Australian sculptor, composer, and
architect Elwyn Dennis, who has produced a remarkable series of sound
works, such as *Wimmera* and *Dry Country*, which explore concepts of sound-
space and time that are quite different from those used in works that do not
have an environmental basis. Dennis insists that still, in this age of material-
ism and media saturation, it is the artist who is responsible for the consciousness of society. Responding to my question of whether his ecologically-based
ideas were not just another form of rugged individualism, Dennis replied that
they were not, but were designed to show the relative unimportance of the
individual in the larger-scale scheme of things. The plea for humility implicit in Dennis's aesthetic is one that perhaps the world of cultural theory might
well heed, and which Zurbrugg would agree with. A criticism that understood
its own (admittedly limited) power and put the forms of that power in perspective would indeed be welcome. The rise of critical conservatism in the past
three decades was not isolated, but was paralleled by a rise in conservatism in
other areas of society as well. The rise of right-wing "economic rationalist"
policies since the 1970s (which has in so many ways affected all of our lives) is
too well-documented to rate any more than a passing mention here, but it is
worth pointing out that there have also been parallel movements in the arts.
The multimedial forms that arose or re-emerged in the sixties, such as electronic music, postmodern dance, conceptual performance, computer art, and
experimental poetry, among others, may have been fun, exciting, and important, but it was not easy for people to figure out how to pay for them. On the
other hand, traditional forms (whatever their content) such as painting on
canvas, ballet, chamber and orchestral music, and linear-narrative novels
already had recognizable support mechanisms, and recognizable ways of being
dealt with, so it was no surprise that conservative critics rallied to the side of
these activities. The survival and thriving of these socially conservative forms
at the expense of the more adventurous forms strikes me as more than just a
desire to stabilize and recuperate after a period of "radical reform" (I can't
agree, for starters, that the "reforms" were all that "radical" anyway!), but
rather as being just one symptom of a colossal and depressing general failure
of societal nerve. It's not for nothing that my colleague, composer and computer scientist Arun Chandra, said to me that he felt postmodernism, with its

interests in recycling older materials, and its anti-originality stance, was "the philosophy of giving up."

(The stalling of the various space programs can be seen as another symptom of this failure of nerve. Whatever one thinks of the politics involved, it's simply true that the momentum of the earlier space programs have been dispersed by a variety of political, economic, and social factors. And in contrast to Baudrillard's complaints about how the postmodern era makes everything "weightless," this exact "weightlessness" was for me and my colleagues, a source of excitement. I remember Randy Cohen, a fellow composition student, shortly after we had first encountered the Moog synthesizer in 1968, saying that here, finally, was a tool where we could indeed escape musical gravity [tonality and the endless beat], and write music that was truly weightless. We then speculated that such music would only really come into its own when people could "dance," or maybe "float" to it, in space stations. Little did we realize how long it would be before this idea, the recreational use of space and weightlessness, would be possible.)

This is not to say that profound and important work has not occurred recently in the more traditional forms (some of my best friends write for orchestra . . .) but simply to point out how conservative economic, artistic, and critical trends have gone hand in hand, creating an environment in the eighties and nineties that was far less exciting than it might have been. Zurbrugg's pointing out how various prominent critics are seriously misinformed about the nature and context of the work they are dealing with, is one attempt to correct this.

However, I would go further than this. If I demand of my creative colleagues that they be open-minded and inclusive in their work, getting, whenever possible, beyond the immediate limits of their own personal tastes (and I do make this demand), then I see nothing wrong with demanding the same of critics. So when I see a semi-conservative literary critic like Roland Barthes paying attention to a semi-conservative writer such as Alain Robbe-Grillet, it is entirely understandable, but disappointing. My desire, however unrealistic, is to see critics being enthusiastic about work which is more than simply a reflection of their own aesthetic and financial interests.

I do sense that things have changed. Around 1993, I began joking that now that postmodernism was over, it was time to get on to more serious work. I even coined a wisecrack name for our new era—the "Paleo-Cyberian." Quickly, however, I realized that what I had coined in jest actually had a serious core, and was an idea worthy of serious consideration. I must admit, though, that I found most of the definitional debates around what constituted postmodernism in the various arts were largely a waste of time. The terms of the debates were never clearly defined, and it largely became a game of "I'm more postmodern than you, so there, nyah nyah!" For example, when I was an undergraduate, from 1967–1971, I thought what I was learning was "modern art." Years later, I realized that everything I was taught about art as process, interaction, and contextuality was actually "postmodern," or even "poststructuralist," and the seeds of the kind of cybernetic interactive work that I am now doing, my "Paleo-Cyberian" work, were already germinating then. Further, the definitional debates often proceeded without a knowledge of the history of the genres involved. As I mentioned earlier, in art music, "appropriation" was taken as a sign of the postmodern. This made no sense to me whatever, because I could see that appropriation was a common thread throughout twentieth-century art music. Early modern composers like Charles Ives, with his collage symphonies of the years 1910–1919 and earlier, later moderns like the young Paul Hindemith with his performing with phonograph records in the 1920s, and neo-classical composers such as Igor Stravinsky, with *Pulcinella* literally composed on top of a copy of an eighteenth-century Giovanni Battista Pergolesi manuscript, had all been involved in appropriation. Further, the 1930s compositional linguistics work of Harry Partch (surely some of the earliest examples of musical postmodernism), the 1950s tape collages of John Cage and Pierre Schaeffer, and the multimedia and sampler work of dozens of composers in the sixties through the nineties, such as Salvatore Martirano (with *L's. G. A.*), John Zorn, or the Tape-Beatles surely formed an unbroken line of working with appropiational ideas. So if appropriation had been used continuously in music since at least the early 1900s, (actually, it's been used continuously since at least A.D. 1000), how was the use of appropriation in music a distinguishing feature of musical postmodernism?

I was grateful then for Zurbrugg's definition of the general dividing line between the modern and postmodern eras as being around the beginning of the Second World War, as shown in his article "Some Further Thoughts on Post Modernism," in which he advances the idea that a succession of cultural ideas in the "modernist" era (1880 through the 1930s) were paralleled by a similar succession of ideas in the "post-modernist" era of the 1930s–1990. To quote Zurbrugg:

Rather than contrasting cultural eras in terms of the mono-dimensional—and usually utterly fictional—conflict between alleged pure order and disorder, it surely makes better sense to consider such eras in terms of re-explorations of *paradoxical sequences* of attitude. In other words, Modernism displays many ideas. Early pessimism and early optimism in the 1880s and 1890s. Riotous confident exploration in the 1900–1918 years. More considered, catastrophe theories and utopian theories in the final decade from 1920–1930. In diagrammatic summary—or in diagrammatic hypothesis:

1880 1900	early pessimism (Nordau)	early optimism (Mallarmé)
1900 1920	relatively accessible "mainstream" experiments (Joyce, Woolf, Eliot)	relatively inaccessible "avant-garde" experiments (Futurism, Dada)
1920 1930	popular late catastrophe theory (Spengler)	obscure late utopian avant-gardism (Marinetti)

... My point here is that Modernism evolves at several speeds and with conflicting values. Some Modernists had a clear sense of design and purpose, such as Piet Mondrian; some explored the laws of chance, such as Kurt Schwitters and Hans Arp. Some were popular and accessible to the intelligentsia, such as James Joyce; others remained mysterious and obscure, such as Hugo Ball and Marcel Duchamp. And so on.

The same categories and conflicts re-emerge very generally in the Post-Modern years in which initial *après-Modern* pessimism (such as Sartre and Beckett's writings of the thirties and forties), and initial *après Modern* optimism (such as John Cage's early work), leads to the relatively accessible Post-Modern experimentation of the fifties and sixties (such as the writings of Samuel Beckett, Günter Grass, Alain Robbe-Grillet, Marguerite Duras, Natalie Sarraute, Doris Lessing, and Jorge Luis Borges), and the still relatively inaccessible avant-gardes of the fifties and sixties (the cut-ups and permutations of William S. Burroughs and Brion Gysin; the concrete poetry movement; the sound poetry movement; multi-media performance). In a way, the "mainstream" and "avant-garde" work

of the fifties and sixties is still more confusing in terms of its dominant structuralist aesthetic; a formal impulse which now seems to have dissolved in the
eighties, but which misleadingly tempts cultural historians to deplore the *neutrality* of Post-Modern creativity. . . . At the same time apocalyptic theorists
such as Fredric Jameson, Jean Baudrillard, and their numerous disciples typify the popular catastrophe theories of the late Post-Modern era. . . .
Catastrophe theory is fun, but the gestures, experiments, and achievements of
the utopian late Post-Modern avant-garde merit serious attention too. As the
following diagram attempts to suggest, Post-Modern culture *as a whole* is as
varied—and in many ways, as *predictable*—as the phases of Modernism. What
we witness is not some crude oppositional relationship, but the contemporary
re-play, re-animation and re-consideration of problems *old* and *new*, with
solutions *old* and *new*.

1930 1950	early pessimism (Sartre, Beckett)	early optimism (Cage)
1950 1970	relatively accessible "mainstream" experiments (Beckett, Duras, Robbe-Grillet, Grass, Lessing)	relatively inaccessible "avant-garde" experiments (Lettrism, Concrete Poetry, Sound Poetry Cut-ups, Multi-media performance art, Minimalism, Cage's collaborations)
1970 1990	popular late obscure catastrophe theory (Baudrillard, Jameson, Virilio)	late utopian avant-gardism (humanistic/ historical/ autobiographical/ multi-medial)[6]

I noticed that Zurbrugg's large-scale time periods were also paralleled by
changes in political and technological conditions, that these eras were not just
cultural, but had political and technological features that also distinguished
them from each other.

First, there was the political situation. The period before World War II was
the one that Lenin characterized as "Imperialism—The Highest Stage of

Capitalism"; that is, the period when the colonialist empires were struggling for supremacy. After World War II, the world divided into two camps, the West and the East, led by two powers, the U.S. and the Soviet Union, who previously had been lesser players on the world scene. After the "fall of communism" (inaccurate, fatuous term though it is) of the early 1990s, the world is now in a much more fluid political position, with only one superpower, a whole host of reemergent nationalisms, and a corporate sector that seems determined to assert itself one way or another as the *true* controller of global destiny. Another way of looking at this political situation is from the perspective of the Third World. Before World War II, they were colonies; after the war, they were the Third World. Now, they are the "emerging nations." (In all three cases though, the fate of their people remains the same: they're being screwed.) Second was the technological situation as reflected in the means of communication. The period before World War II was the period where cinema, telephone, radio, and newspapers were the dominant media. After the war, we saw the rise of television as the primary communications media. Currently, we're seeing the rise of global computer linkups such as the Web, and the increased use of portable communications media such as cellular phones and modems. Where previously the computer had been an adjunct to peoples' lives and communications, now it was becoming central, and omnipresent.

According to one set of ideas, cultural periods move hand in hand with economic and social periods, sometimes reflecting them, sometimes moving in advance of them. It seemed only logical to me that if the "modernist" explorations of, say, Charles Ives, Kasimir Malevich, Isadora Duncan, Kurt Schwitters and Frank Lloyd Wright had paralleled the political and technological developments of the early twentieth century, and the postmodern era of TV and two superpowers had been paralleled by the work of, for example, Robert Ashley, Mario Merz, Trisha Brown, Jas Duke, and Philip Johnson, then the current changed political and technological climate would both produce, and be articulated (and even predicted) by a different set of artistic concerns and techniques. (Guy Debord's ideas of "the spectacle," which might be seen as the archetypical understanding of media life under postmodernism, seem to me to encompass the whole of the century, with different means of controlling and promulgating (and even subverting) "the spectacle" being offered by different media.) Seeing as how it's impossible to go "post-post-" anything without appearing silly, I decided to name my new era based on its primary technology, the computer. And seeing as how the level of technology, still, in 1997, is so damn primitive, I decided that this must be the old computer era. Having a Paleo-Cyberian era, an *old* computer age, implies a Neo-Cyberian era, a new computer age. (Presumably, this will be when all this damn cyberjunk begins to work.)

So given the idea that we're at the beginning of a new cultural period, perhaps I can sense the depression and frustration expressed in Zurbrugg's essays beginning to lift, as changed conditions promote a new flowering of radical ideas, or at least a new recognition of the consistently important work of radical thinkers throughout the century. This recognition will, in all likelihood, not come from the generation of critics Zurbrugg criticizes. He would like, I believe, to change the views of the theorists of the seventies and early eighties who have set the terms of a more conservative critical discourse in motion. On this, I remain more pessimistic than he does. I don't think that these critics will change. I think that a new kind of criticism will more likely come from a new generation of writers and academics, who, thoroughly sick of the pessimism and hopelessness of the current generation of critics, create a new criticism, one that is completely comfortable with the new technological tools and cultural expressions at hand, and which understands the value of curiousity over condemnation, of openmindedness over dismissiveness, of exploration over classification, and of the necessity of cultural work (even revolutionary political and cultural work) over ennui and defeatism.

For this generation, the work of such critics as Zurbrugg will provide a guide to the cultural riches of their predecessors—who actually never went away, even in the darkest days of their work being ignored and marginalized. In making ideas about their work (and in his curatorial roles, actually making the work itself) available, Zurbrugg is one of a number of cultural heroes, who make sure that work that they consider important is not ignored or dismissed. Zurbrugg's complaint, then, is twofold: first, that many of the current generation of critics are so blinded by their own pessimism and critical languages that they are incapable of evaluating the interesting work that goes on around them, and that, second, these critics, in refusing to broaden the canon (often promoting their own writing and discourse at the expense of this work, which they do not even recognize), produce erroneous critical perspectives and cultural models. Zurbrugg's vastly more important celebration, however, is that this important work exists, and is more than worthy of our attention. Hallelujah.

II

Praiseworthy as these essays are, I still have some problems with them. These problems may arise from my viewpoint as an observer who is also a participant in the arts described. My knowledge of the "nuts and bolts" of the art may color my perception of writing about it. In "Marinetti, Boccioni, and Electroacoustic Poetry: Futurism and After," for example, in the very first sentence—"One of the most difficult tasks for the comparatist is the definition and categorization of successive phases in the art of the contemporary avant-garde"—problems arise. Why, for example, is this definition and categorization necessary? Admittedly, if we are going to take the avant-garde work of this century seriously, we're going to need some kind of framework to approach it—some set of conceptual tools to deal with the wide variety of expression we will encounter. I just wonder, however, if "definition and categorization of successive phases" is the right framework for such an initial approach to take. A more valuable approach might be what Zurbrugg refers to as suspension of theoretical disbelief, in that almost any theory so far advanced will only be able to deal with a portion of the work produced by this century's avant-gardes. (Perhaps, like Russian art music and improvising composers, who developed the notion of "poly-stylism" in the 1980s, we need a notion of "poly-theorism" to come to terms with the rich artistic heritage of our recent past.)

The very next sentences of the article set the tenor for the rest of the essays, as Zurbrugg then identifies a critic who not only fails to comprehend the work he wishes to draw our attention to, but actually dismisses it out of hand, and, from a position of cultural power, actually prevents us from finding out about the work in question. In this case, the critic in question is D. J. Enright, who is in the "powerful" position of being the editor of *The Oxford Book of Contemporary Verse*.[7] This immediate dealing with adversaries of the work, rather than the work itself, quickly establishes that we are here dealing with a world, not of artistic productions, but of the reception of those productions, and questions of who controls access to those productions.

Taking a cynical insider's view for a moment, it may be that such concerns are misplaced. If I want to find out about contemporary experimental poetry, it would never occur to me to go to such a limited collection as *The Oxford Book of Contemporary Verse*. The very name Oxford would warn me away, reeking as it does of establishment validation. If I wanted to find out about more radical poetic activities, I'd go to my local experimental poet, or small press knowledgeable bookshop, and find out from them. Or I might even go to a larger library and find out if they have back-issue copies of *Stereo Headphones*, the journal Zurbrugg edited for many years. Zurbrugg's point is that the Oxford collection should be the place where one can discover interesting work. My view, based on years in the field, is that institutions like the Oxford collections are largely a lost cause, anyway, and the really interesting work, whether conservative or radical, is always going to take place in the margins. (I still feel this, even though I recently contributed an article on electronic music to *The Oxford Companion to Australian Music*!) The problem, of course, with such a cynical insider's view is that it is just that, a view from the inside, from one who already knows where to find interesting contemporary activity. For the vast majority of, say, literary undergraduates, I suspect that if they have any interest in the subject at all, for the most part they would be encouraged by their conservative and remarkably un-curious teachers (who, relying on the critics that Zurbrugg is taking to task, will also be unaware of the avant-garde work of this century) to look in just such establishment collections as those of Oxford.

My own quests for experimental musical activity while I was still in high school in the mid-1960s bear witness to this. Early on, I knew I was interested in something that was different. In hindsight, I call this my "search for the weird," though I doubt that I thought of it that way then. Rock and roll seemed too staid and rhythmically uninteresting, Broadway too trite, and "classical" music seemed only to be written by dead people. As a kid who had been to the New York City Ballet every summer season, and had seen most of the Stravinsky-Balanchine collaborations by the time I was fifteen, I knew that this was not the case. The Stravinsky works (especially *Agon* and the *Huxley Variations*) seemed marvelous, and were pointers to a world that only existed as glimpses in my upstate New York high school world. But a search of the local public library only turned up two records of interest—Stravinsky's *Persephone* (surely one of his more minor works), and Messiaen's *Trois Petite Liturgies* (whose onde martinot solos I found absolutely compelling). It was only when I reached university a few years later, and was, in that university, lucky enough to find nonconservative people who made the stuff, that I realized that simultaneous with my high school searching, and only 150 miles south, in New York, the musics I had been searching for existed: among these would be included both the late, ecstatic, improvisatory work of John Coltrane, and the beautifully austere middle-period indeterminate electronic, instrumental, and dance works of John Cage and David Tudor.

I was lucky. I found what I was looking for after only a few years of searching. For those who weren't so lucky, their sources of information might indeed be things like the Oxford collections, and they would remain sadly unknowing of important work that might excite them. So Zurbrugg's concern over Enright's conservatism is, from a pedagogical point of view, entirely justified. And his articulating of the "key problems attending anyone attempting to analyse avant-garde literature: the frequent inacessibility of exemplary works and the absence of any conceptual framework for their analysis" strikes me as almost, but not quite, spot on. Not quite because I would point out that if there were such a "conceptual framework" already existing, the work in question might fail to be "avant-garde" (or whatever term we're going to feel comfortable with to describe cutting-edge work). Again, only a few paragraphs later, Zurbrugg writes "What is the best way of defining such a bewildering movement, still 'in the making'?" His solution is to trace the history of the genre carefully. This tracing might hopefully eventually lead the reader even beyond the limits of the history as given in the essay, allowing them to assemble their own history from a plethora of carefully documented examples.

It is important to not present such a collection of examples as a disconnected field. Connections do exist, and a well presented history can show this. Zurbrugg's describing Henri Chopin's work as a postmodern avant-garde realization of a modernist avant-garde aspiration is a case in point. To show that radical works do not exist in a void, but are part and parcel of an ongoing web of knowledge investigation and creation is important work.

We should be careful not to take this sort of thing too far. For example, the connections between the American composer, sound-sculptor, music-theorist, and music-theater director Harry Partch and the Irish poet W. B. Yeats are clear. We have letters and writings from both of them about their meetings in the 1930s, and the sensitive observer can clearly hear a Yeatsian strain in Partch's vocal works, at least through the *11 Intrusions* of 1950. However, to then observe that Yeats was a member of the occult group The Golden Dawn, and to try to extrapolate some sort of connection between that and the seemingly mystical, but actually practical, music-making numerology of Partch's just intonation tuning theories is probably taking things a bit far.

It is also true that much of the multimedial work Zurbrugg discusses is confusing. For people accustomed to putting art into neat boxes labeled "poetry," "music," "drama," the work of someone like Henri Chopin, which participates in all of the above, can indeed be confusing. If you have developed one way of responding to poetry, and another way of responding to music, work that lives in an uneasy middle ground between the two can seem either alienating or deliciously disorienting, depending on one's attitude toward encountering the unexpected.

This disorientation can also be a product of venue, that is, where one encounters the work. For example, contemporary sound-poetry might be encountered in a poetry reading, or it might be encountered in the "weirdos night" at the local pub that puts on experimental events, at a computer music event in an art gallery or a university, or in a performance art event.

In each of these cases, the venue the work appears in will probably focus our attention on it in different ways. Faced with a confusion like this artists themselves have adopted a number of strategies. A practical solution was Australian linguistic performance artist and event-organizer Chris Mann's decision to consider himself a "composer," even though he mostly dealt with words and speech because a) the rates of pay in music were slightly better, and b) he found that there was at least a conceptual framework for people to deal with what he did as "composition," whereas this framework was missing in the more formal world of "poetry." A more philosophical solution was philosopher-composer Herbert Brun's all-embracing definition of a "composer" as someone who "brings about that which without him cannot happen," which allows for practically any activity to be considered under the rubric of "composition."[8] The aim of these strategies is to find a place for the work to exist, so that people can discover and enjoy it. A delightful fringe benefit of these strategies is that they tend to expand one's outlook and output, allowing an inclusively wide variety of activities in one's work.

Zurbrugg's essay on electroacoustic poetry strikes me as one of his most valuable pieces. And yet, I find several points where, if I do not totally disagree with him, I feel there are alternative views to the ones he expresses. For example, he is surely correct when he states that Boccioni's and Marinetti's views partially, but not wholly, help one understand the work of such technological sound poets as Bernard Heidsieck and Charles Amirkhanian. And his quoting of Lázló Moholy-Nagy, who states that the guidance for the student of modernist literature can be acquired by being "acquainted . . . with . . . the tendencies of contemporary composers" is also accurate. However, guidance could also be found by using any of a number of perceptual strategies, which, even without acquaintance with other works, could prove helpful.

For example, Denis Smalley, in "The Listening Imagination: Listening in the Electroacoustic Era" deals with two main modes of listening: autocentric and allocentric.[9] Autocentric listening focuses on emotional responses to sound, including the feelings of pleasure and displeasure. Allocentric listening is more focused on the structures and features of the sound itself; enjoyment is gained through concentration on these structures and features. Although both modes of perception are often used by listeners, the emphasis on allocentric modes of listening can often be helpful, allowing perceptions and insights that might not occur if a strictly historically based mode of perception were being used.

Similarly, when Zurbrugg states that "when considered in terms of Marinetti's associations, Boccioni's distinctions and Chion's categories," the surprises of contemporary electroacoustic poetry will make sense, he is correct. However, even without those categories, the works could still make sense if one used a "beginner's mind" approach—that point of emptiness and openness discussed in both Zen and Christian mysticism—experiencing a work as if it were the first of its kind, looking and listening clearly to what the work was, rather than what one wanted it to be. This is an important point, one that composers such as Cage and Gaburo were insistent on: that even the most radical work could "make sense" if it was approached in this way. Classificatory schemes such as the ones given in this essay are extremely valuable, but they are not the only way one can meaningfully encounter such work. There are other philosophies of reception/perception that offer insights equal to the Western intellectual/critical one.

Another valuable thing that I think this essay offers is its pointing out of cultural behavior patterns. One of these is shown in the Boccioni quotation that states that the Futurists are not tainted with the "archaism" that led the French artists of the period to study, for example, African sculpture. This pointed out to me how many artists go through a first rejective phase followed by a later embracing, integrative phase. That these patterns keep being repeated strikes me as both bizarre and tedious. When will people simply learn to accept and integrate right from the start? While admitting that trial and error does have its value, I keep wondering why the errors of the past (such as fascism) keep being brought back for new trials. Why a continual repetition, generation after generation, of the same silly patterns? Isn't there another way to learn?

Another such pattern is pointed out in Michel Chion's identifying of a phase in the history of electroacoustic music where artists attempted to gain a "certificate of cultural nobility" for their efforts by imitating established forms. This concern with validation is, as has already been noted, a leitmotiv in Zurbrugg's essays. Whether it is the artists themselves seeking validation by writing, say, electroacoustic symphonies, or whether it is Zurbrugg's (and others') concern that the work is both not available to those who might be interested in it and not recognized by those whose works might have the potential of reaching those who might be interested, the concern is the same. Understandable as this is, I wonder if we might not also come to accept the view that, except financially, a concern with validation is a sign of intellectual weakness. (That is, after working this racket for twenty-seven years, I would be really happy if I could have an income greater than upper-level poverty/lower middle class (please note—I'm considered a success by my colleagues!), and it would be nice if I could get copies of the work to those who were interested in it, but as for being liked and/or feted and praised by the critical establishment and/or the academy, well, as Benjamin Boretz says, "that's only for simps anyway."[10] To have relied on critics for information in this period would have been dangerous. To have relied on them for reputation would have been suicidal.

Finally, it should be pointed out that this essay was published in 1982, and that things have moved on since then. For example, the French electroacoustic sound poet Henri Chopin could, in the 1960s, talk about the tape-recorder allowing the poet's voice "infinite possibilities of orchestration." True at the time, it was also amazing how quickly so many of us came to the limits of these "infinite possibilities" and then, like one of Zurbrugg's beloved Burroughsian junkie characters, needed more, more, and still more. Although the tape-recorder gave us many new possibilities, we quickly learned to hear very many of these as part of a larger category called "tape-manipulated sounds" and began to look for other vocal modifications that didn't sound like that. This "categorical perception," which seems to be yet another of those predictable human behavioral patterns, can frequently blind us to subtlety, and we find that we are continually having to retrain our perceptions in order to stay aware of those subtleties. And then, eventually, the analog tape-recorder became obsolete, and harder and harder to find. The techniques it did make available were, in some cases, replaced by the capabilities of newer computer-based systems, but in some cases, were lost. For example, with two analog tape-recorders placed several meters apart, extremely long delays of sound repetitions, of up to a minute's duration or more, could be easily accomplished. Today, with digital delays, these extremely

long delays are not available. Computer-based systems can sometimes imple-
ment these delays, but the level of expertise (and expense) required to accom-
plish them is far greater than that required to simply put two tape-recorders a
few meters apart and run the tape from one machine to the other. A simple
mechanical skill was replaced by a more complex software skill, and yet the
result is almost the same. Almost, but not quite—the decay of sound quality produced by multiple analog tape generations, which tended to "sweeten" the
sound, has been replaced by the harsher "granulation" of digital sound process-
ing. Each new generation of equipment has, it seems, its own artistically useful
inadequacies, which reveal the true nature of the equipment, but the general
trend of the engineering profession is, in the name of simplification, to make
things more and more complex.

III

Zurbrugg's reformist impulses are shown most clearly in his valuable "The
Limits of Intertextuality," in which he clearly reveals the limitations of an excessively literary approach to contemporary cross-media work. One way he does
this is by constantly inserting quotes from William S. Burroughs, quotes which,
at first reading, seem jarringly inappropriate. On later readings, I began to
appreciate them for what they were, quotes from a literary wild man chosen to
show just how wide the social gap is between the freewheeling creativity of the
radical artist and the "po-faced" seriousness of the world of literary criticism.

In his cogent analysis of Barthes's work, showing how Barthes's ideas
evolved, and giving us an inkling as to where they came from, Zurbrugg criticizes
a number of contemporary critics who have taken Barthes's ideas far too literally and used them as the basis for constructing whole edifices of critical theory. Unfortunately, except for Jonathan Culler, none of these acolytes are
mentioned by name. Perhaps this was for libel reasons, or out of professional
courtesy, but I feel that it's a pity. I would have liked to have known who these
people were, so I wouldn't have to waste my time dealing with them. (What ever
happened to the notion of criticism as a public service?)

More seriously though, the most valuable parts of this essay for me were
where Zurbrugg showed how once Barthes began to deal with non-literary
areas, his ideas on authoriality had to be revised. After the non-body-orient-
ed world of words on paper (how many people have you seen jogging while

reading?), it is quite a shock for Barthes to attend a concert and realize that as well as the sound, it is the *body* of the performer that is conveying much of the meaning. And as Zurbrugg points out, it's only a short step from this realization to being plunged from the world of words on paper into the world of words as sound—into oral culture. (You've probably seen many more people jogging while listening to "talking books" on their "Walkmen.")

The reintroduction of the body into artforms which were tending to become over-cerebralized is one of the important trends in twentieth-century arts. Harry Partch's insistence on "corporeality" in his music theatre productions, postmodern dance's use of body therapies such as the Alexander Technique and Feldenkreis work as a stimulus for choreography, and a whole host of "body-art" performance artists bear witness to this. The continuing presence of the oral poet, whether in the person of the early-twentieth-century verbal experiments of a Raoul Hausmann or Kurt Schwitters, or in the mid-century ecstacies of more traditional, linear poets like Alan Ginsburg and Gary Snyder, or in the late-century work of performers such as Chris Mann and Amanda Stewart, has been how this reinsistence on the body has manifested itself in literature. This phenomenon has caused a lot of difficulty for literary critics who view words on paper as the most important aspect of literature. (But hey! They're just going to have to learn how to boogie, right?)

A most recent example of this orality is *24 Hours*, a massive book by Melbourne poet Pi O.[11] In this book, the speech of Australian migrants is transcribed faithfully. Accent is extremely critical here, as are fracturings of grammar and syntax. The book, even for someone as enthusiastic about Pi's work as I am, is hard reading. Imagine the difficulties a conservative literary critic would have with it! But it *is* rewarding: once the words are decoded, and the accent is revealed, the words leap off the page with a phsyicality few other poems have. And if you're lucky enough to hear Pi read the work himself, the results are miraculous and joyful. In fact, as marvelous as *24 Hours* is on the page, I feel that it is only in the live reading that it really comes to life. The book here is not the final object, it is more akin to a documentation of a living process.

And this reinsistence on orality is only one small part of the transdisciplinary developments that characterize all contemporary arts. When I first heard of "intertextual" criticism, I naively assumed that this was criticism's version of these transdisciplinary tendencies. And indeed, in the more open of its practitioners, it is. Just as artists were applying ideas from one form to another, so too should critics. A good example of this is Michel Chion's applying of concepts from cinema history to the development of French *musique concrète*.[12] (And it's worth pointing out that Chion is also a very fine composer who *does* know how to boogie.) For the truly "intertextual" critic, anything can, and should, be a text. And for work made in ways that cross traditional genre boundaries, it seems only logical that such boundary crossing would be the ideal method of writing about it. How disappointing, then, to find out that there are a whole legion of critics, some quite well known and powerful, who have chosen to retain narrow boundaries for both the work they choose to deal with, and the ways they choose to deal with that work. I am quite surprised, for example, that Zurbrugg's comparison of Burroughs's and Karlheinz Stockhausen's work would be considered radical. I would have thought that such comparisons would be a matter of course. And I'm equally surprised that literary critics would not have realized that new means of criticism would be required to evaluate texts generated in new ways.

For example, the text of my *Post-Colonialist Poem on the English Language*, a radio piece for two readers and *concrete* sounds, consists of ten pages of computer-generated permutations of the syllables in the phrase "Werribee Mitsubishi Minnesota Bonsai." To apply traditional methods of literary analysis to this admitted non-sense would be unproductive. But rather than dismiss this non-sensical text as "nonsense" (as Zurbrugg implies that many literary critics would), I would have thought that a truly "intertextual" critic would draw upon ideas from radio drama, electronic music, arithmetic, and linguistics (which are among the areas I drew ideas from in making the work) in order to deal with it.

I do wonder about Zurbrugg's assertion, though, that "the fact that such experiments have received negligible attention (or none at all) from most intertextual theorists typifies the way in which a preoccupation with 'prior discourse' has led contemporary intertextuality to neglect contemporaneous discourse." While this may be true, it occurs to me that *as a class*, those practicing and being trained to practice intertextual analysis might just come from classes, or social groups, where just such notions of "contemporaneous discourse" are frowned upon. That is, intertextual critics and transmedia artists might constitute two totally different groups, and the concerns of the one might not be the concerns of the other. (Conservative establishments breed their own successors far more often than they are swept away by generational changes.)

The most important issue, though, that is raised by this essay is the way that the new possibilities offered by new media and tools are unable to be dealt with by a literary theory which, while not denying the possibility of something "new" being created, does its best to suppress such a notion. Barthes's comment that such innovations may be "born technically, occasionally even aesthetically," but have "still to be born theoretically," points this out.[13] That this statement implies the heretical notion that theory follows practice seems to be not noticed by many writers of critical theory. This is a point that Zurbrugg returns to again and again in his essays. Caught in a web of referentiality and mutual influence, many cultural theorists often forget that the stuff they're dealing with has to come from somewhere. One of the many places the stuff comes from is artists, who somehow combine things in a way that hasn't existed before, which is what I, at least, understand as originality.

An example of a technological innovation that has made possible something new is in the field of computer music. Finally, after a century of development, we have the ability to precisely specify the harmonic makeup of each tone we use. It was long thought that certain scales were dissonant, or unpleasant, because of the nature of their intervals. A scale such as thirteen tone equal temperament (placing thirteen notes within the space of twelve on the piano) was thought to be irredeemably unpleasant. Now, however, with the ability to tune each partial of each tone, composer and theorist William Sethares has found that if the partials of a tone are themselves tuned to the pitches of the thirteen tone scale, harmonies made in that scale cease to be dissonant: they sound totally unfamiliar, but very pleasant.[14] Let me make this point emphatically. At no point in history, before the invention of electronic instruments, was it possible to make these tones. This is literally the first time (since, perhaps, Atlantis or some other mythological high-tech past) that these tones and harmonic combinations can be heard. This research has occurred since 1993, and the first articles about it are just now appearing. The world of psychoacoustics is just beginning to deal with it. It will be quite a while before the world of criticism also does so. Eventually, this knowledge will become an accepted part of the composer's repertoire. And the notion of *eventual* understanding implied by this is extremely important. Sometimes a newly made work just needs to sit for a while in order for you to see and hear what it is.

It is also clear that we are dealing here with several notions of "theory." In science, a theory is just one step below a law, and in order to be a theory, has to have some predictive value which can be proven. In music, theory usually describes the "nuts and bolts" of pre-existing compositions, as in "if you use these rules for combining notes, you'll be able to write a piece that sounds something like a choral written by Johann Sebastian Bach." More recently, a field has arisen called "speculative music theory," where tuning and structural concepts that have not yet been tried out are proposed with the aim of finding out what they sound like. And in the field of criticism, "theory" has yet another meaning, being, as far as I can see, speculations about possible structures and connections that might exist among and between works, groups of people, ideas, and so on. And in different fields, there will be different minglings of these kinds of theory. One group of contemporary choreographers in Melbourne, for example, deal extensively with French feminist theory while also pursuing the quite independent and different body-based ideas contained in Mabel Todd's *The Thinking Body*.[15] Both are necessary for the work they currently create.

However, it should also be made clear that each of the above concepts of theory still deals with the idea of rules, of establishing rules of physical behavior, or of trying to find the rules by which a certain work or phenomenon has come into existence. The articulating of these rules is of the greatest service to creative artists, for, once decoded, these rules can act as guides for what *not* to do. As Kenneth Gaburo wrote, "as a composer, the statement: 'a given system is the only tenable one,' constitutes the only challenge necessary to disprove that statement."[16] As a composer, I realize the challenges I am giving music and critical theorists. My recent series of microtonal electronic compositions (1991 to the present) for example, quite consciously uses a different tuning, and a different set of structures in each one.

Faced with this diversity, it is quite understandable if a critic who is concerned with larger scale sets of rules that might exist between works would be baffled by these. Only when the rampant pluralism implied by such a series of works is dealt with will a critic be able, I feel, to approach these works in a meaningful way. For contrary to many trends in contemporary critical thought, I am still primitive enough to believe that the function of an artist is not to follow rules, but to make (and break) them. Artists, no matter how conservative, are essentially anarchists. Critical theorists, by the very nature of the field they choose to deal in, aren't. Experimental artists, moreover, are, in Allan Vizents's words, "problem finders," or, in Chris Mann's, "problem seekers," or in Herbert Brun's formulation, "interested in the art we *don't* like, yet."[17] Thus there is an essential dissonance between the activities and natures of those who make things in a boundary-challenging way, and those who seek to classify them. Those who seek to indulge in both activies, such as Zurbrugg and myself, keenly feel the tensions of such a contradiction.

IV

The position of critical theory, criticism, and the like, in relation to the mass medium of television, is interesting. Canadian comic-book artist Dave Sim has recently identified television, correctly, I feel, as the *only* mass medium.[18] Although many critics have a great affinity for the mass media, and may think of their work as part of it, sales figures show that compared with the billions that television reaches, the few thousands who read any given critical work, and the few tens of thousands that deal with all criticism are very small indeed. In Sim's case, he points out that the twenty to thirty thousand copies he sells a month of his ground-breaking *Cerebus* in no way qualify his work to be considered part of a mass medium, or indeed, to be considered part of that nebulous entity sloppily called "popular culture." (In my case, with sales of my recent CD already in the high tens, this is even more the case)[19].

In "Postmodernity, *Métaphore Manquée,* and the Myth of the Trans-Avant-Garde," Zurbrugg quotes Jean Baudrillard's accurate rephrasing of views earlier expressed by Jerry Mander as to how the mass media neutralizes an image's power and reality until the image bears no relation to any reality whatsoever, and becomes its own pure simulacrum. That this home truth was pointed out by one of the chief cultural theorists of our era was useful. Why, then, did legions of artists and critical thinkers in the eighties and nineties do everything in their power to become part of this mass medium? I knew so many artists in the eighties and nineties who read their Baudrillard and then proceeded to attempt to become part of mainstream popular culture with their absolutely non-mainstream work. Almost to a man or woman, they failed, and were mystified. I, too, was mystified as to why they hadn't realized that the mass medium was a totally separate world with its own rules that would subvert your message more than you could subvert its.

And though I am enthusiastic about this part of Baudrillard's analysis of the mass medium, and also very much in love with his hymn to the Los Angeles freeway system in *Amérique,* I must confess that most of Baudrillard's views are completely alien to me. For example, being involved in music and video/computer-graphics technology as I am, the thirty years from 1967–1997 have been incredibly exciting. A constant stream of new ideas and possibilities has been made available. The pace of change has been breathtaking, and with each new development, ideas that I had years ago, or which my spiritual grandfathers such as Henry Cowell or Percy Grainger once had, now become realizable. When, in 1984, I read Henry Cowell's *New Musical Resources*, written in 1919, I realized that here was an agenda for computer music research for the next ten years.[20] This was, for me, a personal example of the point Zurbrugg makes about much postmodern creativity being realizations of earlier modern aspirations. Therefore, when I read Baudrillard's views about how postmodern technology has become a source of stasis and superficiality, or Achille Bonito Oliva's views on the "collapse" of the technological avant-garde, or Barthes's views on the last century largely being one of reiteration, or Fredric Jameson's associating of the postmodern temper with a schizophrenic experience of signifiers that fail to link up, I am simply bewildered. I mean, I can't even keep up with all the things that I want to do that I now *can* do, and these guys are complaining about *STASIS, COLLAPSE, and THINGS NOT MAKING SENSE*? Whatever *can* these European and American academic boys be talking about? Dunno, but maybe things look different from Paris than they do from Melbourne.

And the further I get into Baudrillard's writings, the less I find that I can even relate to. I mean, I'm a pretty optimistic kind of a guy, and so his nihilism and pessimism cut no ice with me. And when he makes his hyperbolic statements such as "Irony is the only spiritual form in the modern world," I would simply reply, "No, irony is not the only spiritual form in the modern world." (Depends on how you define "spiritual form" and "the modern world," doesn't it?) Or when he writes that "All philosophies of change . . . appear naive. . . . Not only transgression, but even destruction is beyond our reach," having been involved in work which *has* made changes, I can only disagree.[21] Even granting a large amount of literary license, such statements seem simply silly and gratuitous.

So much of *Amérique* seems alien to me. I find it saturated with a European romanticism that I just can't relate too. It makes me wonder, why do we allow certain people, certain ideas, to have power over us? The idea that Europe is an "older world," unable to participate in the excitement of the New World, for example. It manifests a certain sense of need for an other, that I've also seen in the attitudes of many cultivated Europeans who, with all the best intentions, inadvertently reduce the art of such sophisticated and globally aware intellects as Australian Aboriginal artists Leah King-Smith (who makes complex, layered computer graphics dealing with urban Aboriginal ancestry and their relation to their land) and Rover Thomas (who makes powerful, stark, almost [to Western eyes] "abstract" canvas paintings depicting Northern Territory landscapes and dreamings), among many others, to the expressions of "primitive, untainted truths." They might just as well be more honest about the implied, mythologizing racism in these attitudes, and call these major late-twentieth-century artists "noble savages." This clearly shows me how much this type of European needs a concept of wilderness and frontier, and Australia (or, in Baudrillard's case, America) is as convenient a dumping ground for these concepts as any. What relationship this has to the Australia I live in (where, the last time I saw Leah, she was upgrading her computer with the latest version of PhotoShop) is tangential and coincidental at best.

(A German friend visiting Melbourne recently said to me that he found the idea of a European-style city out of place in the Australian landscape. I replied that I found the idea of a European-style city equally out of place in the European landscape. Just ask an Etruscan or a Celt how they felt about being displaced.)

Baudrillard claims that as a European (and it's interesting how his choice of authorial voice makes it appear that he thinks he's speaking for *all* Europeans— who is this royal WE he continually refers to?), he's incapable of participating in radical modernity. And yet, Baudrillard's Europe is filled with institutions and individuals who are participating in precisely that radical modernity that he has to go to America to find. The computer and telecommunications artists of Austria, gathered around Heidi Grundmann and Robert Adrian X, the computer music studios STEIM in Amsterdam and LOGOS in Ghent, the work of many of the choreographers at the European Dance Development Centre are all as close to the cutting edge as anything happening in America. In a world that, thankfully, is becoming more and more decentred (and I *am* writing this in Melbourne, remember), it is bewildering to still encounter people who regard Europe (or Manhattan, or ...) as "the center."

Our mutual acquaintances inform me that Jean Baudrillard is a charming and gracious man, and I, someday would like to have the pleasure of meeting him. Maybe then his writings would make more sense to me, I would understand where he was coming from. This, again, is not a gratuitous point. It's well known, but not discussed much in critical theory, that knowing an artist changes the way you perceive their work. It may be finding out something about their attitude to their work, such as my knowing British composer John White makes me appreciate his neo-tonal piano sonatas of the sixties, seventies, and eighties as ironic musical equivalents of Warhol's silkscreens, rather than as the nostalgic yearnings for a lost past that the equivalent George Rochberg pieces are. (And this knowledge makes White's work exciting for me, while I regrettably find most of Rochberg's current work dull, even when the "sound" of their pieces is similar.) Or it may be just knowing something about their body language, or the quality of their voice, that then forms the way you relate to their output. And I think this sort of personal relating to art is a good thing. I have never been happy with the idea of "objective" views of art, probably because I never had any. It might even be that concepts such as objectivity are a partial result of having work available in print, recordings, scores, films, and so on. If it's possible to experience a work without the artist being present, then strategies for appreciating the work without that presence, like "objectivity," or as a logical extension, "the death of the author," will develop. And in a field such as traditional literary criticism, where the idea of personal presence is almost alien (it all happens in books, you know?), no wonder the myth of objectivity is so rampant. Therefore, I am not being flippant when I say that my further dealing with Baudrillard's work is on hold until I can have a cup of tea with him. I only hope that there is more to establish than a simple confirmation of mutual irrelevance.

As I find that I have great difficulty identifying with the nihilism of Baudrillard, I find I also have a similar lack of points of contact with Fredric Jameson. Almost all of Jameson's statements, as quoted in Zurbrugg's essay "Jameson's Complaint" are completely at variance with what I feel. The art that Jameson finds "impenetrable," for example, I often find too clear, with not *enough* "mess" in it; what he sees as "ceaseless rotation of elements" I find to be a fascinating and refreshing use of permutational forms. He finds Rauschenberg's work to be limited; I find it deep and enlightening. Jameson claims that the use of permutational and random forms cannot produce monumental works, that "metabooks" are somehow inferior to the masterworks of modernism. Yet I find John Cage's *Roaratorio*, surely a "metabook" if ever there was one, to be one of the profound masterpieces of the late-twentieth-century.[22]

More than these simple (and ultimately unproductive) disagreements of taste, however, I find Jameson's work forcing me to ask questions about perception and choice of language. The question, it seems to me, is what do *you* do

when you encounter a new work? What sort of strategies do you employ to perceive it, to process it? And what sort of attention do you *choose* to give that work?
For surely, we can choose how we give attention to a work: we can choose close
scrutiny, bringing to bear a variety of critical tools, or we can choose an open
mode of attention, where we try to perceive what is there with as little regard to
our prejudices as we can manage, or we can choose to treat a work as back-
ground to our own reveries. Jameson, surprisingly, seems unaware of this, or at
least he adopts authorial strategies that suggest he is.

Most telling for me though, is Jameson's admission that his critical language
may be inadequate for dealing with the subject at hand, video art. (And doesn't
he understand that video [or the computer, or ...] is just another tool for artists
to work with?) Yet despite this, he clings to his language because it provides an
"entry ticket to the public sphere in which these matters are debated." Rather
than changing his language to deal with a new artform, he insists on evaluating
the new artform in terms of his old language so he can keep his sense of
respectability. He isn't alone; this sort of thinking was rampant in the 1980s. I
once asked a colleague who had produced a very funny radio piece, and then
written a very prolix paper full of art-theory language about it, why she had done
such a thing. Was she aiming at an ironic contrast between the straightforward
humor of the piece and the complex language of the paper? She replied that that
wasn't the case. She had written the paper using that language because she felt if
she didn't use that language she wouldn't be taken seriously by the art world, and
that for her, being taken seriously by the art world was paramount. Thus are we
formed by our desires for respect. What a trap! As John Lilly observed, during a
lecture he gave in the early 1970s on his dolphin research, "Your communication
is limited by the language you know."[23] And yet, many people find it so difficult
to step outside their languages to deal with work that was clearly not made to
accomodate those languages.

V

It becomes increasingly clear, then, that the worldview of those critics Zurbrugg
takes most seriously (because he gives most attention to them) and the worldview of those artists whose works he admires are almost totally at variance with
each other. Given the almost complete dissonance between those who make it
and those who theorize about it I am increasingly forced to conclude that the

only way the experimental art of this century will get written about in an understanding way will be when the practitioners themselves write about it, or train a new generation of critics to do so. The existing critics and critical theorists have proven themselves incapable of lively, much less understanding, responses. The despair and just plain grumpy-old-man tiredness that emanate from the writings of such critics as Baudrillard and Jameson stands in stark contrast to the sense of wonder of, for example, John Cage. One of my favorite Cage quotes (which I can never find the source of) was from an interview where the interviewer asked about the danger of going to extremes. His reply was typically optimistic, and refreshing: "Unless we go to extremes, we won't get anywhere."

Cage's definition of the avant-garde, quoted in Zurbrugg's article on *Amérique*, is similarly clear: "Without the avant-garde, which I think is flexibility of mind and freedom from institutions, theories and laws, you won't have invention and obviously, from a practical point of view . . . society needs invention." (It should be pointed out, though, that Cage is hardly ambivalent on this point. After all, his father was a rather well known inventor.)

In contrast to Jameson's lamenting of the lack of expressive possibilities in randomly based forms, Cage, in such works as *Cartridge Music* and *Variations II*, shows how randomly based forms can be rigorous, tight, and coherent. Over a period of twenty-five years, I've made about ten realizations of *Cartridge Music*, and about four realizations of *Variations II*, two of Cage's famous "kit" scores from 1960-1961, where the performer is to follow instructions to realize their own version of the piece. In both cases, if the instructions are followed, what results in each case is a unique member of a "family" that constitutes a piece. That is, each realization of *Cartridge Music* sounds different, but the same kinds of structures and sounds recur in each version. If realized carefully, it always results in a "cartridge music," and not, say, a "variations II." And far from being simply random improvisations, the realization of each score is hard work. To realize the version of *Variations II* for toy electronic instruments that Australian composer Ernie Althoff and I performed at the Canberra Contemporary Art Space in August 1996, I worked for about four days, three hours a day, endlessly drawing and measuring the lines between the points and lines that constitute the score. Out of this were assembled precisely timed lists of instructions, which were then performed with the fidelity of any other classical music "score." What Cage had done in *Variations II* was to create a paper and pencil physical model of a kind of random-composing computer program. This was clearly the most practical solution for a gigging musician constantly on the road in 1961. (Today, the conceptual grandchildren of Cage's "kit" scores are such algorithmic composing programs as Kinetic Music Machine and Max.) Working it out by hand took hours. If I had simply wanted "random" sounds from my toy instruments, there would have been far easier ways of achieving that. Making the commitment to realize *Variations II* was a commitment to rigorously explore a very serious stochastic structure.[24]

The process is similar with contemporary video art. Many of the contemporary video works I most admire, such as works by Bill Viola, Woody Vasulka, Martha Rosler, and Robert Randall (to name four extremely different artists) are as rigorously worked out as works in any other media. The cheesy Warholian reworked movie star images in Robert Randall's interactive CD-Rom "Little Gems," for example, are backed up by some of the most complex chaos-equation-generated computer graphics I've ever seen. A critic who only deals with the literary (and in this case, the intentionally and sarcastically stupid) "surface" of this work will clearly miss the point of what's lurking in its depths.

Similar things might be said about the very refined and austere work of Bill Viola, an artist who shares my skepticism about the competence and relevance of contemporary critical theory. In one sense, to even use contemporary word-based critical theory to deal with Viola's work is a mistake. The major sources of Viola's work, as I understand it, are not materialistic, verbal or even contemporary. His major sources are such spiritual disciplines as Zen and medieval Christian mysticism. Han-shan, Zeami, John of the Cross, and Theresa of Avila are more relevant starting points for an understanding of his work than are, say, Freud and Wittgenstein.

In fact, one of the themes of Viola's work, as I understand it (and to a large extent of my work as well), is the primacy, if not the absolute superiority, of nonverbal modes of intelligence, such as sound, smell and color/shape/image, over word-based expressions. A recent major work of his, *I Do Not Know What It Is I Am Like*, deals at length with the notion of the nonverbal forms of animal consciousness. For my part, verbal descriptions are an inferior mode of expression, their so-called precision being precisely what renders them so vague. But a smell, ahh, there's no mistaking what's "meant" by that. I had an epiphany a few weeks ago: two colleagues and I argued critical theory in a local coffeehouse for about two hours. Upon leaving the place, I passed a *pitosporum,* one of the most fragrant of Australian native trees. It was not yet in blossom, not for about four months yet, but its bark already gave off its distinctive, sweet, intoxicating odor. I can assure you that that one moment of nasal experience was far more meaningful to me than all the words we had expended in the previous two hours. Emphatically I realized that, for me, words were indeed inferior.

This insistence on keeping words in their place was also shared by John Cage. In the fifties, he was asked what he was trying to say in one of his works with Merce Cunningham. His reply was "We are not, in these dances and music, saying something. We are simple-minded enough to believe that if we were saying something, we would use words. We are rather doing something. The meaning of what we do is determined by each one who sees and hears it."[25] It is important, I feel, to keep making this separation between *doing* and *saying*.

And this is a perception that has been shared by many artists throughout the century. In contrast to Wittgenstein's pronouncement that what cannot be spoken of must be passed over in silence, the American composer, musicologist and semiotician Charles Seeger pointed out that what cannot be spoken of may have already be danced, painted, sculpted, or sung for centuries.[26]

It becomes clear that the work of many contemporary critical theorists is as irrelevant to our artistic concerns as our work is to theirs. Surely we, as artists, and as intelligent perceivers of the richness of the contemporary environment, have the right to demand interesting, lively, broad-minded, and informed responses from, and dialogues with, our critics and cultural theorists. And if they fail to measure up to these criteria, surely we have the right to be as contemptuously dismissive toward them, and their works, as they have been toward ours.

notes

notes to introduction

1 W. H. Auden, "The Word and the Machine," *Encounter* 2, no.4 (April 1954): 3.

2 William S. Burroughs, *Dead Fingers Talk* (London: John Calder, 1963), 68.

3 See Warren Burt, "Zurbrugg's Complaint," in this volume. All references to Burt in this preface refer to this essay.

4 Germaine Dulac, "The Essence of the Cinema: The Visual Idea" (1925), trans. Robert Lamberton, in *The Avant-Garde Film: A Reader of Theory and Criticism*, ed. P. Adams Sitney (New York: Anthology Film Archives, 1987), 36.

5 Germaine Dulac, "The Avant-Garde Cinema" (1932), trans. Robert Lamberton, in Sitney, ed., *The Avant-Garde Film*, 43.

6 Roland Barthes, "The Third Meaning" (1970), in his *Image-Music-Text*, trans. Stephen Heath (Glasgow: Collins, 1977), 67.

7 William S. Burroughs, "William Burroughs: Grandpa From Hell," interview with Nicholas Zurbrugg (1993), *World Art* 1, no.2 (1994), 73.

8 Félix Guattari, *Chaosmosis: An Ethico-Aesthetic Paradigm* (1992), trans. Paul Bains and Julian Pefanis (Sydney: Power Publications, 1995), 132.

9 *Ibid.*, 106.

10 Félix Guattari, "Postmodernism and Ethical Abdication," Interview with Nicholas Zurbrugg (1993), trans. Nicholas Zurbrugg, in *The Guattari Reader*, ed. Gary Genosko (Oxford: Blackwell, 1996), 16.

11 Hal Foster, *The Return of the Real: The Avant-Garde at the End of the Century* (Cambridge, MA: MIT Press, 1996), xiv, and 208.

12 *Ibid.*, xiv. Félix Guattari, "The Postmodern Dead End," trans. Nancy Blake, *Flash Art* 128 (May/June 1986): 41.

13 Foster, *The Return of the Real*, xiv.

14 Roland Barthes, *Camera Lucida : Reflections on Photography* (1980), trans. Richard Howard (New York: Hill and Wang, 1981), 51, 53. Jacques Derrida, "*Ja, or the faux-bond* II," Interview with D. Kambouchner, J. Ristat, and D. Sallenave (1977), in *Points . . . : Interviews, 1974–1994*, ed. Elisabeth Weber, trans. Peggy Kamuf (Stanford: Stanford University Press), 48–49.

15 Foster, *The Return of the Real*, 14–15.

16 Dulac, "The Essence," 36.

17 Charles Baudelaire, "The Universal Exhibition of 1855" (1855), in his *Selected Writings on Art and Literature*, trans. P. E. Charvet (London: Penguin, 1992), 117–18.

18 Baudelaire, "The Salon of 1845" (1845), and "The Painter of Modern Life" (1863) in his *Selected Writings*, 35 and 402, respectively.

19 Baudelaire, "The Universal Exhibition," 118.

20 Foster, *The Return of the Real*, xiv.

21 Fredric Jameson, "Reading without Interpretation: Postmodernism and the Video-text," in *The Linguistics of Writing: Arguments between language and literature* eds. Nigel Fabb, Derek Attridge, Alan Durant and Colin MacCabe (Manchester: Manchester University Press, 1987), 200.

22 *Ibid.*, 208, 221.

23 See chapter two of this volume.

24 Brion Gysin, to Nicholas Zurbrugg 24 September, 1984.

25 Jameson, Reading without Interpretation, 200, 208, 200.

26 *Ibid.*, 200.

27 William S. Burroughs, "On Coincidence," in his *The Adding Machine: Selected Essays* (New York: Seaver Books, 1986), 103.

28 William S. Burroughs, *The Ticket That Exploded* (Paris: Olympia, 1962), 172–74.

29 "Jean Baudrillard, "The Ecstasy of Photography," interview with Nicholas Zurbrugg, trans. Nicholas Zurbrugg (1993), *Jean Baudrillard: Art and Artefact*, ed. Nicholas Zurbrugg (London: Sage, 1997), 38. Guattari, *Chaosmosis*, 90–91.

30 Marshall McLuhan, *Understanding Media: The Extensions of Man* (New York: Signet, 1964), 70–71.

31 F. T. Marinetti, "Destruction of Syntax—Imagination without Strings—Words-in-Freedom" (1913), trans. R. W. Flint, in *Futurist Manifestos*, ed. Umbro Apollonio (London: Thames and Hudson, 1973), 97.

32 William S. Burroughs, "Remembering Jack Kerouac" (1979), in his *The Adding Machine*, 176.

notes to chapter one

1 D. J. Enright, Introduction to *The Oxford Book of Contemporary Verse 1945–1980*, edited by D. J. Enright (Oxford, 1980), xix–xxii and xxv-xxvi. Henceforth cited in the text by page number.

2   See for example: Matei Calinescu, *Faces of Modernity* (Bloomington, 1977); Christopher Butler, *After the Wake: An Essay on the Contemporary Avant-garde* (Oxford, 1981); Allan Rodway, "The Prospects of Postmodernism," *London Magazine* 20, nos. 11 and 12 (February/March 1981): 52–61.

3   Walter Benjamin, *Illuminations* (London, 1970), 239. Henceforth cited in the text by page number.

4   László Moholy-Nagy, *Vision in Motion* (Chicago, 1947), 351. Henceforth cited in the text by page number.

5   Michael Kirby, *Futurist Performance* (New York, 1971), 3. Henceforth cited in the text by page number.

6   See such journals as *The Drama Review, Performing Arts Journal,* and *Live.*

7   Arrigo Lora-Totino, *Futura: poesia sonora* (Milan, 1978); Henri Chopin, *Poésie sonore internationale* (Paris, 1979).

8   Umberto Boccioni et al., "Prefazione al catalogo delle esposizioni di Parigi, Loudra, Berlino, Bruxelles, Monaco, Amburgo, Vienna, ecc. (1912)" in Umberto Apollonio, *Futurismo* (Milan, 1970), 95, trans. Robert Brain et al. As *Futurist Manifestos* (London, 1973), 49. With the single exception of Marinetti's "La Radia," of 1933, all subsequent quotations from Futurist manifestos, and from their translations, are followed in the text by page references to these books.

9   As might be expected, Dadaist manifestos are ambiguous in their response to technology. Raoul Hausmann envisioned "la peinture électrique" (electric painting) in his "PREsentisme" manifesto of 1921, collected in *Courier Dada* (Paris 1958), 98. But other Dadaists such as Hugo Ball and Tristan Tzara appear to have imitated the "archaic" primitivism of African poetry, as Jerome Rothenberg emphasizes in "Changing the Present, Changing the Past: A New Poetics," in *Talking Poetics from Naropa Institute* (Annals of the Jack Kerouac School of Disembodied Poetics), vol. 2, ed. Anne Waldman and Marilyn Webb (Boulder, 1979), 279–82.

10   Jerome Rothenberg, "A Dialogue on Oral Poetry with William Spanos," *Boundary 2* 3, no. 3 (Spring, 1975), 528.

11   Jerome Rothenberg, ed., *Technicians of the Sacred* (New York, 1968).

12   Jerome Rothenberg, "Changing the Present," 277, 259.

13   Jerome Rothenberg, "New Models, New Visions: Some Notes Toward a Poetics of Performance," in *Performance in Postmodern Culture*, ed. Michel Benamou and Charles Caramello (Madison, 1977), 11.

14   Jerome Rothenberg, "Old Man Beaver's Blessing Song: Notations for a Chant," *Panjandrum* 4 (Fall, 1975): 85.

15   Rothenberg discusses the way in which texts form a "simplification" of his reading in "Changing the Present," 286

16   F. T. Marinetti, "Distruzione della sintassi Immaginazione senza fili PAROLE IN LIBERTA' La sensibilitaà futurista" (1913), 142–53.

17   Henri Chopin, "Lettre ouverte aux musiciens aphones," *OU* 33 (1968): 24; trans. Jean Ratcliffe-Chopin as "Open Letter to Aphonic Musicians," Ibid., II.

18   Henri Chopin, "Machine Poem," *OU* 20/21 (1964): n.p. My translation, as are all other translations unless otherwise specified.

19 Chopin's later works, such as "Le Temps Aujourd'hui," of 1976, employ the semantic values of language quite explicitly. A record of this work is in *Stereo Headphones*, 8–9–10 (Spring, 1982).

20 Henri Chopin, *Poésie sonore internationale*, 173.

21 Bengt-Emil Johnson, "Fylkingen's Group for Linguistic Arts and Text-Sound Compositions," *Fylkingen International Bulletin* 2 (1969): 15.

22 Marinetti's "La Radia," of October 1933, is reprinted from the *Gazzetta del popolo*, in *Sintesi del FUTURISMO storia e documenti*, ed. Luigi Scrivo (Rome, 1968). Printed between pages 204 and 205, this text is inexplicably unpaginated. Accordingly, references to this text remain unpaginated. Though briefly mentioned by Kirby, "La Radia," is neither collected nor printed in full in his *Futurist Performance;* nor indeed does it appear in Apollino's *Futurismo* and *Futurist Manifestos*, or in *Marinetti: Selected Writings*, edited by R. W. Flint (London, 1972). (Objection over-ruled! Stephen Sartarelli's translation of "La Radia" appears in *Wireless Imagination: Sound, Radio, and the Avant-Garde*, ed. Douglas Kahn and Gregory Whitehead (Cambridge, MA, 1992), 265-8.

23 Translations of "La Radia," by Joseph Gioscio and Nicholas Zurbrugg.

24 Bengt-Emil Johnson, "Fylkingen's Group," 15.

25 Bernard Heidsieck, "La Poinçonneuse," *Stereo Headphones 7* (Spring, 1976): 20–24; recorded on "*Troi biopsies*" & "*Un passe-partout*" (Multi-Techniques L. P.: Paris, 1971).

26 Gérald Gassiot-Talabot, "Bernard Heidsieck: Notes et Contresens," *Opus International* 40–41 (January 1973): 66.

27 Bernard Heidsieck, Gérard-Georges Lemaire, and Philippe Mikriammos, "Quatrième entretien," in William S. Burroughs and Brion Gysin, *Le Colloque de Tanger* (Paris, 1976), 364. Henceforth cited in the text by page number.

28 Ulrich Weisstein, "Collage, Montage, and Related Terms: Their Literal and Figurative Use in and Application to Techniques and Forms in Various Arts," *Comparative Literature Studies* 15, no. 1 (March 1978): 131.

29 Larry Wendt, quoted by Ellen Zweig, in Zweig, "Performance Poetry: Critical Approaches to Contemporary Intermedia," doctoral dissertation presented to the University of Michigan, 1980, 54. Larry Wendt's work is discussed later in this article.

30 See *Boundary* 2, 3, no. 3 (Spring, 1975). *New Literary History* 8, no. 3 (Spring, 1977) discusses similar issues.

31 Michael Benamou, "Presense and Play," in Benamou and Caramello, eds. *Performance in Postmodern Culture*, 5.

32 Charles Amirkhanian, letter of 1971 to Nicholas Zurbrugg, published as untitled statement in *Stereo Headphones*, 5 (Winter, 1972), 35.

33 Charles Amirkhanian, "dutiful ducks," published with inserted notes to Amirkhanian's LP *Lexical Music*, Record S-1779, 1750 Arch Records, 1979.

34 Charles Amirkhanian, quotations from statement about "dutiful ducks" in unpaginated booklet accompanying the tape cassette *Variety Theater: An Anthology of Sound Poetry* (San José, 1977).

35 See, for example, the now-defunct French review *Musique en jeu;* the late Gregory

Battcock's anthologies entitled: *New Artists Video* (New York, 1978) and *Breaking the Sound Barrier: A Critical Anthology of the New Music* (New York, 1981).

36 Michel Chion, "Vingt années de musique électroacoustique ou une quête d'identité," *Musique en jeu* 8 (September, 1972): 19–28. Henceforth cited in the text by page number.

37 For recorded examples of authorial readings by Hausmann, Schwitters, Cobbing, Jandl and Dufrêne, see—or hear—the LP *Phonetische Poesie,* Luchterhand Schallplatte F 60 379, Germany.

38 A recording of Schwitters reading the "scherzo" of this poem appears on the LP *Phonetische Poesie.* Pierre Henry's "Le Voyage," incorporating Dufrêne's "crirythmes," appears in the Philips Perspective xxie siècle series, on LP 936/899 DSY. Paul de Vree's "Vertigo Gli" appears on a record in the review *OU* 28/29 (1966).

39 Example of Chopin's "purist" work appear on his record *Audiopoems,* TCS 106 (Tangent LP: London, 1971); on *Phonetische Poesie;* and on several of the records issued with his review *OU.*

40 While work like that of Heidsieck and Amirkhanian moves from relatively "purist" modes to a final hybrid phase at the end of an evolutionary pattern roughly following Chion's outline, it must also be acknowledged that certain poets have almost continuously worked within a hybrid phase. Jackson MacLow exemplifies this permanent hybrid approach in his interview in *The Craft of Poetry,* ed. William Packard (New York, 1974), 225–63.

41 Sten Hanson, "Henri Chopin, the Sound Poet," in *Stereo Headphones,* 8–9–10 (Spring 1982); quoted from French translation by Jean Ratcliffe-Chopin, in Henri Chopin, *Poésie sonore international,* 124.

42 Larry Wendt, interview with Nicholas Zurbrugg, San José, 15 May 1981. This interview has been edited without attempting to alter its conversational style. John Giorno's "reel-time" work appears on several of his Giorno Poetry Systems Institute LPs, including: *William S. Burroughs—John Giorno* (GPS 006–007); and the anthology *Big Ego* (GPS 012–013). This LP not only collects work by Giorno, Wendt, and Heidsieck, but additionally contains related work by musicians like Philip Glass, rock groups like The Fugs, and punk singers like Patti Smith, demonstrating the strange convergences between the avant-garde and popular arts.

43 Typical of this group are Wendt and Stephen Ruppenthal, who both have work on the aforementioned tape, anthology *Variety Theater* (see note 34) significantly, both work at West Coast universities and have access to electronic music studios.

44 The Swedish Fylkingen radio station is particularly important in this respect, having organized sound poetry festivals, opened its studios to poets, and issued LP anthologies of resultant works. By comparison, the BBC's few collaborations with poets leave much to be desired.

45 Eugene Jolas, "From 'Jabberwocky'" to 'Lettrism'," *Transition Forty-Eight* I (January 1948); 104. "The Revolution of the Word" was the war cry of Jolas' magnificent review, *Transition.*

46 This phrase appears anonymously in an advertisement for Philippe Lejeune's *Je est un autre,* on the back cover of *Poétique* 42 (April 1980).

notes to chapter two

1   William S. Burroughs, *The Book of Breeething* (1974), in *Ah Pook Is Here and Other Texts* (London: John Calder, 1979), 102.

2   Brion Gysin, interviewed by Terry Wilson, in Wilson et al., *Here to Go: Planet R-101* (San Francisco: Re/Search Publications, 1982), 65. Unless otherwise indicated, all quotations from Gysin in this article are from this collection of interviews, and page references will hereafter appear in the text.

3   Roland Barthes, "The Death of the Author," in *Image-Music-Text*, trans. Stephen Heath (New York: Hill and Wang, 1977), esp. 142–48. Unless otherwise indicated, all quotations from Barthes are from this collection of essays, and page references will hereafter appear in the text.

4   See chapter one, note 36

5   Burroughs, *The Naked Lunch* (New York: Grove Press, 1959), 150. All page references hereafter are to this edition and will appear in the text.

6   Burroughs, *Exterminator!* (London: Calder and Boyars, 1974), 106.

7   Burroughs, "Statement on the Final Academy," in *The Final Academy: Statements of a Kind*, ed. Roger Ely (London: The Final Academy, 1982), 1. Catalog to accompany Burroughs's "Final Academy" readings in London, 29 Sept–2 Oct. 1982.

8   Burroughs reads from *The Naked Lunch* and *Nova Express* on the record *Call Me Burroughs*, published in Paris by Gaît Frogé's English Bookshop (1965). A more accessible example of his readings is the record *William S. Burroughs/John Giorno*, GPS 006–007, published by Giorno Poetry Systems, 222 Bowery, New York (1975); subsequent Giorno Poetry Systems anthologies provide other examples. Such records illustrate the ways in which technology reveals and records the "grain" of the authorial voice.

9   Jonathan Culler, *Structuralist Poetics: Structuralism, Linguistics, and the Study of Literature* (London: Routledgc and Kegan Paul, 1975), 139. All page references are to this edition and will hereafter appear in the text.

10   Culler, *The Pursuit of Signs: Semiotics, Literature, Deconstruction* (Ithaca: Cornell University Press, 1981), 38. Unless otherwise indicated, all quotations from Culler are from this book, and page references will hereafter appear in the text.

11   Julia Kristeva, *La Révolution du langage poétique* (Paris: Editions du Seuil, 1974), 59; my translation, as are all subsequent translations unless otherwise indicated.

12   Laurent Jenny, "La Stratégie de la forme," *Poétique* 27 (1976): 265. Page references will hereafter appear in the text.

13   Jenny, "Sémiotique du collage intertextual, ou la littérature à coups de ciseaux," *Revue d'Esthétique* nos. 3–4 (1978): 168 (issue subtitled *Collages*). Page references will hereafter appear in the text.

14   Dieter Freundlieb "Understanding Poe's Tales: A Schema-Theoretic View," *Poetics* 11 (1982): 25–44.

15   Barthes, *S/Z*. trans. Richard Miller (London: Jonathan Cape, 1975), 28–30. Page references will hereafter appear in the text.

16   See Ellen Zweig, *Performance Poetry: Critical Approaches to Contemporary Intermedia*, Ph.D. diss., Michigan, 1980. A number of new journals (such as *Alive, ArtCom, High*

Performance, Performing Arts Journal and Performance Magazine) now document and analyze performance art and its analogue, performance poetry. These new genres are usefully exemplified in *High Performance* 4, no. 4 (1981–82); this includes scores for performance and an article by Lewis MacAdam, "Nightclubbing with William S. Burroughs, John Giorno and Laurie Anderson" (38–42), which discusses Burroughs's readings with the performance poet John Giorno and the performance artist Laurie Anderson.

17 Samuel Beckett, "Proust in Pieces," *The Spectator,* 22 June 1934, 975.

18 Beckett, *Watt* (1953; rpt. London: John Calder, 1963), 73.

19 Marcel Proust, *A la recherche du temps perdu,* ed. Pierre Clarac and André Ferré (Paris: Gallimard, 1954), I, 553.

20 For discussions of these technological modes of creativity, see my articles "Beyond Beckett: Reckless Writing and the Concept of the Avant-Garde within Post-Modern Literature," *Yearbook of Comparative and General Literature* 30 (1981): 37–56, and "Marinetti, Boccioni, and Electroacoustic Poetry: Futurism and After," reprinted in this volume.

21 Burroughs, in Daniel Odier, *The Job: Interview with William Burroughs* (London: Jonathan Cape, 1970), 46, 48. Page references will hereafter appear in the text.

22 Claudio Guillén, *Literature as System: Essays Toward the Theory of Literary History* (Princeton: Princeton University Press, 1971), 61.

23 Brion Gysin, "Statement on the Cut-Up Method and Permutated Poems" (1958), published as "Cut-Ups Self-Explained," in Burroughs and Gysin, *The Third Mind* (London: John Calder, 1979), 34.

24 In order to demonstrate that poets do not "own" their words, Gysin's permutated poem "no poets don't own words" systematically liberated the semantic and sonic potential the words "no/ know," "poets," "don't," "own" and "words" by mixing them in a sequence of some 120 permutations. Yet far from constituting an anonymous and mechanical text, Gysin's first recording of the poem in 1960 (an abbreviated version consisting of twenty permutations and published on a record in *Revue-Disque OU,* nos. 23–24 [1965]) is informed by the rich "grain" of Gysin's highly individual reading, a quality less evident in the 1981 recording *Brion Gysin: Orgy Boys* (New York: Hat Haut Records, 1982).

25 Gysin, "Statement on the Cut-Up Method," 34.

26 The term "intermedia" was coined and defined by the American poet and Fluxus artist Dick Higgins in an article of the same title (1965), collected in his *A Dialectic of Centuries: Notes Towards a Theory of the New Arts* (New York: Printed Editions, 1978), 12–17. The article begins: "Much of the best work being produced today seems to fall between media."

27 Burroughs, *Nova Express* (London: Jonathan Cape, 1968), 52.

28 Few Anglo-American intertextual critics have attempted to relate literary and artistic variants of montage, or the new literary and extraliterary occupants of technological discursive spaces (such as that of recorded creativity). The *Collages* issue of the *Revue d'Esthétique* 3–4 (1978) documents the efforts of French and Italian critics to relate literary and extraliterary variants of collage.

29 Mihai Nadin vainly attempts to analyze Pierre Garnier's poem "cinema" in terms of prior poetic discourse ("Sur le sens de la poésie concrete," *Poétique,* No. 42 [1980], 253),

   although Garnier's play with the optical effects peculiar to the typeface of the typewriter are best explicated in the context of "op art" works by Bridget Riley and Jesus Rafael Soto.

30 Burroughs, "The Art of Fiction xxxvi," interview with Conrad Knickerbocker, *The Paris Review* 35 (Fall 1965): 24.

31 Burroughs, *Electronic Revolution* (1971), in *Ah Pook Is Here and Other Texts*, 125–26.

32 Burroughs, "An Introductory Text for Henri Chopin's book on 'Poésie sonore,'" in *Chopin, Poésie sonore internationale* (Paris: Jean-Michel Place, 1979), 9.

33 The term "interNONtextuality" was coined by the editors of *New York Literary Forum* no 2 (1978: viii (issue subtitled *Inter-textuality: New Perspectives in Criticism*). I use the term "intercontextuality" to denote the attempt to explicate literary texts (particularly, radical contemporary literary texts) by analogy with extraliterary discursive practices.

34 Culler, *The Pursuit of Signs*, 80–118, summarizes Riffaterre's, Jenny's, and Bloom's intertextual systems, with particular reference to Michael Riffaterre, *Semiotics of Poetry* (Bloomington: Indiana University Press, 1978), Jenny, "La Stratégie de la forme," and Harold Bloom, *The Anxiety of Influence: A Theory of Poetry* (New York: Oxford University Press, 1973), *A Map of Misreading* (New York: Oxford University Press, 1975), and *Poetry and Repression: Revisionism from Blake to Stevens* (New Haven: Yale University Press, 1976). See also Ann Jefferson, "Intertextuality and the Poetics of Fiction," *Comparative Criticism: A Yearbook* 2 (1980): 235–50.

35 See Claus Clüver, "Brazilian Concrete: Painting Poetry, Time, and Space," in *Literature and the Other Arts*, Proceedings of the Ninth Congress of the International Comparative Literature Association, ed. Zoran Konstantinović et al. (Innsbruck: Innsbruck University Press, 1981), III, 207–13. See also my article, "Dada and the Poetry of the Contemporary Avant-Garde," in *Dada: Studies of a Movement*, ed. Richard Sheppard (Chalfont St Giles: Alpha Academic, 1980) 121–43.

36 Burroughs, "Forward Note" to *Nova Express*, 5.

37 Starting in the late fifties, Burroughs conducted a number of tape-recorder experiments during his years in Paris at the "Beat Hotel." Gysin recalls: "Burroughs was busy punching to death a series of cheap Japanese tape recorders, to which he applied himself with such force that he could punch one of them to death inside a matter of weeks, days even" (195). A selection of these experiments appears on Burroughs's record entitled *Nothing Here Now but the Recordings*, IR 0016 Industrial Records (1981; distributed by Rough Trade, 137 Blenheim Crescent, London). Burroughs's experiments with projections are discussed in "How to Be Humphrey Bogart," in *The Job*, 179–84. He describes some that led to the film *Bill and Tony* (1966), made in collaboration with the film-maker Antony Balch, in an interview with Robert Palmer in *Rolling Stone* no. 108 (11 May 1972): 48–53. Balch's account of the experiments and collaboration is in his interview "Breakthrough in Grey Room ... Towers Open Fire," *Cinema Rising no.* 1 (April 1972), 10–13. Burroughs, Gysin, Batch and Ian Somerville also collaborated on the films *Towers Open Fire* (1963) and *The Cut-Ups* (1968).

38 Andy Warhol and Pat Hackett, *Popism: The Warhol '60s* (London: Hutchinson, 1981), 280.

39 Jean Ricardou, "Claude Simon," Textuellement," in *Claude Simon: Colloque de Cerisy*, ed. Jean Ricardou (Paris: Union Général d'Editions, 1975), 11.

40 Burroughs, "An Introductory Text," 9.

41 Karlheinz Stockhausen, "Electronic and Instrumental Music," in *Postwar German Culture: An Anthology,* ed. Charles E. McClelland and Steven P. Scher (New York: Dutton, 1974), 361. (Translated by Ruth Hein from Stockhausen's *Texte zur Elektronischen und Instrumentalen Musik,* 1 [Cologne: DuMont Schauberg, 1963].)

42 Gysin, "Statement on the Cut-Up Method," 34.

43 John Weightman, "High Priest of Modernism," *The Observer* (Review Section), 24 Oct. 1982, 34.

44 Burroughs, quoted in Alan Ansen, "Anyone Who Can Pick up a Frying Pan Owns Death," in Burroughs, *White Subway* (London: Aloes, n.d. [1965?]), 71.

notes to chapter 3

1 For further discussion of this periodization of modernism (1880–1930) and post-modernism (1930–1980), see my article "Beyond Beckett: Reckless Writing and the Concept of the Avant-Garde within Post-Modern Literature," *Yearbook of Comparative and General Literature* no. 30 (1981): 37–56.

2 This term is formulated by Laurent Jenny in his article "La Stratégie de la Forme." *Poétique* no. 27 (1976): 259.

3 László Moholy-Nagy, *Vision in Motion* (Chicago: Theobald, 1947), 10.

4 Jean Baudrillard, "The Ecstasy of Communication," trans. John Johnston, in *The Anti-Aesthetic: Essays on Postmodern Culture,* ed. Hal Foster (Port Townsend, WA: Bay Press, 1983), 132. Page references will hereafter appear in the text.

5 Jean Baudrillard, "The Precession of Simulacra," trans. Paul Foss and Paul Patton, in *Simulations,* trans. Paul Foss, Paul Patton, and Philip Beitchman (New York: *Semiotext(e),* Foreign Agents Series, 1983), 4. Page references will hereafter appear in the text.

6. Ross Gibson, "Customs and Excise," in *Seduced and Abandoned: The Baudrillard Scene,* ed. André Frankovits (Glebe, Australia: Stonemoss, 1984), 50.

7 Michel Chion, "Vingt années de musique électro-acoustique, ou une quête d'identité," *Musique en jeu* no. 8 (1972): 19–28.

8 For further discussion of these experiments, see my article "Marinetti, Boccioni and Electroacoustic Poetry: Futurism and After," reprinted in this volume.

9 Jean Baudrillard, "The Implosion of Meaning in the Media and the Implosion of the Social in the Masses," trans. Mary Lydon, in *The Myths of Information: Technology and Postindustrial Culture,* ed. Kathleen Woodward (Madison, WI: Coda Press, 1980), 142; emphasis mine. Page references will hereafter appear in the text.

10 Max Nordau, *Degeneration,* trans. George L. Mosse (New York: Howard Fertig, 1968), 42, 27, and 31, respectively. Page references will hereafter appear in the text.

11 Marinetti, "Manifesto del teatro sintetico" (Synthesist Theatre Manifesto), trans. R. W. Flint, in *Futurist Manifestos,* ed. Umberto Appollonio, trans. Robert Brain et al. (London: Thames and Hudson, 1973), 194.

12 William S. Burroughs, interview of 1978, quoted by Victor Bockris in *With William Burroughs: A Report from the Bunker* (New York: Seaver Books, 1981), 127.

13 William S. Burroughs, quoted by Daniel Odier in *The Job: Interview with William Burroughs* (London: Jonathan Cape, 1970), 19. Page references will hereafter appear in the text.

14 For further discussion of Burroughs's technological experiments, see my article "The Limits of Intertextuality," reprinted in this volume.

15 See William S. Burroughs, *Electronic Revolution* (1971)in *Ah Pook Is Here and Other Texts* (London: John Calder, 1971). Burroughs discusses *Electronic Revolution* in this quotation from an interview with Dan Georgakas in London, summer 1970, in *Something Else Yearbook, 1974,* ed. Jan Herman (Barton: Something Else Press, 1973), 22.

16 William S. Burroughs, "An Introductory Text for Henri Chopin's Book on 'Poésie Sonore,'" in Henri Chopin, *Poésie sonore internationale* (Paris: Jean-Michel Place, 1979),9.

17 William S. Burroughs, interview with Nicholas Zurbrugg, 22 November 1983, Lawrence, Kansas.

18 William S. Burroughs, interview with Nicholas Zurbrugg, 6 October 1983, Minneapolis, Minnesota.

19 William S. Burroughs, interview with Robert Palmer, *Rolling Stone* no. 108, 11 May 1972, 49.

20 James Joyce, "The Dead," *Dubliners* (Harmondsworth, England: Penguin, 1971), 220.

21 Marcel Proust, "Les nuages" (Clouds), ca. 1885–86, in *Contre Sainte-Beuve, precédé de Pastiches et mélanges, et Suivi de Essais et articles* (Paris: Gallimard, 1971), 329; translation mine.

22 Fredric Jameson, "Post-Modernism and Consumer Society," in *The Anti-Aesthetic: Essays on Postmodern Culture,* ed. Hal Foster (Port Townsend, WA: Bay Press, 1983), 119.

23 Samuel Beckett, *Dream of Fair to Middling Women* (Dublin: Black Cat Press, 1992), 241.

24 Marcel Proust, *A la recherche du temps perdu,* ed. Pierre Clarac and André Ferré, (Paris: Gallimard, 1968-69), 838; translation mine.

25 William S. Burroughs, interview with Conrad Knickerbocker, *Paris Review* no. 35 (Fall 1965): 23.

26 William S. Burroughs, *Dead Fingers Talk* (London: John Calder, 1963), 169.

27 See Hans Richter, *Dada: Art and Anti-Art* (London: Thames and Hudson, 1970),206–07; and Raoul Hausmann, "Dadaism and the Avant-Garde," *Times Literary Supplement,* 3 September 1964, 800–801.

28 Walter Benjamin, "The Work of Art in the Age of Mechanical Reproduction," in *Illuminations,* trans. Harry Zohn (Glasgow: Fontana/Collins, 1977), 239. Page references will hereafter appear in the text.

29 For further discussion of these conceptual shifts, see my article "Towards the End of the Line: Dada and Experimental Poetry Today," in *Dada Spectrum: The Dialectics of Revolt,* ed. Stephen Foster and Rudolf Kuenzli (Madison,WI: Coda Press, 1979), 226–48.

30 Jean Baudrillard, "On Nihilism," extract translated and quoted by Paul Foss in "Despero Ergo Sum," in *Seduced and Abandoned: The Baudrillard Scene,* ed. André Frankovits (Glebe, Australia: Stonemoss, 1984), 10.

31 This was the title of a paper given by Jean Baudrillard at the *Futur-Fall: Excursions into Post-Modernity* Conference, Sydney, Australia, 28 July 1984.

32 Roland Barthes, "The Third Meaning," trans. Stephen Heath, in *Image-Music-Text* (Glasgow: Fontana/Collins, 1977), 67.

33 Jean-François Lyotard, "Answering the Question: What is Postmodernism?," trans. Régis Durand, in *Innovation/Renovation: New Perspectives on the Humanities*, ed. Ihab Hassan and Sally Hassan (Madison, WI: University of Wisconsin Press, 1983), 340–41; emphasis mine.

34 Achille Bonita Oliva, *Trans-Avantgarde International*, trans. Dwight Gast and Gwen Jones (Milan: Giancarlo Politi Editore, 1982). Page references will hereafter appear in the text.

35 Reviews of this exhibition, and an interview with its organizer, Frank Popper, appear in *Domus* no. 646 (January 1984): 75–80.

36 Roland Barthes, "Objective Literature," in his *Critical Essays*, trans. Richard Howard (Evanston, IL: Northwestern University Press, 1972), 14; emphasis mine.

37 Alain Robbe-Grillet, *The Voyeur*, trans. Richard Howard (London: John Calder, 1959), 6.

38 Marcel Proust, *A la recherche du temps perdu*, III, 885. English translation by Samuel Beckett, in his *Proust* (London: Chatto and Windus, 1931), 57.

39 Roland Barthes, *Camera Lucida: Reflections on Photography*, trans. Richard Howard (New York: Hill and Wang, 1981), 51. Barthes italicizes "punctum" and "studium" throughout.

40 Jean Baudrillard, interview with Sam Mele and Mark Titmarsh, 18 January 1984, Paris; quoted by Ross Gibson, "Customs and Excise," 48.

41 Renato Poggioli, *The Theory of the Avant-Garde*, trans. Gerald Fitzgerald (Cambridge, MA: Harvard University Press, 1968), 137.

notes to chapter four

1 Charles Baudelaire, "Correspondances" in *Les Fleurs du Mal* (1857), French text with translations by R. Howard (Boston; David R. Godine. 1982), 193 (translation modified).

2 Jean Baudrillard, interviewed by Sylvère Lotringer in "Forget Baudrillard," collected in *Forget Foucault*, trans. P. Beitchman, L. Hildreth and M. Polizzotti (New York: Semiotext(e), 1987), 130. Baudrillard comments: "The secret of theory is that truth doesn't exist. . . . The only thing you can do is play with some kind of provocative logic" (129–30). This "logic" is applied to American culture in the main subject of this article: *Amérique*. Baudrillard's poetic writings are exemplified by his poems in *L'ange de stuc* (Paris: Galilée, 1978).

3 Baudrillard, *Amérique* (Paris: Bernard Grasset, 1986). Page numbers cited hereafter refer to this book. All translations are my own.

4 Baudelaire, "L'Invitation au voyage, op. cit., 235.

5 Baudrillard, "L'Amérique comme fiction," interview with Jacques Henric and Guy Scaparta, *Art Press* 103 (May 1986): 41–42. My translation of this interview appears in *eyeline* 5 (June 1988): 24–25.

6 The research by Burroughs and Gysin is documented in their book *The Third Mind* (London: John Calder, 1979), whereas that of Frank J. Malina and his fellow artists is documented in his *Kinetic Art: Theory and Practice* (New York: Dover, 1974).

7   Robert Wilson has produced stage versions of Heiner Müller's *Hamletmachine and Quartet.* Both plays appear in Müller's *Hamletmachine and Other Texts for the Stage,* ed. and trans. Carl Weber (New York, *Performing Arts Journal* Publications, 1984. For further discussion of Heiner Müller's collaborations, see my article "Postmodernism and the Multimedia Sensibility: Heiner Müller's *Hamletmachine* and the Art of Robert Wilson." Reprinted in this volume.

8   Heiner Müller quoted by Arlene Akiko Teraoka in *The Silence of Entropy or Universal Discourse: The Post-Modern Poetics of Heiner Müller* (New York: Peter Lang, 1985) 106.

9   Ibid., 100.

10 Umberto Eco, *Travels in Hyperreality,* trans. William Weaver (New York and London: Harcourt Brace Jovanovich 1986), 149, and 147, respectively. Page numbers given in later quotations refer to this text.

11 Umberto Boccioni, Carl Carrà, Luigi Russolo, Giacomo Balla, Gino Severini, "*The Exhibitors to the Public*" (1912) in *Futurist Manifestos,* ed. Umbro Apollonio, (London: Thames & Hudson, 1973), 49; emphasis in the original.

12 Letter to the *Village Voice* (Jan. 1966), in *John Cage,* ed. Richard Kostelanetz (London: Allen Lane, 1974), 167.

13 Letter to Paul Henry Lang (22 May 1965), Ibid., 118.

14 John Cage comments, "Well, long live the technology to come!" at the end of his conversations with Daniel Charles, in *For the Birds,* (London, Marion Boyars, 1981), 238.

15 "After antiquity," conversation with Peter Gena, in *A John Cage Reader,* Peter Gena and Jonathan Brent, (New York, C. F. Peters, 1982), 170–71.

16 Interview with Nicholas Zurbrugg, *eyeline* 1 (May 1987): 6–7.

17 Joris-Karl Huysmans, *Against Nature* (1884), trans. Robert Baldick, (Harmondsworth, England: Penguin, 1968), 35.

18 "L'Amérique comme fiction," 41.

19 Charles Dickens, *Hard Times* (New York: Signet, 1961), 14.

20 Heiner Müller, "Reflections on Post-Modernism," *New German Critique* 16 (Winter 1979): 56.

21 George Eliot, "The Natural History of German Life" (185), in *The Portable Victorian Reader,* ed. Gordon S. Haight (Harmondsworth, England: Penguin, 1976), 609.

22 Müller, "Reflections," 57.

23 English modification by Baudrillard, from "L'Amérique comme fiction," 41.

24 "Forget Baudrillard," 135, and 134, respectively.

25 Baudrillard, "L'Amérique comme fiction," 42.

26 William Wordsworth, "Above Tintern Abbey" (1798), in *The Norton Anthology of English Literature,* vol. 2, ed. M. H. Abrams (New York: Norton, 1986), 154.

27 G.–Albert Aurier, "Symbolism in Painting: Paul Gauguin" (1891), in *Theories of Modern Art: A Source Book by Artists and Critics,* ed. Herschel B. Chipp (Berkeley: University of California Press, 1968), 91.

28 Comte de Lautréamont (Isidore Ducasse), *Les Chants de Maldoror,* trans. Guy Wernham (New York: New Directions, 1965).

29 Baudelaire, "L'Invitation au voyage," 235.

30 Paul Éluard, "L'amoureuse" (c. 1923), trans. Samuel Beckett in *Collected Poems in English and French* (London: John Calder, 1967), 67.

31 William S. Burroughs, *The Western Lands* (New York: Viking, 1987) 181–82. All

subsequent page references to this novel appear in the text. Here as elsewhere, Burroughs's fiction parallels (and anticipates) the general tone of much of Baudrillard's writing.

32 Huysmans, *Against Nature*, 97.

33 cf. Baudrillard, "L'Amérique comme fiction," 41.

34 Burroughs, *Nova Express* (London: Panther, 1968), 97.

35 Letter to Paul Henry Lang, in Kostelanetz, ed., *John Cage*, 116.

36 John Cage, "Experimental Music" (1955), in *Silence* (Middletown, CT: Wesleyan University Press, 1983), 12.

37 William Carlos Williams, "A Point for American Criticism," in *Our Exagimination Round His Factification for Incamination of Work in Progress* (London: Faber & Faber, 1972), 179.

38 Voltaire, *Candide, or Optimism* (1759), trans. John Butt (Harmondsworth, England: Penguin, 1985), 35.

39 This transition is nicely exemplified by the collection of the Museum für Gegenwartskunst in Basel, Switzerland, which has successively purchased extensive holdings of both minimal art and trans-avant-garde "spaghetti-expressionism."

40 Interview with Catherine Francblin, *Flash Art*, 130 (Oct-Nov 1986): 55.

41 Raoul Hausmann, "Dadaism and Today's Avant-Garde," *Times Literary Supplement* (3 Sept. 1964), 801.

42 Interview with Catherine Francblin, 55.

43 For further discussion of video installations at Documenta 8 see my article "Adventures in Techno-Space: Documenta 8," *Praxis M* 19 (May 1988): 23–27.

44 Quoted by Alan Ansen, in *The Burroughs File* (San Francisco: City Lights, 1984), 19.

45 From a conversation (concerning the potential of television) with Nicholas Zurbrugg in Paris, 21 December 1987.

46 *Nova Express*, 42; italics in original.

notes to chapter five

1 William S. Burroughs, "St Louis Return," *The Paris Review* 35 (1965): 57.

2 Walter Benjamin, The Work of Art in the Age of Mechanical Reproduction," *Illuminations,* trans., Harry Zohn (Glasgow: Collins, 1979), 239.

3 Umberto Eco, "The Multiplication of the Media" (1983) and "A Photograph" (1977), in *Travels in Hyperreality,* trans. William Weaver (London: Picador, 1987), 149, 147, and 214–15.

4 Charles Jencks, *Post-Modernism: The New Classicism in Art and Architecture* (London: Academy Editions, 1987), 12.

5 Ibid., 20.

6 Jean Baudrillard, *Amérique* (Paris: Bernard Grasset, 1986) 74, my translation.

7 Jean Baudrillard, interviewed by Nicholas Zurbrugg, *Eyeline*, no. 11 (1990): 6.

8 Fredric Jameson, interviewed by Anders Stephanson, *Flash Art* international edition, no. 131 (1986/7): 72.

9 Fredric Jameson, "Postmodernism and Utopia," in *Utopia Post Utopia: Configurations of Nature and Culture and Recent Sculpture and Photography* (Boston: The Institute of Contemporary Art, 1988), 18.

10 Fredric Jameson, "Reading without Interpretation: Postmodernism and the Video-text," in *The Linguistics of Writing: Arguments Between Language and Literature,* ed. Nigel Fabb et al.(Manchester: Manchester University Press, 1987). All references to this essay appear henceforth as unattributed page numbers in my text.

11 Roland Barthes, "The Death of the Author," trans. Stephen Heath, in *Image-Music-Text* (Glasgow: Collins, 1977), 142–48. Where appropriate, all subsequent references to this essay appear in my text.

12 Jean Baudrillard, "*L'Amérique comme fiction,*" interview with Jacques Henric and Guy Scaparta, *Art Press* no. 103 (1986): 41. My translation in *Eyeline* no 5 (1988): 24.

13 Luis Buñuel, *My Last Sigh,* trans Abigail Israel (New York: Knopf, 1983), 108, 110.

14 Luis Buñuel, "Notes on the making of *Un Chien andalou,*" in *The World of Luis Buñuel,* ed. Joan Mellen (New York: Oxford University Press, 1978), 153.

15 Jean Baudrillard, untitled interview from the French "La Sept" television channel program l'objet d'art à l'âge électronique (8 May 1987), translated by Lucy Forsyth in *Block* no 14 (1988): 9.

16 Roland Barthes, "Objective Literature," in his *Critical Essays,* trans. Richard Howard (Evanston, IL: Northwestern University Press, 1972), 14, 16.

17 Ibid., 16–17.

18 Robbe-Grillet dismisses Barthes's conclusions as "a simplification" of his work. "Confessions of a voyeur," interview with Roland Caputo, *Tension* (September–October 1986): 10–11.

19 Roland Barthes, *Camera Lucida,* trans. Richard Howard (New York: Hill and Wang, 1981), 22–27.

20 Roland Barthes "Deliberation," in *The Rustle of Language,* trans. Richard Howard (New York: Hill and Wang, 1986), 366–67.

21 Emphasis mine.

22 Emphasis mine.

23 John Cage, letter to Paul Henry Lang (22 May 1956) in *John Cage,* ed. Richard Kostelanetz (London: Allen Lane, 1971), 118.

24 Alexei Gan, "Constructivism," trans. John Bowlt, in *The Tradition of Constructivism,* ed. Stephen Bann (London: Thames and Hudson, 1974), 35–36.

25 Roland Barthes, "The Death of the Author," 147.

26 Jean Baudrillard, "Requiem for the Media," trans. Charles Levin, in *Video Culture: A Critical Investigation,* ed. John G. Hanhardt (New York: Gibbs M. Smith, (1987), 128.

27 Baudrillard, "The Precession of Simulacra," in *Simulations,* trans. Paul Foss and Paul Patton (New York: Semiotext(e), 1983), 55.

28 Jean François Lyotard, "Answering the Question: What is Postmodernism?" trans. Régis Durand, in *The Postmodern Condition: A Report on Knowledge,* trans. Geoff Bennington and Brian Massumi (Manchester: Manchester University Press, 1984), 81.

29 Jameson, interview with Anders Stephanson, 72.

30 Jameson, "Postmodernism and Utopia," 16.

31 Jameson, interview with Anders Stephanson, 72.

32 John G. Hanhardt, "Video in Fluxus," *Art and Text* no. 37 (1990): 86.

33 Ibid., 91.

34 Marita Sturken, "Video in the United States," in *Video,* ed. René Payuat (Montreal: Artextes, 1986), 57.

35 Nam June Paik, "Afterlude to the Exposition of Experimental Television 1963, March, Galerie Parnass," in *Ubi Fluxux ibi Motus,* 1990–1962, ed. Achille Bonito Oliva (Milano: Mazzotta, 1990), 387.

36 John Cage, interviewed by Nicholas Zurbrugg. Geneva, 12 September 1990.

37 Jameson, "Postmodernism and Utopia," 16; "Postmodernism or the Cultural Logic of Late Capitalism," *New Left Review* no. 146 (1984): 57.

38 John Cage, *Silence* (Middletown, CT: Wesleyan University Press, 1973), 16.

39 Paik, "Afterlude," 386.

40 Rosalind Krauss, "Video: the Aesthetics of Narcissism," in *New Artists Video: A Critical Anthology,* ed. Gregory Battcock (New York: Dutton, 1978), 45.

41 Paik's *Self-Portrait* (1970) is illustrated in Battcock, 122; Acconci's *Face-Off* (1972) is illustrated, 118; and *Morris's Exchange* (1973) is illustrated, 19.

42 Mona da Vinci, "Video: The Art of Observable Dreams," in Battcock, ed. *New Artists Video,* 17.

43 Paik's *Nam June Paik, Edited for TV* (1976) is illustrated in Battcock, 22.

44 Cage, *Silence,* 93.

45 Kraus, "Video," 45.

46 René Magritte's *Reproduction Prohibited (Portrait of Mr James)* (1937) is illustrated on the front cover of Dawn Ades, *Dada and Surrealism* (London: Thames and Hudson, 1974).

47 Campus's *Shadow Projection* (1974) is illustrated in Battcock, 101.

48 Paik's *TV Bra for Living Sculpture* (1969) and *Concerto for TV Cello and Videotapes* (1971) are illustrated in Battcock, 124 and 126. Paik's comments on *TV Bra* appear in his essay (coauthored with Charlotte Moorman) "TV Bra for Living Sculpture," Battcock, 129.

49 Gregory Battcock, "Disaster in New York," in Battcock, 133.

50 Heiner Müller, "The Walls of History," interviewed by Sylvère Lottinger, *Semiotext(e),* 4, no 2. (1982): 37.

51 See Baudrillard, *Amérique,* 146. For further discussion of Baudrillard's use of this concept see my "Baudrillard's *Amérique,* and the 'Abyss of Modernity,'" reprinted in this volume.

52 Jameson, "Postmodernism and Utopia," 27 and 29. Jameson's conclusions elaborate the overstatements of the Italian art critic Achille Bonito Oliva. For further discussion of Oliva's conclusions see my article "Postmodernity, *Métaphore Manqué,* and the myth of the Trans-avant-garde," reprinted in this volume.

53 Louis Aragon, "Open Letter to André Breton" (2 June 1971), trans. Linda Moses, in program to Wilson's production of Heiner Müller's *Hamletmachine* (London: Almeida Theatre, 1987), unpaginated.

54 See my "Baudrillard's *Amérique,* and the 'Abyss of Modernity.'"

55 William S. Burroughs, "On Freud and the Unconscious," in *The Adding Machine* (New York: Seaver Books, 1986), 89.

56 Stefan Brecht, *The Theatre of Visions: Robert Wilson* (Frankfurt am Main: Suhrkamp, 1978), 271.

57 Eco, *Travels in Hyperreality,* 213.

58 Cage, Letter to the *Village Voice* (January 1966), in Kostelanetz, ed. *John Cage,* 167.

59 Georg Lukács, The *Meaning of Contemporary Realism,* trans. John and Necke Mander (London: Merlin, 1963), 33.

60 Renato Poggioli, *The Theory of the Avant-Garde* (Cambridge, MA: The Belknap Press of Harvard University Press, 1968), 137.

61 Alexei Gan, "Constructivism," in Stephen Bann, ed. *The Tradition of Constructivism*, 36 and 35; Kasimir Malevich, title of painting of 1917, cited by Aaron Scharf, "Suprematism," in Tony Richardson and Nikos Stangos, *Concepts of Modern Art* (Harmondsworth, England: Penguin, 1974), 139. As Scharf comments, Malevich's suprematist compositions appear to aspire to "the final emancipation: a state of nirvana."

62 Robert Wilson, "Robert Wilson: Current Projects," interview with Laurence Shyer in *Robert Wilson: the Theater of Images* (New York: Harper and Row, 1984), 113 and 111.

63 Nam June Paik, interviewed by Nicholas Zurbrugg, Sydney, 10 April 1990, *Scan* + no. 3 (November 1990): 14.

notes to chapter six

1 Publicity brochure for *Hamletmachine,* issued by the Almeida Theatre, London. The London season of Wilson's production opened on 4 November 1987. Jean Jourdheuil's world premiere of the play opened at the Théâtre Gérard Phillipe, St. Denis, near Paris, on 30 January 1979.

2 Robert Wilson, quoted by Robert Hewison, "A Pioneering Space Explorer," *The Sunday Times,* 1 November 1987, 61.

3 Ibid.

4 Robert Wilson, quoted by Christopher Granlund, "Pinball Ruins," *The Guardian,* 23 October 1987, 18.

5 Robert Wilson, quoted by Kevin Jackson, "Listen with Your Eyes," *The Independent,* October 1987, 9. Arlene Akiko Teraoka suggests that Heiner Müller's theater obeys a similar impulse, insofar as "the breakdown or distortion of models/orders (defined as forms of drama, literary works, literary and historical characters, or quotations) essential to the author's project of overcoming "entropy" is not purely deconstructive, but creates a *new* ordering." Teraoka argues that Müller's use of montage or collage "takes specific meaningful elements (quotes, figures, images, etc.) from established literary works or historical events, thereby destroying the original contexts ('entropy'), and juxtaposes these selected elements in a disharmonious way (as the 'universal discourse') within a new framework," thereby "claiming a total openness to other texts and other voices." *The Silence of Entropy or Universal Discourse: The Postmodernist Poetics of Heiner Müller* (New York, 1985), 179. I think Teraoka probably exaggerates the "openness" of Müller's predominantly literary montages and collages. As I shall suggest, Wilson's work generates more revolutionary modes of extraliterary collage and montage, exploring the openness of multimedia theatre.

6 Robert Wilson, quoted by Granlund, *The Guardian.*

7 See Harold Hobson, "Samuel Beckett: Dramatist of the Year," *International Theatre Annual* 1 (London, 1956): 153, and Beckett's letter to Alan Schneider of 21 June 1956, in *Disjecta: Miscellaneous Writings and a Dramatic Fragment,* ed. Ruby Cohn (London, 1983), 107.

8   Tom F. Driver quotes Beckett's wish to "find a form that accomodates the mess" in "Beckett by the Madeleine," *Columbia University Forum* 4 (1961): 23.

9   John Cage, "Experimental Music" (1957), in *Silence* (Middletown, CT, 1983), 12.

10 John Cage, unpaginated notes accompanying *Indeterminacy: New Aspects of Form in Instrumental and Electronic Music* (New York, 1959), FT 3704.

11 Janny Donker, *The President of Paradise: A Traveller's Account of Robert Wilson's 'the CIVIL warS'* (Amsterdam, 1985), 87.

12 Ibid.

13 Heiner Müller, quoted by Teraoka, *The Silence of Entropy*, 100.

14 Ibid., 106.

15 "Something Rotten in the State of Germany," *New Statesman,* 6 November 1987, 24.

16 Quoted by Jackson, *The Independent.*

17 Irving Wardle, "A Mechanistic Solution," *The Times,* 5 November 1987, 18.

18 Michael Billington, "Images for an Age of Anxiety," *The Guardian,* 6 November 1987, 28.

19 Heiner Müller, *Hamletmachine* (1977), trans. Carl Weber (1984), unpaginated text, published in the Almeida Theater's program for *Hamletmachine* (London, 1987). All subsequent references to *Hamletmachine* refer to this text.

20 Peter Kemp, "Rude Mechanicals," *The Independent,* 6 November 1987, 15.

21 Untitled statement on *Hamletmachine* of 30 April 1986, in the Almeida Theater program.

22 Bonnie Marranca, "Robert Wilson, Byrd Hoffman School for Byrds," in *The Theatre of Images* ed., introductory essays, by Marranca (New York, 1977), 43 and 40.

23 Ibid., 48.

24 Stefan Brecht, *The Theatre of Visions: Robert Wilson* (Frankfurt, 1978), 271.

25 Ibid.

26 Robert Wilson, 1970 interview with Stefan Brecht; Ibid., 29. 27. Production Notes on *The King of Spain;* Ibid., 223.

28 Billington, *The Guardian.*

29 Eric Shorter, "Hamlet without the Bard," *The Daily Telegraph,* 4 November 1987, 16.

30 Statement on *Hamletmachine*, Almeida program.

31 Shorter, *The Daily Telegraph.*

32 As Denis Calandra points out, Müller applauds Antonin Artaud's disturbance of "business as usual" in the theatre; see *New German Dramatists* (London, 1983), 128.

33 David E. Wellbery praises this scene as one of Müller's "most memorable" evocations of the "link between domination and phantasms of authority," and as a dramatic fusion of "extremes of parody and ritual seriousness": "Postmodernism Europe: On Recent German Writing," in *The Postmodern Moment: A Handbook of Contemporary Innovation in the Arts,* ed. Stanley Trachtenberg (Westport, CT: 1985), 236. Somewhat similarly, Wellbery praises the "elaborate and uncanny dance of male and female identity" in *Hamletmachine* (237). Considered on the page, Müller's naked female clones of Marx, Lenin, and Mao appear a rather obvious joke. Significantly, Wilson's production made no attempt to revive this hackneyed visual reversal, transforming it into a more striking verbal contradiction as his three women "at table" fleetingly glide from their respective intonations—

elocution-exercise, Southern belle, and Minnie Mouse—into Marxist, Leninist, and Maoist diction.

34 Quoted by Jackson, *The Independent.*

35 Quoted by Granlund, *The Guardian.*

36 Speech introducing *Freud,* in Brecht, *The Theatre of Visions,* 421.

37 Cynthia Goodman, *Digital Visions: Computers and Art* (New York, 1987), 89.

38 Quoted by Goodman, 89.

39 I am thinking in particular of European and American sound poets. See Henri Chopin, *Poésie sonore internationale* (Paris, 1979), for a general introduction to their work.

40 John Gill discusses the visionary quality of Wilson and Cage in "Robert Wilson," *Time Out,* 4–11 November 1987, 31.

41 Nicholas Zurbrugg, "A Conversation with Allan," *Praxis M* 16 (1987): 11. Vizents discusses developments in sound poetry at the Soundworks Festival during the 1986 Sydney Biennale.

notes to chapter seven

1 Jean Baudrillard, quoted by Mike Gane in "Ironies of Postmodernism: Fate of Baudrillard's Fatalism," *Economy and Society,* 19 (1990): 331.

2 Arthur Kroker, *The Possessed Individual: Technology and Postmodernity* (London: Macmillan, 1992), 62.

3 Steven Best and Douglas Kellner, *Postmodern Theory: Critical Interrogations* (London: Macmillan, 1991), 111.

4 Marshall Berman, "Why modernism still matters." in *Modernity and Identity,* ed. Scott Lash and Jonathan Friedman (Oxford: Blackwell, 1992), 45.

5 Jean Baudrillard, quoted in *Baudrillard Live: Selected Interviews,* ed. Mike Gane (London: Routledge, 1993), 166.

6 Ibid., 171.

7 Christopher Norris, "Lost in the Funhouse: Baudrillard and the Politics of Postmodernism," in *Postmodernism and Society,* ed. Roy Boyne and Ali Rattansi (London: Macmillan, 1990), 140.

8 Arthur Kroker, Marilouise Kroker, David Cook, *Panic Encyclopedia: The Guide to the Postmodern Scene* (London: Macmillan, 1989), 265.

9 Fredric Jameson, *Postmodernism, or, The Cultural Logic of Late Capitalism* (Durham: Duke University Press, 1991),419, emphasis in the original.

10 Best and Kellner, *Postmodern Theory,* 140, 143.

11 For further information, contact David Blair, PO Box 174, Cooper Station, New York, NY 10276. Richard Kadrey reviews *WAX* in *MONDO 2000,* (Summer 1992): 104–5, as "a new video-based artform" in which "video cinematography blossoms from new digital image-processing tools" (105), which takes narrative compression to "a whole new level," attaining "the effect of a novel . . . in 85 retina-battering minutes" (104). Discussing the conceptual and compositional *advantages* of current technology, Blair comments: "Fortunately, I discovered a non-linear editing system in New

York that had been made available for artist use. The other artists had no idea what the hell they could use it for, but I went to see it, and realized this was exactly what I was trying to do. You could have 2000 pairs of digitised frames available, each pair representing the first and last frames of a shot. These were all lined up, and by pushing buttons, you could rearrange their order, like rearranging a collage on paper. Then you could order the machine to play the shots represented by these virtual stills, in the order they were arranged. Editing became so fast, it really was just like composition. And I could really try out every possible combination before I chose the sequence that I really wanted" (unpublished interview with the author, Sydney, 1992).

12 I discuss my concepts of the "B-effect" and the "C-effect" in more detail in *The Parameters of Postmodernism* (Carbondale: Southern Illinois University Press, 1993).

13 "Postmodernism and Ethical Abdication," Félix Guattari interviewed by Nicholas Zurbrugg, in *The Guattari Reader*, ed. Gary Genosko (Oxford: Blackwell, 1996), 116.

14 Dick Higgins, unpublished interview with the author, Barrytown, NY, July 5, 1993.

15 The concept of "Extreme Phenomena" appears in the title of Jean Baudrillard's *The Transparency of Evil: Essays on Extreme Phenomena,* trans. James Benedict (London: Verso, 1993). Baudrillard's notes on delusion appear on page 1.

16 Gene Youngblood, "The New Renaissance: Art, Science and the Universal Machine," in *The Computer Revolution and the Arts*, ed. Richard L. Loveless (Tampa: University of Southern Florida Press, 1989), 14.

17 Ibid.

18 Marcel Janco, "Dada at Two Speeds" (1966), trans. Margaret Lipp, in *Dadas on Art.* ed. Lucy R. Lippard (Englewood Cliffs, NJ: Prentice-Hall, 1971), 37–38.

19 Jürgen Habermas, "Modernity versus Postmodernity," trans. Seyla Ben-Habib, *New German Critique* 22 (Winter 1981): 7.

20 Gane, *Baudrillard Live,* 74.

21 Ibid., 64.

22 Jean Baudrillard, "The Anorexic Ruins," trans. David Antal, in *Looking Back on the End of the* World, ed. Dietmar Kamper and Christopher Wulf (New York: Semiotext(e), 1989), 43.

23 I elaborate my reservations regarding Jameson's accounts of postmodern culture in "Jameson's Complaint: Video Art and the intertextual 'time-wall,'" reprinted in this volume, and question Huyssen's interpretation of the impact of mass-media culture in *The Parameters of Postmodernism,* 129–37.

24 Jean Baudrillard, "The Ecstasy of Photography," Interview with Nicholas Zurbrugg (1993), in *Jean Baudrillard: Art and Artefact,* ed. Nicholas Zurbrugg (London: Sage, 1997), 32-42.

25 See Max Nordau, *Degeneration* (New York: Howard Fertig, 1968). The other prime "panic" cartographers of the postmodern condition are of course Arthur Kroker, Marilouise Kroker, and David Cook, authors of the alarming *Panic Encyclopedia* (London: Macmillan, 1989).

26 See Stéphane Mallarmé, "'Music and Literature" (1894), in *Debussy's "Prelude to 'The Afternoon of a Faun',"* ed. William W. Austin (New York: Norton, 1970), 113.

27 Baudrillard, "The Ecstasy of Photography," 37.

28 Ibid., 39. Barthes discusses *punctum* in *Camera Lucida: Reflections on Photography* (New York: Hill and Wang, 1981).

29 Marcel Proust, "John Ruskin," in *Mélanges (1900–1908)*, collected in *Contre Sainte-Beuve* (Paris: Gallimard, 1971), 129.

30 Edward Dorn, *Gûnslinger 1 & 2* (London: Fulcrum, 1970), 77.

31 Baudrillard, "The Ecstasy of Photography," 41. See Baudrillard, *Transparency of Evil*, 174.

32 Gane, *Baudrillard Live*, 55.

33 Ibid., 82.

34 Habermas, "Modernity versus Postmodernity," 11 and 9.

35 Stjepan G. Mestrovic, *The Coming Fin de Siècle: An Application of Durkheim's Sociology to Modernity and Postmodernism* (London: Routledge, 1991) 211–12.

36 Don DeLillo, *White Noise* (London: Picador, 1986), 326.

37 Mestrovic, *The Coming Fin de Siècle*, 210.

38 Ibid., 212.

39 Gane, *Baudrillard Live*, 63.

40 Ibid., 66.

41 Ibid., 82.

42 Ibid., 75.

43 Ibid., 48.

44 Ibid., 44.

45 See Mestrovic, *The Coming Fin de Siècle*, 210-12; Jean-François Lyotard, "Answering the Question: What is Postmodernism?" trans. Régis Durand, in Lyotard, *The Postmodern Condition: A Report on Knowledge,* trans. Geoff Benningon and Brian Massumi (Manchester: Manchester University Press, 1986), 82; Berman, "Why Modernism Still Matters," 54; Linda Nicholson, "On the Barricades: Feminism, Politics, and Theory," *Postmodernism and Social Theory: The Debate over General Theory,* ed. Steven Seidman and David G. Wagner (Oxford: Blackwell, 1992), 87–91.

46 Tristan Tzara, "Lecture on Dada," (1924) in *Theories of Modern Art: A Source Book by Artists and Critics,* ed. Herschel B. Chipp (Berkeley: University of California Press, 1968), 386, 389.

47 Tzara, "Lecture on Dada," (1924), 386–87.

48 Gane, *Baudrillard Live*, 68.

49 Ibid., 37.

50 Ibid., 34.

51 Ibid., 159.

52 Roland Barthes, "From Work to Text" (1971), in Barthes, *Image-Music-Text,* trans. Stephen Heath (London: Fontana, 1977), 159, emphasis in the original; Jacques Derrida, *Positions,* trans. Alan Bass (Chicago: Chicago University Press, 1981), 27; Michel Foucault, *The Archaeology of Knowledge and The Discourse of Language,* trans. A. M. Sheridan-Smith (New York: Pantheon, 1972), 5; Gilles Deleuze and Félix Guattari, "Rhizome," trans. John Johnson, in Deleuze and Guattari, *On the Line* (New York: Semiotext(e), 1983), 50.

53 Walter Pater, "Conclusion" (1868), in Pater, *Studies in the History of the Renaissance*

(1873), in *The Modern Tradition: Backgrounds of Modern Literature,* ed. Richard Ellmann and Charles Feidelson, Jr., (New York: Oxford University Press, 1965), 183–84.

54 Stéphane Mallarmé, "Crisis in Poetry" (1880–95), trans. Bradford Cook, in Ellman and Feidelson, eds. *Modern Tradition,* 111.

55 Virginia Woolf, "Modern Fiction" (1919), in Ellmann and Feidelson, eds. *Modern Tradition,* 124 and 123.

56 Joris-Karl, Huysmans, *Against Nature* (1884), trans. Robert Baldick, (Harmondsworth, England: Penguin, 1979), 198–99.

57 Jean Baudrillard, *Les Stratégies Fatales* (Paris: Bernard Grasset, 1983).

58 Gane, *Baudrillard Live,* 38.

59 Habermas, "Modernity versus Postmodernity," 10, 12, 10, and 6.

60 Mestrovic, *The Coming Fin de Siècle,* 211.

61 William S. Burroughs, "On Freud and the Unconscious," in Burroughs, *The Adding Machine: Selected Essays* (New York: Seaver Books, 1986), 119.

62 Jean Baudrillard, *America,* trans. Chris Turner (London: Verso, 1988), 86.

63 See, e.g., Baudrillard's allusions to microphysics, television screens, contact lenses, assorted networks and circuits, and the domain of Telecomputer Man in his *Transparency of Evil.*

64 Gane, *Baudrillard Live,* 105.

65 Raoul Hausmann, "Dadaism and Today's Avant-garde," *The Times Literary Supplement* (Sept. 3, 1964), 801.

66 Michel Foucault, "Preface" to Gilles Deleuze and Félix Guattari, *Anti-Oedipus: Capitalism and Schizophrenia,* trans. Robert Hurley, Mark Seem, and Helen R. Lane (New York: Viking, 1977), xii.

67 The term "astronauts of inner space" derives from Alexander Trocchi's formulation "cosmonaut of inner space," first used at the 1962 Writers' Conference in Edinburgh. William S. Burroughs refers to this occasion in "Alex Trocchi, Cosmonaut of Inner Space," his introduction to Trocchi's *Man at Leisure* (London: Calder and Boyars, 1972), 9; emphasis in the original. Jeff Berner, ed., consequently titled a collection of avant-garde texts and manifestos *Astronauts of Inner Space* (San Francisco: Stolen Paper Review Editions, 1966).

68 Foucault, "Preface" to *Anti-Oedipus,* xii.

69 Henri Chopin, interview with Nicholas Zurbrugg, in *Henri Chopin,* ed. Nicholas Zurbrugg and Marlene Hall (Brisbane: Queensland College of Art Gallery, 1992), 41.

70 Bernard Heidsieck, "Poésure et Peintrie," interview with Nathalie de Saint Phalle, *Galeries Magazine* 53 (Feb.–Mar. 1993): 54. See the encyclopedic catalog accompanying the exhibition "Poésure et Peintrie" (Marseilles: Musées de Marseilles-Réunion des Musées Nationaux, 1993). Henry M. Sayre's *The Object of Performance: The American Avant-Garde since 1970* (Chicago: University of Chicago Press, 1989) and Jean-Yves Bosseur's *Sound and the Visual Arts: Intersections between Music and Plastic Arts Today,* trans. Brian Holmes and Peter Carrier (Paris: Dis Voir, 1993) both similarly emphasize what Sayre terms "a modernism that might be said to be founded in dada and futurism" (xi), and what Bosseur associates with "experiments carried out by Futurists and Dadaists or, more recently, by John Cage" (5).

71 Gane, *Baudrillard Live,* 168.

72 Baudrillard further discusses his photography in "Cover Story Baudrillard," interview with Serge Bramly, *Galeries Magazine* 53 (Feb.–Mar. 1993) 78–87, 125. See also Corrina Ferrari, "L'occhio esclusivo," in the catalog *La Biennale di Venezia: XLV Esposizione Internazionale d'Arte—Punti cardinali dell'arte* (Venice: Marsilio, 1993), 574.

73 Jean Baudrillard, "Xerox and infinity," trans. Agitac (London: Touchepas, 1988), unpaginated.

74 Diamanda Galas, "I Dominate my Electronics," interview with Carl Heyward, *Art Com* 22 (1983): 23. Galas comments: "There is a stupid concept that electronics have us evolving to this unfeeling inhuman state. I dominate my electronics. "

75 Baudrillard, "Xerox and Infinity," n.p.

76 The conclusion to this essay (first published as "Le Xerox et l'Infini," in *Traverses* 44–5 [Sept. 1988]: 18–22) is modified in the version in Jean Baudrillard's *La Transparence du Mal: Essai sur les phénomènes extrêmes* (Paris: Galilée, 1990), 58–66 and in the version translated as *Transparency of Evil*, 51–59. An abbreviated variant of the essay's original final lines (significantly lacking the affirmation, "Again this is interesting"), serves as conclusion to the essay "Superconductive Events," Ibid., 36–43.

77 John Cage, letter to the *Village Voice* (Jan. 20, 1966), in Richard Kostelanetz, ed., *John Cage* (London: Allen Lane, 1971), 167.

78 John Cage, "Experimental Music" (1958), in Cage, *Silence: Lectures and Writings* (Middleton, CT: Wesleyan University Press, 198 3), 12. While Best and Kellner claim that Baudrillard's scientific metaphors are often "not appropriate or particularly illuminating" (*Postmodern Theory*, 138) I would argue that the particularly illuminating qualities of Baudrillard's thought is its *poetic* impetus and its *heuristic* momentum as thought self-consciously looking beyond the precise analysis that Best and Kellner would prefer.

79 Habermas, "Modernity versus Postmodernity," 6.

80 Gane, *Baudrillard Live*, 189.

81 Ibid., 202.

82 Nicholson, "On the Barricades," 89.

83 Gane, *Baudrillard Live*, 56.

84 Ibid., 38.

85 Ibid., 39.

86 Ibid., 125.

87 Ibid., 75.

88 Kathy Acker, interview with Nicholas Zurbrugg, quoted in Zurbrugg, *The Parameters of Postmodernism*, 148.

89 Nicholson, "On the Barricades," 89.

90 Gane, *Baudrillard Live*, 66.

91 Ibid., 45.

92 Ibid., 24.

93 Ibid., 14.

94 Ibid., 168.

95 Nicholson, "On the Barricades," 89.

96 Renato Poggioli, *The Theory of the Avant-garde*, trans. Gerald Fitzgerald (Cambridge, MA: The Belknap Press of Harvard University Press, 1968), 32.

97 Ibid., 137.

98 Gane, *Baudrillard Live,* 168.

99 Jean Baudrillard, interview with Catherine Francblin, *Flash Art* 130.

100 See "Baudrillard's *Amérique* and the 'Abyss of Modernity,'" reprinted in this volume.

101 Baudrillard, *America,* 5, 103.

102 See Louis Aragon, *Paris Peasant* (1926), trans. Simon Watson Taylor (London: Picador, 1980).

103 Acker, interview with Zurbrugg, *Parameters of Postmodernism,* 146.

104 Baudrillard, *America,* 36–37.

105 Ibid., 13.

106 Gane, *Baudrillard Live,* 63.

107 Ibid., 135.

108 Ibid., 187.

109 Baudrillard, *America,* 63.

110 Huysmans, *Against Nature,* 142.

111 Gane, *Baudrillard Live,* 182.

112 Berman, "Why Modernism Still Matters," 54.

113 Ibid., 55; emphasis in the original.

114 Lyotard, "Answering the Question: What is Postmodernism?," 81.

115 Ibid.

116 Gane, *Baudrillard Live,* 125.

117 Ibid., 22.

118 Burroughs, "On Coincidence," *The Adding Machine,* 102; emphasis in the original.

119 Gane, *Baudrillard Live,* 61.

120 Ibid., 56.

121 Barthes, "The Third Meaning," *Image-Music-Text,* 67.

122 Henri Chopin, "Open Letter to Aphonic Musicians," trans. Jean Ratcliffe-Chopin, *OU* 33 (1968): 11.

123 Henri Chopin, Reply of July 17, 1979 to a questionnaire on " 'Advances' and the Contemporary Avant-garde," *Stereo Headphones* 8–9–10 (1982). See Chopin's more detailed consideration of the specific qualities of sound poetry in his history of the genre, *Poésie Sonore Internationale* (Paris: Jean-Michel Place, 1979). For more recent studies of the genre see Vincent Barras and Nicholas Zurbrugg, eds., *Poésies Sonores* (Geneva: Contrechamps, 1993).

124 Achille Bonito Oliva, unpaginated *Press Release* for the 45th Venice Biennale, 1993.

125 William S. Burroughs, *Cities of the Red Night* (London: John Calder, 1981), 332.

126 Gane, *Baudrillard Live,* 39.

127 Ibid., 25.

128 Ibid., 81.

129 Ibid., 170.

130 Ibid., 135.

131 Baudrillard, "Xerox and Infinity," n.p.

132 Gane, *Baudrillard Live,* 37.

133 Ibid., 44.

134 Baudrillard, "The Anorexic Ruins," 40.

135 Huysmans, *Against Nature,* 220.

136 Gane, *Baudrillard Live*, 80.

137 Michel Foucault, "The Birth of a World" (1969), interview with Jean-Michel Palmier, in Sylvère Lotringer, ed., *Foucault Live: (Interviews, 1966–84)*, trans. John Johnston (New York: Semiotext(e), 1989), 60.

138 For further discussion of Situationism as an early postmodern movement see my article "'Within a Budding Grove': Pubescent Postmodernism and the Early *Evergreen Review*," *The Review of Contemporary Fiction* 3 no. 10 *(Fall* 1990): 150–61.

139 Umberto Boccioni, Carlo D. Carri, Luigi Russolo, Giacomo Balla, and Gino Severini, "The Exhibitors to the Public" (1912), in Chipp, *Theories of a Modern Art*, 297. Here, as in other Futurist manifestos, these artists claim to be "primitives" of the machine age.

140 Walter Benjamin, "The Work of Art in the Age of Mechanical Reproduction" (1936), in Benjamin, *Illuminations*, trans. Harry Zorn (Glasgow: Collins, 1979), 239.

141 Chopin, Reply of July 17, 1979, 74.

142 Howard Rheingold, "New Tools for Thought: Mind-Extending Technology and Virtual Communities," in Loveless, *The Computer Revolution and the Arts*, 23; emphasis in the original.

143 Burroughs, *Cities of the Red Night*, footnote 49; Rheingold, New Tools for Thought," 23.

144 Baudrillard, "Xerox and Infinity," n.p.

145 Youngblood, "The New Renaissance: Art, Science, and the Universal Machine," 15; Morris Berman, "The Cybernetic Dream of the Twenty-first Century," in Richard L. Loveless, ed., *The Computer Revolution and the Arts* (Tampa: University of Southern Florida Press, 1989), 94; emphasis in the original.

146 Best and Kellner, *Postmodern Theory*, 28.

147 Roland Barthes, "The Third Meaning," 67. I am thinking here of various kinds of experimental technological postmodern creativity which overtheorized analysis frequently marginalizes out of existence (refusing to recognize that which it cannot categorize) and which overfictionalized theory frequently exaggerates out of existence (as discourse supposedly beyond all "real" and "genuine" exchange). Qualitative recognition seems to offer the first step toward subsequent theoretical definition of such innovative practices. Discussing the sound poet Henri Chopin's semi-abstract composition "La Peur" (collected on Chopin's LP *Audiopoems*, TCS 106 [London: Tangent Records, 1971]) the composer Sten Hanson emphasizes its thematic validity and its technological intensity as a "40-minute poem about how man mobilises all his inner resources to analyse and fight his fear—of destruction, of living, of dying," in which "The combination of the exactness of literature and the time manipulation of music makes it possible to penetrate and influence the listener more deeply and more strongly than any other artistic method" (Hanson, "Henri Chopin, the sound poet," *Stereo Headphones*, 8–9–10 (1982): 16) In much the same way, the medievalist Paul Zumthor's discussion of "La Peur" concludes: "Chopin's sonic variations on the word 'fear' constitute, to my mind, one of the most powerful poems of our time" (Zumthor, "Une poésie de l'espace," in Barras and Zurbrugg, *Poésies Sonores*, 12). My point here is that Hanson's and Zumthor's *identification* of qualitatively significant postmodern technological creativity both oversteps the reserva-

tions of cautious orthodox theory, and avoids the apocalyptic overstatement of spec-ulative fictional assertion, laying tentative claim—as it were—to new discursive fields requiring further analysis. Without such initial sensitivity to emergent practices aris-ing within—and making reference to—what Morris Berman terms "real situations," the terms of cultural analysis seem fated to become indistinguishable from the kind of self-contained simulacra that too many critics mistake for the substance of the postmodern condition, and the objects of cultural analysis—as Jameson discovers— "all turn out to be 'the same' in a peculiarly unhelpful way" (Jameson, "Reading with-out interpretation: Postmodernism and the Video-text," in *The Linguistics of Writing: Arguments between Language and Literature*, ed. Nigel Fabb et al. [Manchester: Manchester University Press, 1987], 222).

148 Foucault, "The Masked Philosopher" (1980), interview with Christian Delacampagne, in Lotringer, *Foucault Live,* 198.

149 Gane, *Baudrillard Live,* 125.

references for chapter eight

Aragon, Louis, 1987. "Open Letter to André Breton (2 June 1971)," trans. Linda Moses with Jean-Paul Lavergné and George Ashley. Program for Robert Wilson's produc-tion of Heiner Müller's *Hamletmachine,* Almeida Theatre, London.

Barthes, Roland, 1981. *Camera Lucida: Reflections on Photography,* trans. Richard Howard. New York: Hill and Wang.

Baudrillard, Jean, 1990. *Cool Memories,* trans. Chris Turner. London: Verso.

———, 1993(a). *Baudrillard Live,* ed. Mike Gane. London: Routledge.

———, 1993(b). *The Transparency of Evil,* trans. James Benedict. London: Verso.

———, 1993(c). "Cover Story: Jean Baudrillard," interview with Serge Brainly, trans. Brian Holmes. *Galeries Magazine* no.53, February-March 1993.

———, 1997(a). "The Ecstasy of Photography," interview with Nicholas Zurbrugg (1993), in *Jean Baudrillard: Art and Artefact,* ed. Zurbrugg. London: Sage.

———, 1994(a). *The Illusion of the End,* trans. Chris Turner. Oxford: Polity Press.

———, 1997(b). "The Art of Disappearance," trans. Nicholas Zurbrugg, in *Jean Baudrillard: Art and Artefact,* ed. Zurbrugg. London: Sage.

Benjamin, Walter, 1974. "The Work of Art in the Age of Mechanical Reproduction," in Benjamin, *Illuminations,* trans. Harry Zorn. Glasgow: Collins.

Breton, André, 1971. "What is Surrealism?" trans. David Gascoyne, in *Theories of Modern Art,* ed. Herschel B. Chipp. Berkeley: University of California Press.

Burroughs, William S., 1983. Unpublished interview with Nicholas Zurbrugg, Minneapolis, 6 October 1983.

———, 1985. "Robert Walker's Spliced New York," *Aperture* no. 101, Winter 1985.

———, 1986. *The Adding Machine: Selected Essays.* New York: Seaver Books.

———, 1991. "Robert Wilson," in *Robert Wilson's Vision,* ed. Trevor Fairbrother. New York: Abrams.

———, 1992. *Painting and Guns.* New York: Hanuman.

Callas, Peter, 1994. "Peter Callas Interviewed by Nicholas Zurbrugg," *Continuum* 8, no. 1, 1994.

Dorment, Richard, 1994, "Towards the Unknown Realm," review of Bill Viola's *Nantes Triptych, The Daily Telegraph*, 30 November 1994, 16.

Eluard, Paul, 1984. *Lady Love,* trans. Samuel Beckett, in Beckett's *Collected Poems 1930-1978*, ed. Samuel Beckett. London: John Calder.

Guattari, Félix, 1996. "Postmodernism and Ethical Abdication," interview with Nicholas Zurbrugg, in *The Guattari Reader*, ed. Gary Genosko. Oxford: Blackwell.

Gysin, Brion, 1973. "Cut-Ups Self-Explained," in *Brion Gysin Let the Mice In*, ed. Jan Herman. West Clover, VT: Something Else Press.

Stein, Gertrude, 1939. *Picasso.* London: B.T. Batsford.

Virilio, Paul, 1991. *The Aesthetics of Disappearance,* trans. Philip Beitchman. New York: Semiotext(e).

————, 1996. "A Century of hyper-violence," interview with Nicholas Zurbrugg, *Economy and Society* 25, no. 1, 111–260.

Wilson, Robert, 1991. Unpublished interview with Nicholas Zurbrugg, Boston, 5 February 1991.

Youngblood, Gene, 1989. "The New Renaissance: Art, Science and the Universal Machine," in *The Computer Revolution and the Arts,* ed. Richard L. Loveless. Tampa: The University of South Florida Press.

notes to chapter nine

1   Bill Viola, "Between How and Why," in his *Reasons for Knocking at an Empty House, Writings 1973–1994* (Cambridge, MA: MIT Ptress, 1995), 257.

2   Jean Baudrillard, *The Perfect Crime,* trans. Chris Turner (London: Verso, 1996), 103. All subsequent page references to this book appear as numbers within the text.

3   Bill Viola, interview with Nicholas Zurbrugg, 1996. Unless otherwise indicated, all subsequent statements by Viola are taken from this interview.

4   Umberto Boccioni (with Carlo Carrà, Luigi Russolo, Giacomo Balla, and Gino Severini), "The Exhibitors to the Public" (1912), trans. R. W. Flint, in *Futurist Manifesotos*, ed. Umberto Apollonio (London:Thames and Hudson, 1973), 49; emphasis mine. F. T. Marinetti, "Destruction of Syntax—Imagination without Strings—Words-in-Freedom,"trans. R. W. Flint, in Apollonio, ed., *Futurist Manifestos,* 97.

5   Wyndham Lewis, *Blasting and Bombardeering* (1937), (London:John Calder, 1982), 35.

6   William S. Burroughs, *Nova Express* (London:Panther, 1968), 62.

7   Walter Pater, Conclusion, *Studies in the History of the Renaissance* (1873), in *The Portable Victorian Reader,* ed. Gordon S. Haight (Harmondsworth, England:Penguin, 1981), 631–32.

8   William S. Burroughs, "On Coincidence," in his *The Adding Machine:Collected Essays* (London:John Calder, 1985), 135–37, 102; emphasis in the original.

9   Jean Baudrillard, "Fractal Theory" Interview with Nicholas Zurbrugg (1990), in *Baudrillard Live:Selected Interviews*, ed. Mike Gane (London:Routledge, 1993), 168.

10. John Giorno, Interview with Nicholas Zurbrugg, 1996. All subsequent statements by Giorno are taken from this interview.

11 Viola, "In Response to Questions from Jörg Zutter," in his *Reasons*, 251.

12 Viola, "The Porcupine and the Car," and "Between How and Why," in *Reasons*, pages 65, and 257, respectively.

13 Viola, "Between How and Why," 257.

14 Dick Higgins, interview with Nicholas Zurbrugg, 1993.

15 Viola, "Statement 1989," in *Reasons*, 174.

16 Viola, "Will There Be Condominiums in Data Space?," in *Reasons*, 106.

notes to chapter ten

1 Warren Burt, ed., "Post-Modernism" issue, *Sounds Australian* 33 (1992).

2 Warren Burt, "Australian Experimental Music 1963–1990," *Leonardo Music Journal* 1, 1 (1991): 5–10.

3 Kenneth Gaburo, *The Beauty of Irrelevant Music* (unpaginated pamphlet) (La Jolla, CA: Lingua, 1976). Now available from Frog Peak Music, P.O.Box 1052, Lebanon, NH 03766, USA.

4 Warren Burt, "Do We Really Need More Arts Coverage?", *Sounds Australian* 26 (1990):10–11.

5 Guy Davenport, *The Geography of the Imagination* (London:Picador, 1984). Suzi Gablik, *The Re-Enchantment of Art*, (London:Thames and Hudson, 1993). Fredric Jameson, *Postmodernism, or the Cultural Logic of Late Capitalism* (Durham, NC:Duke University Press, 1991).

6 Nicholas Zurbrugg, "Some Further Thoughts on Post-Modernism," *Sounds Australian* 33 (1992): 25–27. All other Zurbrugg essays cited in this commentary are reprinted in this volume.

7 D. J. Enright, ed., *The Oxford Book of Contemporary Verse 1945–1980* (Oxford:Oxford University Press, 1980).

8 Herbert Brun, *Compositions*, 3 LPs and unpaginated booklet (Champaign, IL: Non-Sequitur, 1983).

9 Denis Smalley, "The Listening Imagination: Listening in the Electroacoustic Era," in *The Companion to Contemporary Musical Thought*, ed., J. Paxuter et al. (London and New York: Routledge, 1992), 514–54.

10 Benjamin Boretz, "Interface, Part 2," in *Perspectives on Musical Aesthetics*, ed. John Rahn (New York:Norton, 1994), 121–24.

11 Pi O, *24 Hours* (Melbourne:Collective Effort Press, 1996).

12 Michel Chion, *Credo Mambo*, CD (Fontaine, France: Metamkine, 1992).

13 Roland Barthes, cited in Zurbrugg's "The Limits of Intertextuality," reprinted in this volume.

14 William Sethares, "Local Consonance and the Relationship Between Timbre and Scale," *Journal of Acoustical Society of America*, 94, 3 (1993): 1218–28.

15 Mabel Todd, *The Thinking Body* (New York:Dance Horizons, 1972).

16 Kenneth Gaburo, *The Beauty of Irrelevant Music*, n.p.

17 Herbert Brun, *Compositions*, n.p.

18 Dave Sim, "Comics and the Mass Medium," *Cerebus Comics* (Kitchener, Ontario: Aardvark-Vanaheim, 1996–1997) issues 213–16.

19 Warren Burt, *39 Dissonant Etudes*, CD (Sydney:Tall Poppies, 1996).

20 Henry Cowell, *New Musical Resources* (Cambridge:Cambridge University Press, 1996).

21 Jean Baudrillard, *The Perfect Crime*, trans. Chris Turner (London:Verso, 1996), 13, 84.

22 John Cage, *Roaratorio*, CD (Mainz, Germany: Wergo, 1994).

23 John Lilly, *The Mind of the Dolphin*, Audiotape (San Rafael, CA: Esalen Institute Tapes, 1971).

24 For an excellent analysis of the structure of *Variations II*, see Thomas DeLio, *Circumscribing the Open Universe*, (Lanham, MD:University Press of America, 1984).

25 John Cage, *Silence* (London:Marion Boyars, 1961).

26 Charles Seeger, *Tractatus Esthetico-Semioticus in Current Thought in Musicology* (Austin:University of Texas Press, 1976).

sources

The essays collected in this volume originally appeared in earlier versions in the following publications. Editing and referencing conventions vary accordingly.

"Marinetti, Boccioni, and Electroacoustic Literature: Futurism and After" originally appeared in *Comparative Criticism,* no. 4 (1982): 193–211.

"The Limits of Intertextuality: Barthes, Burroughs, Gysin, Culler" originally appeared in *Southern Review* (Adelaide), 16, no. 2 (July, 1983): 250–73.

"Post-Modernity, *Métaphore Manquée,* and the Myth of the 'Trans-avant-garde'" originally appeared in *Sub-Stance,* vol. XIV, no. 3 (1986): 68–90.

"Baudrillard's *Amérique* and the 'Abyss of Modernity'" originally appeared in *Art and Text,* no. 29 (June–August 1988): 40–63.

"Jameson's Complaint: Video Art and the Intertextual 'Time-Wall'" originally appeared in *Screen,* vol.32, no.1 (Spring 1991): 16–34.

"Post-Modernism and the Multimedia Sensibility: Heiner Müller's *Hamletmachine* and the Art of Robert Wilson' originally appeared in *Modern Drama,* vol.XXI, no.3 (September 1988): 439–53.

"Baudrillard, Modernism and Postmodernism" originally appeared in Douglas Kellner (ed.), *Baudrillard: A Critical Reader* (Oxford: Blackwell, 1994): 227–55.

"'Apocalyptic?' 'Negative?' 'Pessimistic?'—Baudrillard, Virilio, and Technoculture," originally appeared in Stuart Koop (ed.), *Photography/Post-Photography* (Melbourne: Centre for Contemporary Photography, 1995): 93–14.

"Baudrillard, Giorno, Viola and the Technologies of Radical Illusion" originally appeared in *Performance Research,* vol.1, no.3 (Autumn 1996): 1–5.

index

C

G

Gablik, Suzi: for Burt, ecological antidote to Jameson's text-based theories, 180-81.

Gaburo, Kenneth: Burt on Gaburo's and Wunder's affirmative teaching practices, 177; Burt on resistance to 'given' systems, 198.

Galas, Diamanda: on art's capacity to dominate technology, 134.

Gan, Alexei: constructivist critique of metaphysical culture and Jameson's more extreme materialist perspective, 90; parallels between Gan's rejection and Malevich's defense, and Jameson's rejection and Wilson's defense of spiritual value, 103.

Gassiot-Talabot, Gérald: on Chekhovian register of Heidsieck's sound poetry, 8.

Giacometti, Alberto: and early postmodern anxiety, 49; and trans-avant-garde painting, 58.

Gibson, Ross; on parallels between Baudrillard's model of simulation and Pogiolli's definition of phases of avant-garde, 42-3.

Ginsberg, Allen: and Baudrillard's images of American freeways, 76; and rhetoric of Müller's *Hamletmachine*, 111, for Burt, example of 'corporeality' of poetic performance, 195.

Giorno, John: Wendt on impeccable timing, 15; on *Eh Joe* as 'visceral' video-theater, 170-71; on sound poetry and multimedia performing skills, 171.

Godard, Jean-Luc: Baudrillard's defense of Godard's 'modernism', 129.

Goodman, Cynthia: on Warhol's use of digital imagery, and Wilson's multimedia aesthetic, 115-16.

Grosz, George: and Baudrillard's neo-expressionist images of NY, 68.

Grundmann, Heidi: Burt on Grundmann, Adrian X, Baudrillard and vitality of European communications art, 201.

Guattari, Félix: on postmodern thought's ethical and aesthetic abdication, xii, 122, 162; on 'structuralist straitjacket', xiii; defense of 'aesthetic machines', xvii; and modernist register of poetic theoretical rhetoric, 130-31.

Guillén, Claudio: on new work as deviation from and confirmation of past norms, 28.

Guys, Constantin: for Baudelaire, specific example of 'modernity', xiv.

Gysin, Brion: and limits of intertextual theory, xv, xvii, 17-40; parallels between Gysin's and Barthes's initial critiques of authoriality and subsequent re-identification of authorial presence and 'third meanings', 29-30, 38-9; on writing 'fifty years behind painting', 30, 150-1; on art's advanced exploration of 'space', 149; on sound poetry and 'machine poetry', 32-3; and 'futurist' postmodern avant-garde experimentation, 44, 67.

H

Haacke, Hans: as exception to Jamesonian paradigms, 93.

Habermas, Jürgen: on 'project of modernity' and defense of 'communicative rationality', 124; as antithesis to Baudrillard's logic of extremes, 127, 131; on 'hopeless surrealist revolts', 131.

Handhardt, John: on Paik's and Vostell's use of video to critique TV culture, 94.

Hanson, Sten: on literary/musical impact of sound poetry, 14.

Haring, Keith: on general neglect of Warhol's originality.

Hausmann, Raoul: as 'primitive' modernist sound poet, 13; critique of neo-Dadaism and cultural 'Renaissances' 53, 83, 132; Chopin on Parisian intelligentsia's neglect of Hausmann, 133; and Baudrillard's moderate poetics, 141; for Burt, example of 'corporeality' of poetic performance, 195.

Heidegger, Martin: Baudrillard's sympathy for concept of 'stellar' mystery, 173.

Heidsieck, Bernard: and continuities between Futurist experiments and postmodern sound poetry, 5, 7-11, 191; Gassiot-Talabot, on Chekhovian register of 'La Poinçonneuse', 8; Wendt on impeccable timing, 15; and Wilson's 'loose-end' multimedia art, 117; on Parisian neglect of Dadaist and Futurist innovation and need for 'different history', 133.

V

W

Warhol, Andy: on avoidance of new realities, 36; echoed by Müller's *Hamletmachine*, 111-12; on Warhol's use of digital imagery, and Wilson's multimedia aesthetic, 115-16; Haring of Warhol's influence, 116; for Baudrillard, example of 'absolute anti-mystic', 169-70.

Weightman, John: on Barthes's authoriality, 40.

Weisstein, Ulrich: and Heidsieck as 'artist engineer', 8.

Wendt, Larry: on Chopin as postmodern technological 'barbarian' mastering early tape-recorder, 8, 15-16; on immaculate timing of Giorno's and Heidsieck's live sound poetry performances, 14-16.

Wilde, Oscar: and Baudelaire, Huysmans, Wilde and decadent rhetoric of Baudrillard's *America*, 72, 79-80, 131, 138, 141.

Williams, Raymond: and Jameson on television as 'total flow ... without interruption', 89.

Williams, William Carlos: and American modernism's contradictory 'mixing of categories', 81.

Wilson, Robert: and Burroughs, Cage and 'harmony' of chance composition, 81; as quintessential example of the postmodern avant-garde, 86; Aragon on *Deafman Glance* as multimedia realization of surrealism's dream, 101; Brecht on Wilson's 'non-verbal, arational communication', 102, 112-13, 117; parallels between Gan's rejection and Malevich's defense, and Jameson's rejection and Wilson's defense of spiritual value, 103; on Wagner and artificiality of naturalism, 103; on antipathy to 'ping pong' naturalism 114, 159; and Müller, 69, 105-118; parallels with Beckett's systematic structures and ambiguous content, 106; parallels with Cage's incongruous juxtapositions, 106; and video-editing, 108, 113, 115; on *The King of Spain* and the compatibility of the dissimilar, 113; neo-Dadaist and neo-Surreal reversals and Buñuelesque images in *Hamletmachine*, 114-15;

Hamletmachine as fusion of live-end and dead-end postmodernism, 116; and Anderson, and problem of evaluating 'loose-end' multimedia art, 116-17; and Proust's Breton's, Aragon's, and Virilio's, concepts of 'another logic', 158-9; for Burroughs, creator of 'life-saving dream images', 159; enthusiasm for Burroughs as writer breaking codes and creating new languages, 160; on Mozart as precursor for Burroughs's textual variations, and *King Lear* as example of art's open impact as 'continuum', 160; on postmodern rediscoveries of the 'classics', 160.

Wittgenstein, Ludvig: Burt on irrelevance of Wittgenstein, Freud, and word-based theory to Viola's video art, 205-6.

Woolf, Virginia: 'Modern Fiction' as precursor for poetic poststructuralist rhetoric, 131, 141.

Wordsworth, William: and romantic register of Baudrillard's *America*, 76.

Wunder, Al: Burt on Wunder's and Gaburo's critiques of evaluative criticism, 176-8.

X

X, Adrian: Burt on X, Grundmann, Baudrillard and vitality of European communications art, 201.

Y

Yeats, William Butler: Burt on Yeats, Partch and simplistic cultural connections, 190.

Youngblood, Gene: on Baudrillard's nostalgia for 'aura', 123; and Berman on compatibility of virtual culture and 'real' situations, 142; and Burroughs, on the 'numbing' effects of pseudo-scientific dogma, 148.

Z

Zorn, John: Burt on C20th lineage from modernist musical appropriation to Cage's, Shaeffer's and Zorn's postmodern sampled collages, 183.